Important Telephone Numbers

Veterinarian: _____
  Address: _____
  Phone: _____
Emergency Clinic or
  Veterinary Hospital: _____
Poison Control Center: _____
ASPCA (Humane Shelter): _____

Your Dog's Records

Name_____ Breed_____ Breeder_____

Sire_____

Birthdate _____ Registration number _____ Dam _____

	7-14 wks.	6 mos.	1 yr.	2 yrs.	3 yrs.	4 yrs.	5 yrs.	6 yrs.	9-14 yrs.
DHLP									
Rabies									
Stool sample									
Heartworm test									
Teeth cleaning									

DHLP	Distemper, Hepatitis, Leptospirosis, Parainfluenza. A puppy series and *yearly* boosters throughout life are needed for full protection.
Rabies	Vaccination at four to six months. Boosters at one- to three-year intervals are required by law.
Tetanus	The tetanus bacteria is common around horse stables. Your veterinarian may suggest that your dog be protected if it is around horses.
Stool sample	Feces should be checked whenever vaccinations are given. Bring a fresh sample to be examined.
Heartworm test	Should be done yearly in most areas.
Teeth cleaning	Should be done every one to three years or whenever tartar collects on the teeth.

ii

Surgery	Date		Complications

Problem or illness	Date	Medication used	Doctor was seen	Used home treatment	Resolved without medicine

In heat	Date bred	Mate:_____Owner:_____ Brucellosis-free?	Number of puppies	Pup mortality

Taking Care of Your Dog

Taking Care of Your Dog

A Complete Guide to Your Dog's Medical Care

Sheldon L. Gerstenfeld, V.M.D.

ADDISON-WESLEY PUBLISHING COMPANY

Reading, Massachusetts • Menlo Park, California
Don Mills, Ontario • Wokingham, England • Amsterdam
Sydney • Singapore • Tokyo • Madrid • Bogotá
Santiago • San Juan

Library of Congress Cataloging in Publication Data

Gerstenfeld, Sheldon L   1943-
    Taking care of your dog.

    Includes index.
    1. Dogs--Diseases. I. Title.
SF991.G47   636.7'08'9   79-2339
ISBN 0-201-03060-8
ISBN 0-201-03061-6 pbk.

Sixth Printing, April 1986

ISBN 0-201-03061-6-P
ISBN 0-201-03060-8-H
FGHIJ-DO-89876

To my dear wife, Traudi, whose love and whole being have expanded my creativity and my sensitivity of the world.

To my dear parents, Sidney and Isabelle, who encouraged their son to pursue his dream to be an "animal doctor."

To our dear Pepe, who recently passed on. He brightened our lives for fourteen wonderful years and will always be remembered.

To the Reader

This book can be of great help to you and your dog. Many veterinarians have reviewed each section and have agreed on the medical recommendations for each problem. The recommendations will not work in every case, however, so here are some qualifications:

1. If your dog is under the care of a veterinarian who gives advice contrary to that given in this book, follow your veterinarian's advice. The individual characteristics of your dog can then be taken into account.

2. You know your dog best; do not hesitate to follow your own judgment as to when to seek professional assistance.

3. If your dog has an allergy or a suspected allergy to a medication, check with your veterinarian, at least by phone.

4. If your dog's problem persists beyond a reasonable period, you should make an appointment with your veterinarian.

Acknowledgments

The sincere help and encouragement of many people made the writing of this book a most pleasurable experience.

First and foremost, I thank my wife Traudi for her very helpful comments and patience, and for providing a loving and creative environment.

Ann Dilworth accepted the manuscript with those three little words that mean so much to an author—"We love it!" The raw manuscript evolved into its most effective form thanks to the teamwork of Doe Coover, Martha Drumm, and Tess Palmer. They helped me rearrange, reword, and delete, studying every word and paragraph until they could almost recite the text verbatim! Lois Hammer deserves a lot of credit for turning my "doctor's handwriting" into a typewritten beauty. John Hackmaster did the marvelous medical illustrations, and Beth Anderson finalized my original cartoons.

Five colleagues took time from very busy schedules to review the manuscript and offer suggestions: Dr. Gus Thornton, Dr. Jean Holzworth, Dr. Robert Brodey, Dr. Donald Patterson, and Dr. Al Kissileff. Encouragement and suggestions were also enthusiastically provided by Eleonore Gerstenfeld, Jack Neifert, Bob and Jill Terranova, and Baxter and Betsy Holland.

I also want to thank Dr. Donald Vickery, Dr. James Fries, and Dr. Robert Pantell for laying the groundwork with **Take Care of Yourself** and **Taking Care of Your Child.**

All my patients' owners deserve a great deal of credit for caring so well and so responsibly for their pets. Their hopes, fears, and needs and their development into well-informed pet owners formed the foundation for this book.

Finally, I want to thank my patients themselves for giving me their unquestioning love and trust.

S. L. G.

Contents

Introduction

Owning a dog is a big responsibility. As the owner, your care is instrumental in helping your animal—whether it be a purebred or a mongrel stray who followed you home one day—live a happy and healthy life. With the information in this book, you will be able to take good care of your pet at home and ensure that professional veterinary care is obtained when it is needed. You will also save time and money.

The writing of this book was a labor of love. I am thankful that I was able to become a veterinarian, to help injured and ill pets, and to be a source of information, comfort, and reassurance for many, many pet owners.

I have been very fortunate in veterinary practice. My pet owners have become *active* partners with me in sharing the responsibility for their pets' well-being and health. **Taking Care of Your Dog** is the result of this wonderful experience.

Your veterinarian is a busy person. A typical day may include reuniting a child with her dog, Jaws, who has mended from serious automobile injuries; watching with pride as an owner gives his diabetic dog its first life-sustaining injection of insulin; performing one or two "Marcus Welby"-type heroics (without a commercial break); giving several well-pet exams, which cover vaccinations and routine tests; and diagnosing and treating illnesses and injuries that require immediate attention. Your veterinarian also sees many minor medical problems that could be called "unnecessary" visits. In human medicine, up to 70 percent of first visits to the doctor have been termed "unnecessary." There is no reason to believe that our pets' illnesses or injuries are any different. You can save money and time and provide the best care for your pet by learning to treat many of your pet's medical problems at home and by learning when it *is* important to visit or telephone your veterinarian. I'm very proud of my pet owners when they handle minor medical problems efficiently at home. They know that I am around if they need reassurance or advice. I'm equally proud when they recognize *early* that their pet's problem requires my help. The step-by-step Decision Charts in **Taking Care of Your Dog** will provide you with enough information to make sound judgments about most of your dog's medical problems.

To help you become an active partner, an aware pet owner, a good consumer, and a constructive critic, the chapters in Part I provide the following useful information:

Selecting a Dog

Taking care of a pet actually starts *before* you choose one (or two). This chapter will help you select and find the proper pet for your life-style, and it emphasizes the *responsibility* of pet ownership.

The Owner's Home Physical Exam: Your Dog's Body and How It Works

You'll be fascinated at the similarities between a person's body and a dog's body. This chapter also shows you how to examine your pet at home.

Keeping Your Dog Healthy, Happy, and Obedient

Many illnesses and injuries are the result of long-term abuse or lack of proper maintenance. Preventive care—grooming, training, good nutrition, annual vaccinations, checking for parasites, and dental care—will keep your pet healthy. The section entitled How Do I Know When My Dog is Sick? describes some general signs that may be the first indication that your pet is not feeling well.

Going to the Veterinarian

Finding a competent and interested veterinarian and being a cooperative, aware, and concerned owner are important for your dog's health. You should understand and appreciate the procedures that may be necessary for your veterinarian to diagnose and properly treat your pet's health problem.

Your Dog's Home Pharmacy

A first aid kit is a must, and this chapter will help you stock it with the most effective medications for minor medical problems. Included are hints on uses, dosages, and possible side effects for a variety of over-the-counter medications.

Part II provides specific guidance for 60 of your dog's most common medical problems. This section is designed for quick and easy reference. First, identify your pet's primary symptom—for instance, coughing, vomiting, or straining to urinate. Then, to find a discussion of the problem, look it up in the Contents or the Index.

Emergency Procedures

Chapter 6 details the best way to approach injured animals and the things you can do during those first vital minutes that could mean the difference between life and death.

Accidents and Injuries

This chapter goes into common injuries sustained by dogs, listing any appropriate home treatment and what to expect from your veterinarian.

Common Problems and Diseases

Each of the medical problems in this section includes a general discussion, suggestions for home treatment, and pointers to show you when a telephone call or visit to your veterinarian is needed. Information on what to expect at the veterinarian's office is also given to help you be aware of appropriate care. The Decision Charts that accompany each problem provide step-by-step instructions to help you decide whether to use home treatment or to seek professional advice. No medication suggested in this section should be used without knowledge of its dosage and side effects. Most medicines are discussed in Chapter 5, Your Dog's Home Pharmacy. First aid information for handling the most common dog emergencies is provided. Your handling of the emergency at home and knowing what to expect at the veterinarian's office may combine to save your pet's life. Prevention of injuries is also discussed.

Breeding and Reproduction

Breeding, pregnancy, delivery, and nursing are fully discussed. Step-by-step charts on delivery and nursing will give you easy instructions to follow if your help—or the veterinarian's help—is needed.

Cosmetic Surgery

This is a brief chapter discussing the whys and whens of tail docking, ear cropping, and the removal of dewclaws.

Genetics and Hereditary Diseases
Cancer

These two chapters provide you with the latest information on advances in these important health areas.

Euthanasia

In today's world, it is painful to lose the unselfish love and companionship that a pet provides. When that pet is suffering and there is no hope for a cure, euthanasia should be considered an act of love and mercy. It is a very difficult decision to make and should be considered only after discussion with your family and your veterinarian.

I know you will find the book informative and helpful in taking care of your dog. I hope you also find it enjoyable and interesting reading.

Philadelphia, Pennsylvania   S. L. G.

Part I

You and Your Dog

Chapter 1

Selecting a Dog

One of the greatest pleasures human beings can experience is to share their home with a pet. Having a dog or cat can keep you closer to nature. It should also kindle your spirit of reverence for all life on earth, from the ant on your picnic table to your brothers and sisters in every country. Dogs and cats are an unfailing source of companionship during times of sadness or joy. They have a sense of timing, of humor, seen in few human comedians. You'll always remember their body movements, facial expressions, and "one-liners," even after their bodies have departed and their spirits have become part of your memories. A kitten or puppy is a wonderful aid in teaching a child (and even some adults) about responsibility, patience, love, understanding, and self-control.

Dogs have been beloved by their human masters practically since mankind first domesticized them. Senator George G. Vest, in his emotional defense during a Missouri lawsuit involving the killing of a dog, captures the essence of the owner-dog relationship:

> The best friend a man has in this world may turn against him and become his enemy. His son or daughter, whom he has reared with loving care, may prove ungrateful. Those who are nearest to us, those whom we trust with our happiness and our good name may become traitors to their faith. The money that a man has, he may lose . . . when he needs it most. A man's reputation may be sacrificed in a moment of ill-considered action. The people who are prone to

fall on their knees to do us honor when success is with us may be the first to throw the stone of malice when failure settles its cloud upon our heels. The one absolutely unselfish friend that man can have in this selfish world, the one that never deserts him, the one that never proves ungrateful or treacherous, is his dog.

A man's dog stands by him in prosperity and in poverty, in health and in sickness. He will sleep on the cold ground where the wintry winds blow and the snow drives fiercely, if only he may be near his master's side. He will kiss the hand that has no food to offer, he will lick the wounds and the sores that come in encounter with the roughness of the world. He guards the sleep of his pauper master as if he were a prince. When all other friends desert, he remains. When riches take wings and reputation falls to pieces he is as constant in his love as the sun in its journey through the heavens. If fortune drives the master forth [as] an outcast in the world, friendless and homeless, the faithful dog asks no higher privilege than that of accompanying him to guard him against danger, to fight against his enemies, and, when the last scene of all comes, and death takes the master in its embrace and his body is laid away in the cold ground, no matter if all other friends pursue their way, there, by the graveside will be found the noble dog, his head between his paws, his eyes sad but open in alert watchfulness, faithful and true even to death.

JOY AND RESPONSIBILITY

With the joy of owning a dog, however, comes *responsibility*. The lack of responsibility and lack of planning for owning or breeding a pet can be witnessed on the streets and in the humane shelters. Millions upon millions of dogs are put to death yearly; the reasons range from "too much trouble" or "too much money" to "the kids went to college." The recent New York City law requiring residents to pick up their dogs' droppings has also increased the number of dogs turned over to shelters.

Owning a dog takes a commitment of time (as much as ten to fifteen years) and money. You and your family should ask yourselves the following questions before deciding on the new family member:

Do we have time for a dog?
Who will have the responsibility for feeding the dog and caring for its toilet needs? Who will train and exercise it? Does the breed need daily grooming?

Can we afford to keep a dog healthy and well nourished?
The purchase price is small change compared to the maintenance fees: food, accessories, veterinary care, boarding, and grooming (for such breeds as poodles, sheepdogs, and Lhasa apsos).

Food and accessories	
Small dog	$125 per year
Medium-sized dog	$250 to $400 per year
Large dog	$400 to $600 per year
Extra-large dog	$600 to $800 per year

Veterinary care	$50 to $200 per year
Boarding	
Small dog	$3 to $6 per day
Medium-sized dog	$4 to $6 per day
Large dog	$5 to $8 per day
Extra-large dog	$6 to $10 per day
Grooming	$100 to $200 per year

These figures are estimates and will vary in different regions, but they provide a model for figuring your pet's expenses for the year. Be sure that you have a little extra money set aside for unforeseen problems.

Do we have room for a dog?
Is the yard fenced? If you are considering a breed that needs a lot of exercise, a fenced-in yard or run or long, daily romps in a park are needed.

Do we want a male or a female?
See Breeding and Reproduction, page 227 for a discussion that should help with this decision.

What are our favorite breeds?
Selecting a purebred dog or a mutt is a personal choice. Mutts are like us—a product of mixed breeding. For the most part, these unions produce wonderful and beautiful offspring.

Purebred dogs (the term means that there is a record, a pedigree, of the puppy's ancestors for three or more generations) that are raised by responsible private breeders are excellent specimens of their breed. The good breeder looks for outstanding physical and mental qualities, such as soundness, beauty, and good temperament, and is continually trying to improve the line. Responsible breeders prepare their dogs for breeding (see Breeding and Reproduction, page 227) so that healthy and vigorous puppies are produced.

There are 124 dog breeds recognized by the American Kennel Club. You can become familiar with the breeds that interest you by attending dog shows or talking to a neighbor who owns the breed that you like. The specialty magazines listed below are another excellent source of information:*

Dog World
10060 W. Roosevelt Road
Westchester, IL 60153

*Pure Bred Dogs—American
    Kennel Gazette*
51 Madison Ave.
New York, NY 10010

Show Dogs
257 Park Ave., South
New York, NY 10010

---

*From *Dog Catalog,* by Don Myrus (New York: Collier Books, Macmillan Publishing Company, 1978).

There are also several foreign publications:

*The Australasian Kennel
  Review and Dog News*
2 Dale St.
Brookvale, N.S.W. 2100
Australia

Dogs in Canada
59 Front St., East
Toronto, Ontario M5E1B3

Dog World
32 New Street
Ashford, Kent
England

Kennel Gazette
1 Clarges St., Picadilly
London, W1Y8 AB
England

*Revue Officielle de la
  Cynophilie Francaise*
215 Rue Saint Denis
75083 Paris
France

Unser Rassehund
46 Dortmund 1, Postfach 1390
Mallinckrodstrasse 26
West Germany

De Hondenwereld
Emmalaan 16
Amsterdam-Zuid
The Netherlands

I Nostri Cani
21 Viale Premuda
20129 Milan
Italy

The Companian Dog
#1-5 Kanda-Sudacho
Chiyoba-Ku Tokyo
Japan

*Boletin Club-Canofilo
  De Jaslisco, AC*
Ave. Vallarta 1835-20
Guadalajara, Jalisco
Mexico

*New Zealand Kennel
  Gazette*
P.O. Box 19101
Wellington
New Zealand

Hundsport
P.O. Box 1308
11183 Stockholm
Sweden

Your veterinarian can supply advice on the breeds that interest you and help you to answer the final three questions:

What are the positive and negative characteristics of the breed?

Can such a dog adapt to our family?

What are the hereditary or common problems of the breed?

FINDING THE RIGHT DOG FOR YOU

If you have decided that you can afford the time and money to own a dog (and I hope you can), where can you go to select the new member of your family? If a specific breed appeals to you, ask your veterinarian for a list of reputable breeders in the area. You can also check the daily newspapers or the specialty magazines.

If you want a pedigreed pet, avoid outlets. The breeding that produces outlet puppies is often indiscriminate, with no regard for good physical and mental characteristics. Crowding, malnutrition, intestinal parasites, and stress make the puppies vulnerable to many viral and bacterial diseases. The most critical period in the formation of a dog's personality is the first sixteen weeks of life. Outlet puppies are given little love and attention during this time—a tragedy that can affect them for the rest of their lives.

Breeders' home-raised puppies are generally healthy and well socialized because reputable breeders usually follow an established procedure before breeding, during pregnancy, and at nursing that will give the newborns every chance at a healthy and long life. The new puppies are also checked, vaccinated, and wormed (if necessary) by a licensed local veterinarian. Most important, they are handled gently and given lots of love during the critical socialization period.

Breeders' puppies actually cost less, in most cases, than outlet pets, since the breeder does not have high advertising costs and overhead (shipping costs, rent, and employees' salaries). The breeder is not in it for the money but because of a love for fine physical and mental specimens of the breed.

Mutts can be found through newspaper ads, through the neighborhood pipeline, through notices on veterinarians' bulletin boards, or at the local humane shelters. There can be drawbacks to getting a mutt. Since the mother may not have had good prenatal care, the puppies have more "youngster" problems, such as external and internal parasites, and their future temperament is harder to predict unless you can see the home where they were raised and the temperament of the parents. But these are correctable problems, given the help of your veterinarian and a lot of tender loving care and proper training. Remember, "mutts are beautiful!"

The best time to form a human bond with a dog is when the dog is very young, from seven to twelve weeks old. (Anything younger should still be with its mother.) But don't forget that adult dogs, especially at humane shelters, are begging for homes, too. That's where "Sandy" of the Broadway show *Little Orphan Annie* was found.

To help overcome the "They're *all* so cute, which should we take?" syndrome, go through the following checklist:

Is this a good breeder and a good kennel?
Of course, your veterinarian's recommendation is usually adequate, but your own observations are important. A good breeder will keep the kennel clean and orderly. He or she will also be active in dog shows and interested in improving the breed. Do the owners seem to love their dogs? Does the breeder want to know about *you*, your family, and your life-style? A good breeder will not sell his dogs to just anyone. Visit several breeders. This will give you a "feel" for the breed and more information. Be sure to telephone for an appointment. Private kennels are part of the breeder's home and should be respected.

Can we meet the puppy's parents?
Meeting the mother and father will give you some idea of the eventual size and temperament of the puppies. The puppy's parents should be friendly and outgoing, not vicious or shy.

"This is the one we want!"

Select a puppy that seems physically healthy . . .

- no eye or nose discharges
- no black debris in the ears*
- a healthy, glossy coat with no hair loss or reddened, scabby areas
- no fleas* or ticks
- pink gums
- no coughing
- firm bowel movements
- no lump at the belly button (this would indicate an umbilical hernia, which is correctable by surgery or, if small, can be left untreated)

. . . and temperamentally well balanced

- friendly
- responds to your attention
- doesn't mind being held

BUYING A PUPPY

Besides the new puppy, what else should you receive from the breeder at the time of payment? He or she should ask you to take your new pet to a veterinarian of your choice within two days of purchase. The breeder should also offer to let you return the puppy for a refund if it is not in good health.

Purchase Papers

You should receive a **written bill of sale** stating: (a) the aforementioned privilege of return; (b) the date of purchase and any conditions of sale; (c) the price paid; (d) the registration numbers and names of the parents; (e) the litter or individual registration number of the puppy; and (f) its date of birth and description, including breed, sex, and color.

You should also receive **registration papers.** If the breeder has not yet received the papers (sometimes this happens) be sure that the bill of sale states this fact and indicates that the papers will be sent when they are received by the breeder. You should *never* be asked to pay extra for the puppy's registration papers—you have a *right* to them.

Note: In some instances, the breeder may indicate that the puppy is not for breeding purposes and will ask you to sign an agreement to this effect. One copy of the agreement goes to the registry. The breeder is within rights to ask this.

Instructions for Care

The breeder should also give you **written instructions on feeding and care.** Dates of any worming that has taken place, and the type of medicine used, should

---

*The presence of fleas, ticks, or ear mites doesn't necessarily disqualify a puppy for purchase.

be included. You should also receive a statement, signed by a veterinarian, of all vaccinations given and the date of the next scheduled vaccination.

When you take your new puppy home, be sure that it has plenty of time for rest. Have bedding (a blanket or soft pillow), food, and water awaiting your new arrival. Be gentle and patient and always keep in mind your *size*. After all, the puppy has been brought to a strange home to live with "giants," who cannot communicate directly and have new rules. Follow the breeder's instructions for feeding and care until you see your veterinarian. Be sure that you are present when your puppy is with small children. Severe injuries and even death can result from being dropped, hit, or squeezed by a child.

Registries

The American Kennel Club (AKC) is the largest and most widely known dog registry. Its purpose is to "adopt and enforce rules and regulations governing dog shows, obedience trials, and field trials, and to foster and encourage interest in, and the health and welfare of, purebred dogs." Registration does *not*, however, ensure *quality*. As the AKC has stated:

> There is, unfortunately, a widely held belief on the part of the general public that "AKC" of "AKC papers" and quality are one and the same. This is not the case. *AKC registration in no way indicates the quality of a dog.* A registration certificate indicates only that the dog is the product of a registered purebred sire and dam of the same breed. Quality in the sense of "show quality" is determined by many factors, including the dog's health, physical condition, ability to move, and appearance. Breeders trying to breed show stock are attempting to produce animals closely resembling the word description of perfection contained in the breed standard. Many people breed their dogs with no concern for the qualitative demands of the standard (the "model" toward which breeders are striving) for their breed. When this occurs repeatedly over several generations, the animals, while still purebred, can be of extremely low quality in terms of the standard for the breed.

The address of the AKC is:

The American Kennel Club
51 Madison Ave.
New York, NY 10010

The American Field of Chicago, Illinois, registers all breeds but is the main registry for sporting dogs, such as setters and pointers. It also produces the *Field Dog Stud Book*. The United Kennel Club of Kalamazoo, Michigan, registers foxhounds and coonhounds.

Outside the United States, the Canadian Kennel Club is the Canadian version of the AKC. Still operating today, The Kennel Club of England was the forerunner of the North American kennel clubs. It was founded in 1873 by a group of well-known dog fanciers. The Prince of Wales, who later became King Edward VII, was a patron.

Chapter 2

The Owner's Home Physical Exam:

Your Dog's Body and How It Works

A veterinarian often hears a pet owner's surprised exclamation, "You mean that my pet has [diabetes, jaundice, leukemia, etc.]! Why, I didn't even know that [cats, dogs, parakeets, etc.] had a [pancreas, liver, kidney, etc.]!" Yes, pets *do* have the same organs in the same locations, and those organs can malfunction. The same diseases are seen in humans, dogs, and cats—and even in birds, guinea pigs, and snakes.

There is nothing more awe-inspiring than the way a body is put together (*anatomy*) and the way the parts function by themselves and in cooperation with the rest of the body (*physiology*). Even that fly or ant that visits your picnic lunch has a heart and intestines. So what does all this have to do with your dog's health? Health (yours and your pet's) is precious. You should know how the body is put together and how it functions so that you can respect it and do your best to prevent illness. For example, giving your dog a steak bone to chew is disrespectful to its stomach and intestines since, if the bone is swallowed, it can cause serious injury. Vomiting, bloody diarrhea, or constipation may result. A more serious, life-threatening complication, such as an intestinal obstruction, can also occur.

You and your dog share more similarities than differences. You have less body hair, no tail, and a thumb, and you walk on two legs; but this is just about where the physical differences end. People do have more complex thinking centers in their

15

brains (which, it seems, they often don't use very well) but dogs leave human beings far, far behind in the development of the senses of smell, hearing, and sight. Many people go through life without developing these senses to their greatest ability—and some never use them at all. So who is "smarter" in "feeling" life—you or your dog?

The normal appearance and functions of your pet's body should be studied so that by using the Decision Charts and by doing a brief physical exam, you will be better prepared to know when to treat your dog at home and when to see your veterinarian.

It's a good idea to examine healthy dogs about once every six months. If your dog doesn't seem to feel well (see How Do I Know When My Dog Is Sick? page 33), it's advisable to run through it again.

SKIN

A wrapping of fur is not all there is to your dog's skin. It is also a factory for vitamin D production; it protects the internal parts from injury, bacteria, and viruses; and it contains a sensory system that is unsurpassed in efficiency. The network of skin nerve cells goes to work when your dog is cold, has a cut, or receives a pat on the head. In cold weather, the hairs stand erect and form air pockets that will insulate against the cold.

Healthy skin and hair coats are flexible, glossy, and free of excessive oiliness, redness, dandruff, scabs, eruptions, or parasites (see page 165). Run your hand against the hair coat and check for growths or blemishes. There should also be no areas of hair loss. Each dog has its own shedding cycle, which may change from year to year. Some pets shed a small amount all the time, while others may lose large clumps at various intervals. Don't be concerned unless the skin Decision Chart indicates a problem.

Pets can have freckles, concentrations of cells containing the brown pigment called *melanin*. These can be found anywhere on the skin and even in the mouth. Be sure to check the skin's special alterations: the mammary glands, the footpads, the claws, and whiskers.

The *mammary glands* are located on the abdomen. You will see five pairs of nipples. The mammary glands of nursing females enlarge and produce milk tailor-made to the needs of their new puppies. Females experiencing a false pregnancy (see page 231) can have enlarged breasts and produce milk. Once your female dog has passed seven years of age, routinely *palpate* (feel gently) each gland to check for lumps (see page 184). See your veterinarian if you find any.

Check your dog's paws. The thick, pigmented, tough *footpads* are excellent shock absorbers. The pads are named for their location. Pets have sweat glands in the footpad area. If your dog gets excited at the veterinarian's office, you may see sweaty pawprints on the exam table. Check the spaces between the digits. Since your dog walks barefoot and this is a very moist area, the interdigital area can be easily irritated and infected by briars, stones, foxtail, sand, and salt (for melting snow).

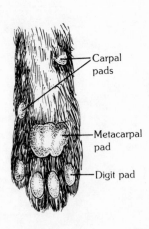

Carpal pads

Metacarpal pad

Digit pad

Whiskers (*tactile hairs*) are long, stiff hairs located on the muzzle, upper eyelids, cheeks, and legs. They are used as feelers and are especially handy for navigation at night or in dark areas.

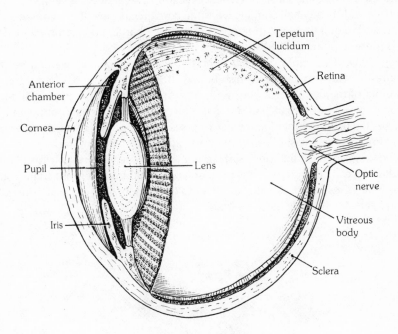

EYES

No other organ in your dog's body contains such an intricate and complex mechanism in such a small structure as the eyes. Without their eyes, your pet's ancestors would not have been able to avoid predators or to capture their food.

The first parts seen when examining your pet's eyes are the upper and lower eyelids—specialized curtains that protect the eyes. Eyelashes are located primarily on the edges of the upper lids. Examine the eyelids; they should be smooth and sharp. The eye margin should not turn in (*entropion*) or turn out (*ectropion*). Be sure the eyelashes and hairs on the nose (especially of Shih Tzus, pugs and Pekingnese) do not rub the eyeball. Sometimes these hairs can be distorted and misdirected and can irritate the eye.

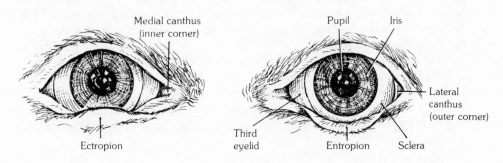

By pulling up on the upper eyelid or pulling down on the lower lid with your thumb, a smooth, pink tissue, called the *conjunctiva*, can be seen covering the inner surface of the lids and continuing onto the eyeball. The conjunctiva helps lubricate the eyeball and protect it from infection. The space between the eyelid conjunctiva and the eyeball conjunctiva is the *conjunctival sac*. If the conjunctiva is red and swollen or if there is a green or yellowish discharge, an inflammation of the tissue is present (see page 188).

Dogs have a structure called the *third eyelid*, or *nictitating membrane*, that contributes to tear formation and distribution. It is light pink and is located at the inner corner of the eye. In sick pets, and sometimes even in healthy pets, the third eyelid may cover more than half the eye. "My pet's eyeball has disappeared," is sometimes the first thought of an owner who sees the third eyelid covering the eye. Don't worry—the eye is still resting comfortably under the membrane.

A gland located on the inner surface of the third eyelid occasionally enlarges. This is known as "cherry eye." It is not dangerous, although it looks frighteningly serious. Mild cases respond to antibiotic-steroid ointment, but surgical removal of the gland is necessary if it stays enlarged.

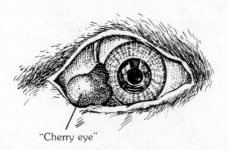

"Cherry eye"

The *cornea* is the clear "front window" of the eye that bends the incoming light rays. The cornea can lose its clarity if it becomes inflamed or injured. Hairs and twigs can injure the cornea, especially in pop-eyed dogs.

The *sclera* is the fibrous coat that gives the eyeball its ping-pong-ball shape and dull white color (this is often called the "white" of the eye). The sclera frequently takes on a yellow color (*jaundice*) in dogs with liver problems.

The *iris* controls the amount of light entering the back of the eye and gives your pet's eye its color. The black hole in the center of the iris is the *pupil*. It *dilates* (gets larger) to let more light enter in dim light and *constricts* (gets smaller) in bright light. Shining a bright light in one eye should constrict both pupils. The pupils should be the same shape and size.

Light rays enter the eye's fluid-filled *anterior chamber*, pass through the pupil, and are further bent by the lens as they continue their journey through the *vitreous body*, a transparent, jelly-like substance that keeps the eyeball firm. The light rays finally hit the "heart" of the eye—the *retina* at the back. This membrane has over 100 million light-sensitive cells, called *rods* and *cones*. These cells set off a flurry of electrochemical activity that transmits the image to your dog's brain by way of the *optic nerve* in about two-thousandths of a second. That's traveling!

Your dog's retina contains a remarkable wedge of reflector tissue, the *tapetum lucidum*. The tapetum makes it possible for your dog to see better than humans in dim light. Light rays are reflected off the tapetum and back to the light-sensitive cells. The bright green *eye* reflection seen in dim light is the tapetum.

Cataracts, white opacities that block the light's passage through the *eye,* can be seen by shining a bright light in the pupil of affected pets. A normal aging process called *senile cataracts,* in which the pupil of older pets takes on a blue-white hue, does not interfere with vision. Senile cataracts, or *nuclear sclerosis,* is caused by a rearrangement of the fibers and a loss of water in the older lens.

Nasolacrimal (tear) canal

Tears cover the eye with each blink. They keep the eyes moist and help protect them from foreign objects, bacteria, and viruses. Tears are formed by the secretion of glands located around the inner lids and behind the third eyelid. They drain from the *eye* through a canal system that runs from the *medial canthus* of the *eye* to the nostrils. (This is why your nose runs when you cry.) The blockage of these canal openings by debris or by an eyelid turning in (*entropion*) can cause excessive tearing (*ephiphora*) and brown staining of the hair around the *eye.*

EARS

A dog's superb hearing ability begins with the sound-gathering flap called the *pinna.* The inner surface of the pinna and the beginning of the ear canal (which you can see) should be a light pink. You may see a small amount of yellow wax and a few

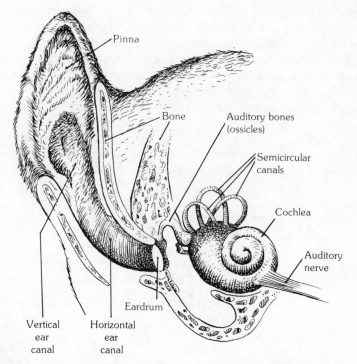

hairs at the canal opening. These act like flypaper, trapping dust, insects, or other potential irritants and guarding against infection. If this area is reddened, foul-smelling, or has a puslike or brown, waxy discharge, an ear infection may be present (see page 190). Your veterinarian can check the rest of the ear with an *otoscope*, a special instrument equipped with a light source and magnifying lens.

The ear canal is L-shaped, going down (*vertical canal*) and then in (*horizontal canal*). The *eardrum* is at the end of the horizontal canal. Sound waves travel down the canal and beat against the eardrum—like a stick beating a drum. The vibrations are amplified in the *middle ear* by three small bones called the *auditory ossicles*, which pass the sound on to the *inner ear's* snail-shaped and fluid-filled *cochlea* via the *oval window* (a vibrating membrane). The waves produced in the cochlea are converted to electrical messages that travel to your pet's brain via the *auditory nerve*. Above the cochlea are three small, fluid-filled *semicircular canals*. These loops of tubing contribute to your dog's remarkable sense of balance.

THE CIRCULATORY SYSTEM

The hardest worker in your dog's body is the heart. It is a top-of-the-line, four-chambered model (just like the human heart) that actually consists of two pumps. The right side of the heart receives the blue blood (depleted of oxygen) that has already dropped off its cargo of oxygen and nutrients and has returned with waste products, such as carbon dioxide, by way of the veins. This blue blood is pumped through the lungs to receive fresh oxygen and to remove the carbon dioxide. The

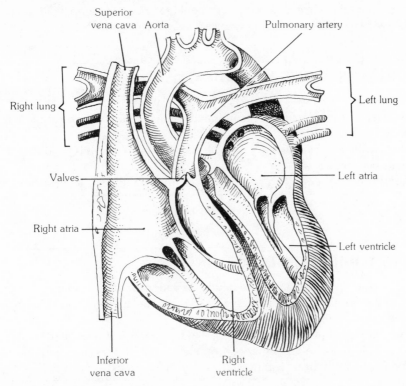

Superior vena cava — Aorta — Pulmonary artery

Right lung

Left lung

Valves

Left atria

Right atria

Left ventricle

Inferior vena cava

Right ventricle

blood then returns to the left side of the heart and is pumped out through the arteries to the trillions of cells in your pet's body.

The normal heart beats about 80 to 100 times per minute in a resting dog. You can feel the heart beat by placing the palm of your hand against your pet's chest, near the left elbow (see Taking Your Dog's Heartbeat, page 22). You may hear the "lub-dup" of the normal heart valves closing by placing your ear there. Panting and breathing may make it difficult for you to hear even with a stethoscope, which you can purchase at a medical supply store. The heart receives its oxygen by way of two branching *coronary arteries* that are about the width of a piece of spaghetti. Fortunately, dogs do not have heart attacks (sudden blocking of the coronary arteries), but after eight years of age they often develop a problem with the heart *valves* (flaps that control the passage of blood through the heart's chambers): The valves do not close properly, and the heart must work harder to pump the blood. It may even fail unless treated with digitalis-like drugs. Your veterinarian (or even you, by using your stethoscope) will detect a heart *murmur* when the valves are closing improperly. A "zsa" sound may be heard between the "lub-dup" of the regular heart beat: "lub-zsa-dup." The regurgitation of blood around "sick" valves is responsible for the "zsa" sound. Not *all* heart murmurs are serious problems. Your veterinarian is the best judge.

The *pulse* and *capillary refill time* will give you some indication of how well the heart and blood vessels are maintaining your pet's blood pressure (see Taking Your Dog's Pulse, page 22). When you press your finger against your pet's gums and then lift it away, the white area produced should return to the normal pink color in one second. This indicates that the capillaries are refilling with blood.

TAKING YOUR DOG'S HEARTBEAT

- Place your palm over your dog's left chest wall.
- Hold this position for fifteen seconds and count the number of beats felt in that time.
- Multiply the number by four. EXAMPLE: 30 beats in 15 seconds $= 30 \times 4 = 120$ beats per minute.
  Note: A normal dog heart rate should fall in the range between 80 and 175.

TAKING YOUR DOG'S PULSE

- Place your fingers lightly in the middle of your pet's upper inner thigh.
- Hold this position for fifteen seconds and count the number of beats felt in that time.
- The number of pulse beats should equal the number of heartbeats.
  Note: The pulse should be easier to detect if the heart is pumping strongly, and fainter if the heart is pumping weakly (as in shock).

What are the *capillaries?* These microscopic vessels serve as the unloading dock for new goods (oxygen, nutrients, antibodies, hormones) and the loading dock for the waste products, such as carbon dioxide. The capillaries are like tiny streams that connect two large rivers (arteries and veins). The capillaries are so tiny that *red blood cells* (the delivery trucks loaded with oxygen) have to travel single file through them. The *white blood cells,* which are important in preventing and fighting infections, and *platelets,* which are vital to patching leaky blood vessels and initiating the clotting mechanism, also flow through these tiny streams. The fluid that keeps all the cells and other components floating is called *plasma.*

The *lymphatic system* is a great helper to the heart and blood vessels. It filters out invaders and transports to the bloodstream, in a watery substance called *lymph,* the *antibodies* and *lymphocytes* produced in *lymph nodes.* These components protect your pet's body against invaders such as bacteria, viruses, and even cancer cells. Three pairs of lymph nodes that may be examined are the *tonsils, prescapular nodes,* and *popliteal nodes.* These may enlarge during infections or in *lymphosarcoma* (leukemia—see page 253). They may be difficult to find, so on your next visit ask your veterinarian to show you where they are. The tonsils are housed in pouches—one on each side of the throat entrance. They are the throat's watchdogs, ready to gobble up any bacteria or viruses with bad intentions. Tonsils rarely have to be removed. Enlargement of the tonsils is usually not a good reason for removing them.

THE RESPIRATORY SYSTEM

Dogs, like people, need to gather oxygen from the air and to expel carbon dioxide (a waste product of metabolism). The *respiratory system*, consisting of the nose, mouth, larynx, trachea, bronchi, lungs, diaphragm, and chest muscles, makes it all possible.

The normal *rate of respiration* is ten to thirty breaths per minute. *Panting*, an increased respiratory rate (as high as 300 breaths per minute), is the primary way that your dog can sweat and thus lower body temperature. Panting is seen in hot weather, after exercise, with lung disease, and even with pain or excitement. Notice also your pet's respiratory *rhythm*. The chest should expand (*inspiration*) and contract (*expiration*) with no difficulty.

A dry, hot nose or a moist, cold nose is not a reliable way to determine your pet's health, but the discharge, if any, might be an indicator of illness. Normally, there is a slight, clear, watery secretion from your pet's nostrils. A bloody or thick yellowish, white, or greenish nasal discharge is abnormal.

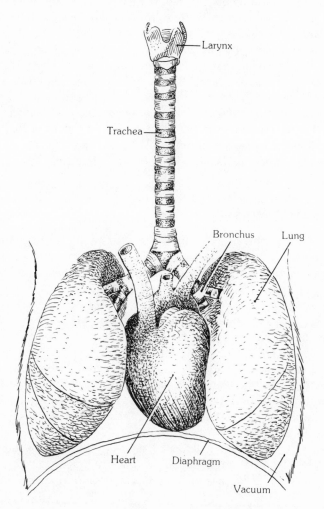

A light pink color to the gums indicates that your pet is getting enough oxygen. A blue or muddy red color to the tongue and gums indicates a serious problem in the respiratory or cardiovascular system. (Chows, by the way, have tongues that are blue; this is normal.) Pale gums may indicate anemia.

The *larynx* (Adam's apple or voice box) can be felt as a hard structure at the top of the windpipe—the same location as the human voice box. The larynx produces your dog's snarls and barks by vibrations of the *vocal chords*.

Air passes through the larynx into the breathing tubes: the windpipe (*trachea*) and its smaller divisions, the *bronchi*. The air is warmed and filtered of dust, bacteria, and viruses by the microscopic hairs and mucus in these tubes until the air finally reaches its destination—the lungs. Your veterinarian uses a stethoscope to hear the passage of air in the breathing tubes and lungs. *Percussion of the chest* is useful in an examination of the respiratory system.

All that dirty air passing down the breathing tubes must be cleaned. The mucus that traps the dust, bacteria, and viruses is expelled through your pet's *cough reflex*. Occasionally, your dog will cough up some mucus. Although owners frequently confuse this with vomiting (expelling food from the digestive system), it's just normal "housecleaning" (see Coughs, page 198), so don't get alarmed.

The lungs don't have any muscles. They expand only when your dog's chest expands and the *diaphragm* (a muscular divider between the chest and abdomen) moves backward. This creates a slight vacuum in the chest, and air is sucked into the lungs. When your dog exhales, the lungs collapse and blow out the carbon dioxide. If air leaked into the vacuum chamber (a condition called *pneumothorax*), or if a tear in the diaphragm allowed intestines to enter the chest cavity (a condition termed *diaphragmatic hernia*), your pet would have a very difficult time breathing. These conditions happen frequently when pets are hit by cars.

THE DIGESTIVE SYSTEM

The most finicky and most delicate part in your pet's body *has* to be the digestive system. Throughout your dog's lifetime it will remind you both that it won't stand for any foolishness. Spicy foods, bones, pieces of wood, and any other garbage will cause a fit of vomiting and/or diarrhea that will send you running to the Decision Charts!

Your dog's digestive system is a food processor par excellence. It puts the Cuisinart® to shame! Not only does the digestive system chop, pulverize, blend, grind, and emulsify food, but it converts carbohydrates, fats, and proteins into easily digested molecules that are then handed over to the bloodstream and lymphatic system for delivery to your dog's cells for energy, growth, and tissue repair.

Digestion begins when food enters your dog's mouth. The tongue positions the food for the shredding and tearing action of the teeth and mixes the food with the saliva to start the digestion of carbohydrates.

Open your dog's mouth as described on page 83. The tongue should be smooth and pink, with no lumps, sores, or discolored areas, although it can be freckled. An exception to the pink rule is a chow's tongue, which is normally a bluish color.

Your pet's teeth are used for protection and for grasping, cutting, and crushing food. Your puppy doesn't have teeth at birth. The "baby" (*deciduous*) teeth appear between two and five weeks of age. The permanent teeth begin replacing the "baby" teeth at four months of age. Dogs have four types of teeth: *incisors, canines, premolars,* and *molars.* The teeth should be white, and the gum line should be pink, not swollen or red (*see* Mouth Odor, page 200).

Some dogs fail to lose all their "baby" teeth (especially an incisor or canine) by eight months of age. In that case, you may see a double tooth. The "baby" tooth should be surgically removed, since it produces a good location for food entrapment and infection and may cause misalignment of the adult teeth.

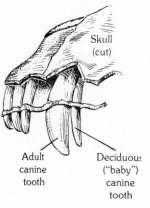

Skull
(cut)

Adult
canine
tooth

Deciduous
("baby")
canine
tooth

A normal bite in dogs has the upper incisors slightly overlapping the lower incisors. A slight overbite (a more marked overlapping) or an underbite (the lower incisors overlap the upper incisors) doesn't seem to cause any problems.

The rest of the digestive system cannot be seen, but with some practice you may be able to palpate some of the organs. Remember, palpate *gently* to avoid injury.

After your dog swallows, the food enters a muscular tube, the *esophagus,* through which it is transported to the stomach by coordinated waves called *peristalsis.* Dogs, since they sometimes eat odd things and fail to chew, can occasionally get blockages in the esophagus, caused by bones, fish hooks, small toys, etc. Early diagnosis and treatment are a must since a perforation in the esophagus can cause a fatal pneumonia. Persistent gulping, difficulty in swallowing, regurgitating (not vomiting) food ("it just seems to come right back out") and excessive salivation are some early signs.

The stomach is the chief active partner in the digestive system, churning food and making it acceptable for the intestines. When your pet's stomach is full of food (or full of gas) it may feel like a doughy bag (feel behind the last rib on the left side). The puppy's stomach can distend considerably after a meal, and this is not necessarily a sign of disease or worms.

Although the liver is the largest organ in your pet's body, it cannot be palpated well in the normal dog because it nestles under the rib cage, probably because it has hundreds of jobs to do and can't be interrupted. The liver makes the proteins that provide strength for your dog's playful jumps, manufactures the clotting agents that stop the bleeding of a cut, and is very important in fat and sugar metabolism. In addition, the liver is the "great detoxifier"—purifying toxins and drugs in your dog's system—and it recycles the bodies of dead red blood cells. Some of its products are used to make new red blood cells; others are used to make *bile,* the green digestive juice stored in the *gall bladder* that, at mealtime, is released to the intestine through the bile duct to help break large fat molecules into smaller ones. Liver disease or the rapid destruction of red blood cells will release large amounts of bile into the blood stream, producing *jaundice* and staining the eyes, gums, and skin yellow.

The *pancreas* resides behind your dog's stomach and also can't be palpated easily. The first job that the pancreas undertakes is to neutralize the acids in the soupy gruel that the stomach passes on to the intestines. These acids are no laughing matter; they could inflict serious damage to the intestines if not neutralized. Your dog's pancreas also produces an impressive array of enzymes that are important in sugar, fat, and protein digestion. If the pancreas becomes inflamed (as in

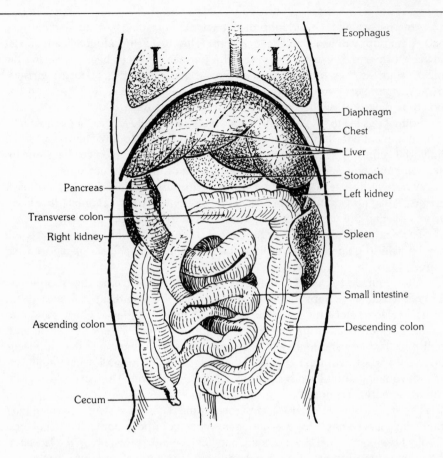

pancreatitis), some of these enzymes leak from the cells into the bloodstream. The pancreas is best known, however, for its manufacture of *insulin,* which ensures that all your pet's cells get *glucose,* a simple sugar, for their energy needs.

All nutrients are absorbed in the *small intestine,* which then passes them to the bloodstream and lymphatic systems. By gently grasping the abdomen between the thumb and fingers, you may feel the small intestine as a slippery tube. In larger dogs, place one hand on each side of the abdomen and slowly and gently press in with your finger tips. The last stop on the way is the *large intestine,* where water is extracted for your pet's use and the *feces* (the stool) become firmer. You may be able to feel the large intestine by gently palpating high in the posterior abdomen. Any problems in this organ can produce diarrhea, sometimes mixed with blood or mucus (see page 210).

All indigestible material has to leave the body by way of the *anus.* The entire trip takes about twenty hours. Your pet's normal feces should be firm and brown in color. If the feces are loose, black, clay-colored, bloody, streaked with mucus, have a foul odor, or are extremely large in volume, see the Decision Chart, page 211. Anal sacs are discussed on page 216.

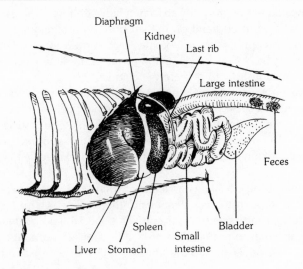

THE UROGENITAL SYSTEM

Your pet's urinary system is the main waste-disposal plant. The paired kidneys clean and filter the blood continuously as it passes through them. It regulates the amount of salt, potassium, and water that is needed in the body. The excess is passed on with the waste products of metabolism through two tiny tubes called *ureters* to the storage tank, the *bladder*. When your pet's bladder fills with enough urine, a signal is sent to the brain for your pet to head for the nearest tree or ask to be let out. The urine exits to the outside by a thin tube called the *urethra*, located in the vagina of the female and the penis of the male.

The one important time for you to examine your pet's urinary system at home is if your dog is straining to urinate or has blood in the urine (see page 218). A large bladder accompanied by frequent attempts to urinate is a very serious problem.

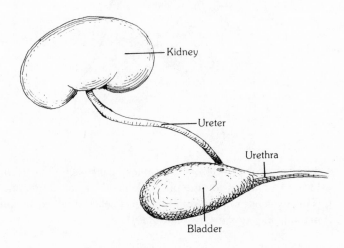

The bladder is located in the posterior abdomen between the rear legs. Using *very* gentle pressure, with your left hand on the left posterior abdomen and your right hand on the right posterior abdomen, you may feel a firm, round ball that varies in size from a ping-pong ball to an orange. During your next visit, you should ask your veterinarian to show you how to palpate the bladder.

The sperm factories of your male dog are the *testes*. There should be two testes located within paired sacs called the *scrotum*, situated between the thighs. The testicles should be present in the scrotum at birth. If only one testicle is present, your pet is called a *monorchid;* if neither testicle is in the scrotum, your pet is a *cryptorchid*. This condition is hereditary (see page 252) and may be the source of a tumor in later life.

When your male dog ejaculates, millions of sperm (enough to repopulate the whole world) travel through the *vas deferens* to the urethra, where a very special fluid from the *prostate* mixes with the sperm. This special fluid contains proteins, fats, sugars, and enzymes to nourish and protect the fragile sperm on their hazardous journey out of the penis and up the female's reproductive system to meet the egg.

The male dog's *penis* is housed in a *prepuce* (foreskin) on the belly, just in front of the rear legs. To examine the penis, stand on the dog's left side and place your right hand between your dog's rear legs. Push forward and, at the same time, pull the fleshy fold backward with your left hand. The dark pink penis should appear at the opening of the prepuce.

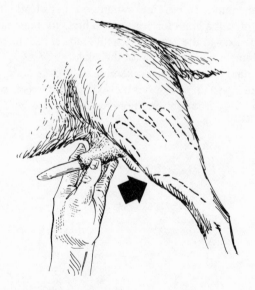

Every veterinarian receives one or two panicky calls each year from worried owners who just found a "tumor" on the penis. Actually, it's a normal part of your dog's anatomy. This swelling, seen during mating, is called the *bulbus glandis*. It is responsible for maintaining the *tie* (see page 230).

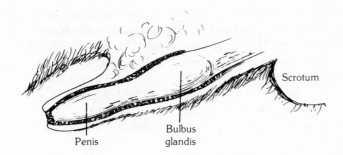

Scrotum

Penis

Bulbus
glandis

   The only readily visible portions of the female dog's reproductive system are
the soft, pliable *labia* (lips of the *vulva*) that form a vertical slit a few inches below
the anus. By gently separating the lips, the pink *vestibule* of the vagina is seen.
Urine exits through the urethral orifice located inside the vestibule.
   Again, the internal parts of the female dog's reproductive system are the same
as in the human: ovaries, fallopian tubes (or *oviducts*), uterus, cervix, and vagina.
The paired ovaries produce eggs and female hormones. The eggs are delivered to
the thick-walled uterus through the small, coiled fallopian tubes. After ejaculation,
the male's tadpole-like microscopic sperm, their tails whipping furiously, must swim
a long distance (equivalent to humans swimming about thirty miles), up the vagina
and through the opening of the muscular cervix. Once in the uterus, there is no
guarantee of making contact with the eggs waiting there.

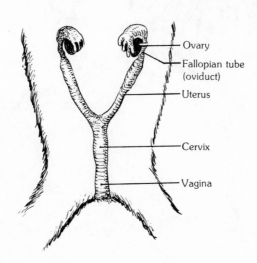

Ovary

Fallopian tube
(oviduct)

Uterus

Cervix

Vagina

THE MUSCULOSKELETAL SYSTEM

Without the support and protection of bones, your dog would collapse into a pile of fur and skin. Most of the two essential minerals calcium and phosphorus are stored in, inventoried by, and distributed when needed from the bones. Without calcium, your pet's heart could not beat, nor could the nerves conduct messages. When your dog is pregnant or nursing, the need for both these minerals is at a peak, to aid in the growth of the fetuses and in milk production (see page 41). Also, old, tired red and white blood cells must be "retired," so replacements are constantly and enthusiastically manufactured by the bones' spongy marrow and sent out into the bloodstream.

The grouping of the 250-or-so bones and the joints, under command of the nervous and muscular systems, makes it possible for your dog to run, jump, and scratch its fleas. The joints of the *cervical* (neck) bones are also very flexible.

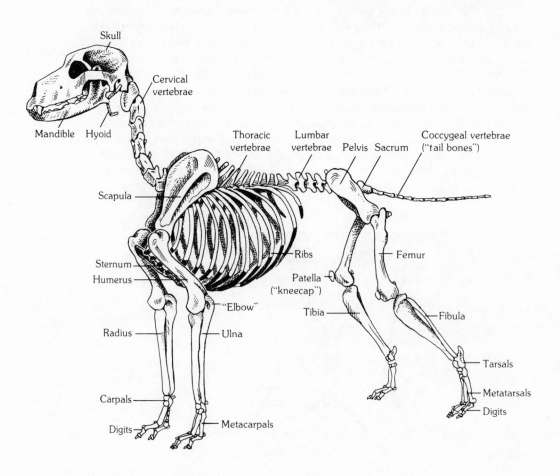

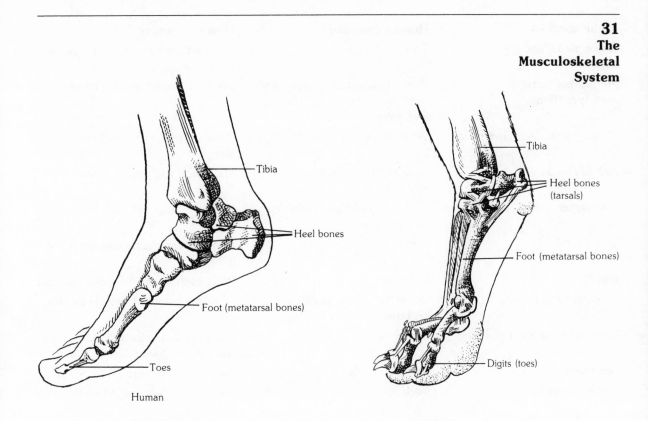

Human

Dogs walk on their "finger tips" and "tiptoes." If you got down in this position, you would find that almost all your bones, muscles, tendons, and ligaments are in the same positions as your pet's. For example, in this position, your heel would be sticking up in the air. Well, so does the "heel" of your dog's rear legs.

The most important time to examine your pet's musculoskeletal system is when you see a lameness (see page 158). If your pet has a lame front leg, its head will bob up when that leg touches the ground; the head will bob down when a sore rear leg touches the ground. A shorter stride and lighter touch are usually seen in the sore leg.

If you notice a lame leg, take the dog's temperature first, since the cause may be a bite wound that has formed an abscess. In that case a fever of 104° to 105° may be seen (see page 182). If the temperature is normal, start the exam. You will be looking for swelling or pain by gently pressing on the bones with your finger or moving a joint. Your pet will exhibit pain by crying or pulling the leg away. If you think you've found a painful area, repeat that part of the exam again to see if you get the same reaction.

To examine the individual areas of your dog's skeletal system, you may find it helpful to locate your own corresponding bones and/or joints first. The chart on the following page is a handy guide to follow. Remember to be gentle.

To be checked	Human equivalent	How to examine
Digits, pads, and spaces between	Toes and fingers	Press on each bone and move each joint
Metacarpal bones and *metatarsal* bones	Bones between the fingers and wrist and between the toes and ankle	Press the length of each bone
Carpal bones and *tarsal* bones	Wrist and ankle	Press on each bone and move each joint
Achilles tendon	Attached between heel bone and muscle	Make sure the tendon is taut
Radius, ulna, tibia, and *fibula*	Forearm bones and lower leg bones	Press the length of each bone
Elbow joint	Same	Press on each bone and move the joint
Patella	Knee cap	Press each bone and move the joint
Humerus and *femur*	Upper arm bone and upper leg bone	Press the length of each bone
Shoulder joint and hip joint	Same	Move the humerus and femur back and forth in their respective joints
Scapula	Shoulder blade	Press on each bone
Cervical bones	Neck	Press each bone and move the neck up and down
Spine	Same	Press the length of the spine and all projections (*dorsal spines*)

That finishes the skeletal system exam. If your dog exhibits pain at any point, by crying out and/or pulling away, repeat that step of the exam to double-check the reaction.

The muscles, after receiving messages from the nerves, move the bones, blink the eyes, and wag the tail. These are the skeletal muscles that your dog can consciously move. Two special types of muscles work day and night involuntarily. The heart (*cardiac*) muscle contracts with less than one-half-second rest between beats throughout your dog's life. Smooth muscle tissue, which moves food along the digestive tract day and night, is also primarily involuntary.

THE NERVOUS SYSTEM

Your dog's brain, the "central computer," coordinates the heavy traffic of messages received from inside and outside the body with the activities the body can perform, via the network of nerves and the spinal cord. The brain is, in fact, your dog. The nervous system, one of the primary controllers of the body's activities, can adjust your pet's body very quickly to environmental and internal changes.

THE ENDOCRINE SYSTEM

People's and dogs' bodies alike contain small chemical factories tucked away in ob-scure corners. These are the *endocrine glands*, whose specialty products are *hor-mones* (from the Greek word meaning "to arouse to activity"). Hormones regulate chemical reactions. The endocrine system primarily regulates processes of long duration, such as growth and reproduction.

Malfunctions of endocrine glands, such as *diabetes* (see page 152), *hypo-thyroidism* (see page 154), and *Cushing's syndrome* are seen frequently in pets. Cushing's syndrome, an overactive adrenal gland, is seen frequently in poodles, dachshunds, Boston terriers, and boxers that are over eight years of age. These dogs will drink a lot more water, urinate excessively, have a symmetrical pattern of hair loss (producing equal bald spots on boths sides of the body or legs), become weak, and get a pot belly. Dogs that are on continuous long-term corticosteroid therapy can also develop Cushing's syndrome.

Many endocrine disorders cause characteristic skin changes. See your veteri-narian if your dog is over eight years of age and has symmetrical hair loss or bald spots but does not scratch. The skin in these areas often becomes brown. Most endocrine disorders are treatable. Your veterinarian will have to perform blood tests and a urinalysis to make the specific diagnosis.

HOW DO I KNOW WHEN MY DOG IS SICK?

The following signs should indicate to you that something is not right:

- Your dog's behavior changes—it becomes less active and withdrawn.
- Your dog exhibits a change in appetite that lasts for a few days. Loss of appe-tite (*anorexia*) or increased appetite (*polyphagia*) may indicate disease.
- Your dog is urinating more or less than normal.
- Your dog exhibits either vomiting or diarrhea for an extended period. Fluid is lost during vomiting and diarrhea, and *dehydration* (depletion of body water), a serious situation, can result.

Is Your Dog Dehydrated?

Pick up a fold of skin in the middle back area. If it snaps back rapidly, your pet is not dehydrated. If it stays up or returns slowly, dehydration is present. Do not test the skin in the neck area; this is normally loose in many animals and will give you false results. If dehydration is present, your doctor will find the underlying cause and will give fluids *intravenously* (in the blood vessel) or *subcutaneously* (under the skin) to replace the water lost.

Is Your Dog in Pain?

Lameness, a stiff neck, reluctance to get up or lie down, or tense abdominal muscles are indicators that your pet is in pain.

What Is Your Dog's Temperature?

A normal temperature is from 101.0°F to 102.5°F. Anything higher indicates a problem that *needs professional attention* (*see* Fever, page 140, for more information). To use a thermometer, follow these steps:

TAKING YOUR DOG'S TEMPERATURE

- To take your dog's temperature, use a *rectal* thermometer, which has a rounded, stubby tip. Shake it down first by holding it between your thumb and index finger and snapping your wrist.
- Apply vaseline or mineral oil to the bulb.
- Restrain the dog (see page 89). *Note:* It is advisable to have someone hold the back end of your pet while you hold the tail and the thermometer, so that your pet cannot move from side to side or up and down and break the thermometer.
- Lift the tail, gently slide the thermometer into the anus, and leave it in for three minutes.
- Remove the thermometer and read the mercury level.

Chapter 3

Keeping Your Dog Healthy, Happy, and Obedient

A dog that is groomed regularly, fed properly, trained well, travels nicely, and sees its veterinarian on schedule for vaccinations, parasite control, and dental care should have a happy and healthy life.

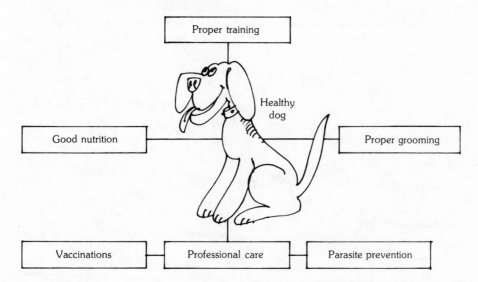

NUTRITION

What is good nutrition and why is it so important? Nutrition is the process of using or transforming food into living tissue. Without a complete and balanced diet, your dog will not grow properly, reproduce, maintain the health of all its body tissues, or fight infection.

The "Great Food Hunt"

Your dog's hunt for a complete and balanced daily food intake is made much easier than its ancestor's hunt of thousands of years ago, thanks to commercial pet foods. The sound of the can opener or the jumbling of the dry food in the bag will awaken the beast inside your dog—it will run from the comfy carpet near the fireplace to the kitchen to devour its neatly packaged and completely nutritious "prey." Your dog's ancestors had to go "shopping." The game they caught provided everything: Protein came from muscle tissue; fats, vitamins, and minerals from organs and bones; carbohydrates were extracted from the vegetable and cereal matter left in the game's digestive tract. Vegetables and cereal starches aren't required by dogs, but they do provide calories and bulk.

Years of research and development by the major pet food companies have produced complete and balanced foods for your modern dog. These products, which are excellent from weaning to old age, eliminate the need for homemade diets that are time-consuming and expensive to prepare and may lack important nutritional requirements. The following discussion will focus on (a) the composition of food, (b) the types of pet foods, (c) how much to feed at different stages of your dog's life, and (d) the advantages and disadvantages of each type of commercial pet food.

FOOD FOR THOUGHT

Fuel needed to keep the heart pumping, the chest expanding, and the legs running is provided by the breakdown of carbohydrates, fats, and proteins. The amount of

energy provided by molecules is measured in *kilocalories* (or *calories*). Fats provide the most energy per unit molecule. Carbohydrates, proteins, fats, vitamins, minerals, and water must be supplied in adequate and balanced amounts. Pregnant or lactating dogs, growing puppies, and all heavily-exercised pets may require up to twice as much energy as the inactive pet.

Carbohydrates

Use	For energy
	For bulk (indigestible cellulose)
	Fiber absorbs water; this bulk stimulates intestinal movements and can prevent constipation
	Spares proteins; since carbohydrate is used for quick energy, protein can be used for body growth and repair
Sources	Primarily well-cooked cereal grains, cellulose, starch, sugars
Amount needed	No more than 65 percent (on a dry weight basis).
	Note: The milk sugar *lactose* may cause diarrhea in many pups and adult dogs, since the amount of *lactase,* an enzyme that breaks up the sugar molecule, may be low
	The large lactose molecule pulls water into the intestines and causes diarrhea
	Remedy: Use little or no milk or milk products if diarrhea develops
	Try yogurt, which has a lower lactose content

Proteins

Proteins are composed of *amino acids,* some of which (*essential* amino acids), cannot be manufactured by the body and must be supplied in the food. Eggs, soybeans, milk, fish meal, and muscle meat contain all the essential amino acids and are therefore said to be of high biological value.

Use	For growth
	Healthy tissue repair and maintenance
	Formation of antibodies that fight infection
	Formation of enzymes and hormones that help in body's chemical reactions
Sources	Meat, eggs, fish, vegetables (especially soybeans), milk and milk products, yeast
Amount needed	About 23 percent (on a dry weight basis)
	Note: Do not feed raw white of egg
	This binds up *biotin* (a B vitamin), which is necessary for growth, but cooked eggs or raw yolk are very good protein sources

Fats

Use	Provide more than twice as much energy per unit molecule than carbohydrates or protein (9.1 calories per gram)
	Transport vitamins A, D, E, K (the fat-soluble vitamins)
	Provide fatty acids (e.g., linoleic) for a healthy skin and hair coat
	An important taste factor (such as marbling in steak)
Sources	Commercial dog food has generally adequate amounts
Amount needed	About 5 percent

Note: If your dog has a dry, lusterless hair coat and scaly skin, consult your doctor

Sometimes the addition of vegetable oil (corn or safflower) is beneficial, but excess oil can decrease the food intake and retard growth

Consult your doctor before starting supplements

Vitamins

Chemically known as *coenzymes,* vitamins are essential for life but are needed in very small quantities. A balanced diet should not let a deficiency develop.

Use	For normal body functioning
Sources	Supplemented commercial pet food has generally adequate amounts

Note: Prolonged diarrhea or vomiting can cause a loss of water *and* water soluble vitamins (such as the B vitamins), which should be replaced with supplements

Minerals

Use	For normal body functioning
	For bone development
Sources	Commercial dog foods have adequate amounts of sodium, potassium, iron, and calcium

Note: Do not use unprescribed calcium-phosphorus preparations

If the calcium-to-phosphorus ratio is altered by unneeded supplements or by an all-meat diet (too high in phosphorus), severe skeletal problems result

Water

Water is essential. It is obtained from the process of *metabolism* (especially of fats) of the foods and liquids that your dog ingests. Your dog also needs constant access to clean, fresh drinking water.

Dogs need about 25 ml. (¾ oz.) water per pound of body weight daily. Lactation, fever, hot weather, exercise, and water loss from vomiting or diarrhea will increase your pet's need. Dry foods (only 10 percent moisture) will increase your pet's water intake, while canned foods (75 percent moisture) will decrease the amount of water it drinks. *Note:* Do *not* allow your pet to drink water from unsanitary sources, such as stagnant pools or streams and toilet bowls.

	Dry	Semimoist	Moist (canned)
Advantages	Most economical	Convenient to feed	Very palatable
	Easy to feed	Very palatable	
	Excellent for self-feeding (see below)	Easily stored	
	Easily stored	No refrigeration needed	
	No refrigeration needed	Convenient to use when traveling	
Disadvantages	None	Expensive	Expensive
		Good taste may lead to overeating	Must refrigerate leftovers
			Spoils if left in bowl all day
			Good taste may lead to overeating
How to feed	Self-feeding—leave daily ration in bowl; dog will eat whenever hungry	Divide daily ration into two equal feedings for less chance of digestive upset	Divide daily ration into two equal feedings
	May be moistened with water or with semimoist or canned food		May be mixed with dry food (up to 25 percent of total daily intake)

Feeding Your Puppy

Since puppies need more calories and more protein, the adult maintenance diets are not adequate. Use any of the complete and balanced commercial foods made especially for puppies, but feed the pup three times daily until six months of age and twice daily thereafter. If you use the dry puppy foods, your job is much easier—just leave the daily amount in the bowl (moistened with water if you like) for self-feeding. If puppy foods are not available, you can supplement the adult

Weight (in pounds)	Calories needed
1	125
5	500
10	850
20	1400
30	1800
40	2300
50	2700
70	3600

maintenance foods with eggs, cooked meat, yogurt, and milk, if it doesn't cause diarrhea. Of course, your puppy should always have access to fresh, clean water.

Feeding Your Adult Dog

Use the following table as a general guide, since each dog's metabolism and amount of daily exercise will change its nutritional needs, as will pregnancy, lactation, and hunting. Being kenneled outside in cold weather increases the number of calories needed to maintain body heat. If your pet is neither too thin nor too fat, is alert and active, and has a glossy hair coat, its diet is adequate. If your dog gets too thin or too fat, increase or decrease the amount of food. *Note:* If your pet gets thin, obese, inactive, or has a dry hair coat, it may *not* be diet-related; use the Decision Charts or call your doctor.

The idea that dogs and bones just naturally go together is a popular one, but I do not recommend it. Bones (especially chicken, pork, and steak bones) splinter easily and can cut the intestines to shreds. If your puppy is teething, or if you have a pet who likes to chew on forbidden items (plants, for instance), try substituting rawhide bones or Nylabones®. If you have to give your dog a bone, use only marrow or knuckle bones that you have first boiled (to remove diarrhea-causing fat and any germs). Take it away as soon as it starts to splinter.

Weight (in pounds)	Calories needed	Dry (cups)*	Daily feeding Semimoist (6 oz. package)†	Canned (16 oz. can)‡
5	250	¾	½	½
10	450	1	¾	1
15	600	1½	1	1¼
20	700	2	1½	1½
25	800	2½	1½	1½
30	900	3	1½ to 2	2
40	1200	3½	2 to 2¼	2½
50	1400	4	2½	3
60	1600	4½	3 to 3⅓	3
90	2100	6	4	4
120	3000	9	5½	6

*These estimates are based on an 8 oz. measuring cup (which, by the way, holds less than 8 oz. of food).

†One 6 oz. package equals about 500 calories.

‡One 16 oz. can equals about 500 calories.

Feeding Your Pregnant Dog

The pregnant dog's nutritional needs (energy and protein requirements) will not increase drastically until the last trimester of pregnancy, which begins on the thirty-fifth day. The fastest growth and calcification of the fetus occurs during this period.

At two weeks, start to increase its food intake by 20 percent. Supplements of cooked eggs, cooked liver, cooked muscle meat, milk, and yogurt are good. At delivery time, the food intake will be 50 to 60 percent higher than the maintenance level.

A high-protein commercial food or supplemental proteins of high biological value (cooked eggs, cooked liver and meats, milk, or yogurt) are very important in late pregnancy to assure a good milk supply.

The fetuses occupy a large area of the abdomen. As pregnancy progresses, the mother's digestive tract will be able to handle only smaller, more frequent feedings.

Feeding Your Lactating Dog

A well-balanced commercial dog food should supply adequate nutrients. Your dog's appearance and milk production are the best indicators of nutritional status; if you notice any change, try supplementing the diet with high protein foods such as milk products and cooked eggs. *Note:* Supplements of vitamins and minerals *should* be given to heavily lactating dogs with large litters.

Although the content of the mother dog's diet won't alter much, the amounts eaten will. A general rule is to feed an additional 100 calories per pound of puppy (you can weigh the babies on an ounce or gram scale). By the end of the nursing period, the mother may be eating three times the prebreeding level (*see* Nursing Period, page 236).

Feeding Your Old Dog

Time passes very quickly. Soon you'll find that the little ball of fur you played with on the living room rug twelve years ago is slow in getting around and stays close by your side as if every minute counted. In old age, everything in the dog's system becomes less efficient. Fewer calories are needed because your old pal is less active and the metabolic rate is slower. The digestive process and absorption of food take longer. If your dog is getting fat, too many calories are being fed, so decrease the daily ration. Unless your dog is a self-feeder, smaller, more frequent feedings will help the old dog digest and absorb the food better. See Special Diets below for further information.

Special Diets

The major pet food companies have special diets for dogs afflicted with the following: allergies, gastrointestinal trouble, kidney or heart problems, and overweight. Your veterinarian will recommend a special diet if your pet's medical condition will benefit from it. *Note:* It is best to avoid any table scraps, especially if they are fatty or highly-spiced. By feeding table food with commercial pet food, you are unbalancing a balanced diet that the pet food industries have spent years perfecting.

VACCINATIONS

In 1879, Louis Pasteur coined the word "vaccination" (from the Latin word for cow), when he realized that his research was based on the same principle that Edward Jenner, an English physician, had observed almost 100 years previously. Dr. Jenner found that cowpox could be used to protect humans against smallpox. Pasteur went on to develop a rabies *vaccine* by drying the spinal cords (thus making the virus noninfectious) of rabbits infected with the rabies virus.

Years later it was discovered that the invading agents, viruses and bacteria (also called *antigens*), cause the body's lymphocytes to produce *antibodies* that fight these foreign invaders. It was also discovered that antigens could be chemically modified to lose their disease-producing quality while still triggering the production of antibodies to fight the disease. The chemically modified antigens together are called an *attenuated vaccine*, and this is what your pet receives in the injections from the veterinarian.

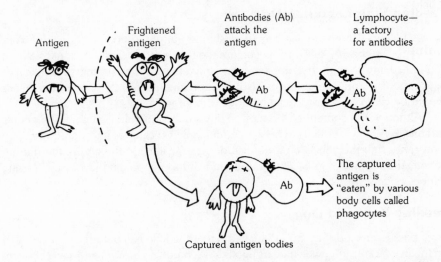

Captured antigen bodies

The body's *amnestic response* ("memory") is the basis for the series of vaccinations given to puppies and for the yearly boosters. Each time a vaccination is given, the body "remembers" its prior experience with these antigens and therefore produces a successively higher number of antibodies (thus affording more protection). Boosters, usually at yearly intervals, are essential to keep the "memory" (and the antibodies) at peak level. (Some dog rabies vaccinations are given at two- or three-year intervals.)

Your pet's immune system must be in good working order to respond to the vaccine. Any stress, such as external or internal parasites or malnutrition, can decrease your dog's manufacture of antibodies. Treating the parasites (see page 47) and correcting the malnutrition (see page 36) are essential for successful vaccinations.

Puppies receive actual antibodies (*passive immunity*) to *canine distemper* while still in the uterus and from the "first milk." These antibodies help protect your puppy for six to twelve weeks after birth. Although they can sometimes interfere with the vaccine, the puppy series of vaccinations should still be initiated early.

On rare occasions, a puppy can get the disease while still receiving the series. It is usually a result of the virus infecting the puppy before the vaccine becomes effective. In some instances (also very rare) the puppy is genetically incapable of producing the necessary antibodies.

The vaccinations should be given only by a *licensed* veterinarian. He or she will use vaccines approved by the Animal Health Inspection Service of the U.S. Department of Agriculture (in Canada and England, by their equivalent departments). All the vaccines are tested for safety and potency. If your veterinarian gives the vaccination, you can be assured that the vaccine was manufactured by a reputable company, that it was refrigerated properly during and after delivery, and that it will be administered to your pet with proper care. *Note:* It is a good idea to sit in the reception area of the hospital for five to ten minutes after the second and third shots, since occasionally a puppy may suffer a severe allergic reaction (collapse and shock). If this happens, an emergency intravenous injection of *epinephrine* (and possibly oxygen) is necessary.

Canine Distemper

What is the nature of the illness?	A viral disease seen in dogs, raccoons, skunks, and foxes
	It does not cause "bad temper"
What are the signs?	Loss of appetite
	Fever
	Diarrhea
	Puslike discharge from nose and eyes
	Coughing
	Pneumonia
	Twitching
	Convulsions
How is it spread?	Airborne transmission
	Direct contact with an infected animal
What is the treatment?	Antibiotics, fluids, forced feeding, anticonvulsants, oxygen (if needed), and vitamins are used in supportive therapy
	With intensive supportive therapy, the cure rate can be 50 to 90 percent
	A permanent twitch or occasional seizure may remain, but the dog can lead a normal life
How is it prevented by vaccination?	Attenuated vaccine is used
	The puppy series begins at six to seven weeks of age and ends between twelve and sixteen weeks

How is it prevented by
vaccination?
(cont.)

A yearly booster is needed

Note: Pregnant bitches should not be vaccinated,
since the vaccine may injure the fetus

Some dogs are sore and sluggish, refuse to eat, and
are slightly feverish for twenty-four hours after vaccination; no treatment is necessary.

Hepatitis

What is the nature of
the illness?

A viral disease that primarily affects the liver

Seen in all members of the canine family

What are the signs?

Weakness

Fever

Loss of appetite

Bloody vomit and diarrhea

Abdominal pain

Eyes seem irritated by light

Note: Newborn pups may die suddenly with no signs
of disease

How is it spread?

By contact with the urine or feces of an infected dog

What is the treatment?

Antibiotics (to prevent bacterial complications), fluids,
vitamins, and blood transfusions (if needed) are used

Intensive nursing and supportive care are important

The cure rate is about 90 percent

How is it prevented by
vaccination?

Attenuated vaccine is used (usually given in the same
injection as distemper vaccine)

Puppy series begins at six to seven weeks of age and
ends between twelve and sixteen weeks

A yearly booster is needed

Dogs may be sore and sluggish, lose their appetite,
and have a slight fever for twenty-four hours after
vaccination; no treatment is necessary

Occasionally, one to three weeks after vaccination,
"blue eye" is seen: The eye becomes cloudy due to
edema (fluid swelling) of the cornea

This condition usually resolves itself without treatment in one or two weeks

Leptospirosis

What is the nature of the illness?	A bacterialike organism that primarily affects the kidney
	Seen in dogs, rats, and cattle
	Note: Infectious to humans
What are the signs?	Fever
	Loss of appetite
	Abdominal pain
	Vomiting and diarrhea
	Weight loss
	Increased water intake and urination
How is it spread?	By direct contact with the urine of an infected dog
	By drinking or swimming in contaminated water, or by contact with rats
	Note: An infected animal can shed the organism for up to one year after the initial infection
What is the treatment?	Antibiotics (penicillin and streptomycin), fluids, vitamins, and *peritoneal dialysis* may be necessary to give the kidneys time to heal
	Intensive nursing and supportive therapy are important
How is it prevented by vaccination?	Two doses of *bacterin,* usually given in the same injection with the distemper and hepatitis vaccines, are administered at two- or three-week intervals.
	A yearly booster is needed; in high-risk areas, six-month boosters are recommended
	Dogs may be sore and sluggish, lose their appetite, and have a slight fever for twenty-four hours after vaccination; no treatment is necessary

Rabies

What is the nature of the illness?	A viral disease that attacks the brain
	Seen in all warm-blooded animals, *especially* skunks, raccoons, foxes, bats, coyotes, dogs, and cats
	Note: Infectious to humans
What are the signs?	Change in behavior
	Extreme restlessness

What are the signs? (cont.)	Dilated pupils
	Extreme shyness or aggressiveness
	Tendency to bite anything in its way
	Paralysis of throat, causing voice changes, salivation, and an inability to eat and drink
	Paralysis of the lower jaw
	Generalized paralysis, coma, and death
How is it spread?	The bite of a rabid animal (virus-laden saliva enters the wound)
	Airborne transmission in caves inhabited by bats has been reported
What is the treatment?	Animals are not treated because of the public health danger and the high (almost 100 percent) mortality rate
	A few humans have reportedly been cured by intensive supportive therapy
How is it prevented by vaccination?	Attenuated vaccines are used
	The first vaccination is given between three and six months of age; boosters at one year and every one to three years thereafter

Tracheobronchitis
("Kennel cough")

What is the nature of the illness?	A virus is an important factor although a bacteria may complicate the infection
	Seen especially in dogs that were boarded at a kennel or dog show three to five days before coughing began
	Note: Highly contagious among dogs
What are the signs?	Loud, deep, harsh cough, usually followed by an unproductive gag, that gets worse after exercise
	Dog seems alert, active and has no fever in most cases
How is it spread?	Probably airborne transmission and by contact with contaminated surfaces
What is the treatment?	With treatment, the disease disappears in about three weeks—without treatment, in about twenty-one days—therefore, unless there is a fever or the cough is weakening the dog, no antibiotics or cough suppressants are necessary

How is it prevented by vaccination?

An attenuated vaccine is used

Many doctors give this vaccine in the puppy series and then give an annual booster

A booster is also recommended before admittance to high exposure areas, such as dog shows or boarding kennels

PARASITES

A parasite obtains its nutrition from your pet and gives nothing in return except possible illness. This one-sided relationship has been under attack by concerned pet owners, veterinarians, pet food manufacturers, and pharmaceutical companies.

As a concerned pet owner, reading this section and the Decision Charts will make you aware of your dogs' parasite problem (if any), whether you can treat it at home or need to visit your veterinarian, and how to prevent the parasite from finding a home on or in your pet's body. First, let me dispel a few old wives' tales:

1. Garlic does *not* cure worms
2. Dogs do *not* transmit pinworms to children
3. Candy does *not* cause worms
4. Worms do *not* always cause disease (many pets live nicely with their parasites)
5. A thin or always-hungry dog does *not* necessarily indicate worm problems.

The worm medicine sold in pet stores and grocery stores should *not* be used unless your pet has roundworms and your veterinarian has advised you to use it. Since other intestinal parasites may be present, it is wiser to have your doctor check for other worms with a fecal sample. In most cases, the adult dog has developed an immunity to the worms (*ascarids*) killed by this medication, so once-a-month worming is not necessary. One stool sample that is negative for worm eggs does *not* mean that your pet has no worms—the worms may not be shedding their eggs at test time.

Veterinary medicine, the pharmaceutical companies, the pet food companies, and concerned pet owners, through good diagnostic methods, specific medicines, and sound hygiene and nutrition, have made it possible for today's pets to live almost free of parasites on or in their bodies.

Heartworms
(Dirofilaria)

Who gets them?	Dogs, foxes, and wolves
	Note: Human infections have been reported but are rare
	A worldwide problem, heartworms are prevalent in warm and tropical areas and in any heavily mosquito-infested areas
What do they look like?	Slender, white roundworms that are five to twelve inches long
How are they spread?	Transmitted by the mosquito
What is their life cycle?	After biting an infected animal, the mosquito hosts the *microfilaria* (noninfective larvae) in its sucking apparatus, where they become infective in two weeks
	A subsequent bite injects the larvae (baby worms) into the skin of another animal
	The larvae migrate through the body and grow into mature worms in the right heart chambers
	The worms produce new microfilaria and release them into the bloodstream, where another mosquito picks them up
Are there any signs to look for?	Weight loss despite a healthy appetite
	Anemia
	Coughing
	Heavy breathing
	Tires easily
	Swollen abdomen and legs
	Severe heart, lung, and liver damage leading to death
How are they diagnosed?	A blood test is necessary
What is the treatment?	Intravenous injections of *thiacetarsamide* kill the adult worms in the heart

What is the treatment? (cont.)	Your veterinarian may take chest X rays and perform an electrocardiogram to see the health of the lungs and heart before treatment
	The liver and kidney will be checked by blood tests before, during, and after treatment, since the chemical can damage these organs and the dead worms can lodge there
	Careful monitoring during hospitalization will minimize the chance of complications
	If everything has gone well, another drug is given about two months later to kill the microfilaria in the bloodstream
Can they be prevented?	Avoid mosquito-infested areas
	Keep your pet screened from mosquitos at night
	Diethylcarbamazine works well to prevent the maturation of larvae into adult worms (a blood test is a prerequisite for this treatment)

Hookworms

Who gets them?	Dogs and cats
	Note: A few cases of development to the adult stage in the human intestine have been reported
What do they look like?	They are too small to be seen with the naked eye
How are they spread?	The larvae penetrate the skin or are swallowed
	Puppies can be infected while in the uterus or by larvae passing in the mother's milk
Are there any signs to look for?	Severe anemia
	Weakness
	Bloody diarrhea
How are they diagnosed?	Check successive stool samples
What is the treatment?	Medication is necessary
	Note: Medication kills only the adults in the intestine, not the larvae migrating through the body, so two or more wormings are usually necessary to kill all the parasites.
	Recent finding: Hookworm larvae can *encyst* (form cysts) in the muscles and survive for long periods of time, and medication is not effective against this stage.

Can they be prevented?	Keep environment sanitary
	Remove feces from your yard
	Wash concrete runs often, with salt or sodium borate (borax), if possible, which may be helpful in killing the eggs and larvae.
	Note: These chemicals can damage or kill grass and other vegetation
	If hookworms are a serious problem in your area, a hookworm preventative called *styrylopyridinium* can be given to your dog daily; ask your doctor

Protozoan - Coccidia

Who gets them?	Dogs and cats
	Note: Mature animals usually build up immunity to this parasite
What do they look like?	They are too small to be seen with the naked eye
How are they spread?	Infected animals shed the parasite in their feces
Are there any signs to look for?	Bloody diarrhea
How are they diagnosed?	Check successive stool samples
What is the treatment?	Sulfa drugs are effective
	Time (allows immunity to develop)
Can they be prevented?	Good sanitation is essential

Protozoan - Toxoplasmosis

Who gets them?	Dogs and cats
	Note: Highly infectious to humans, and birth defects can result from infection
What do they look like?	They are too small to be seen with the naked eye
How are they spread?	The *oocysts* ("egg-sac" stage) are introduced by eating infected raw meat, rodents, or birds, or handling the feces of infected animals
What is their life cycle?	The parasite multiplies in the wall of the intestine
	Sometimes the parasite will spread to other parts of the body
Are there any signs to look for?	Fever
	Loss of appetite
	Weight loss

Are there any signs to look for? (cont.)	Weakness
	Vomiting
	Diarrhea
	Breathing difficulties
	Coughing
	Anemia
	Jaundice
	Note: Most infections do not develop signs or else the signs are very mild
How are they diagnosed?	Special stool and antibody tests
What is the treatment?	Sulfa drugs are effective
Can they be prevented?	Do not feed your dog raw or undercooked meat
	Wash hands well after handling raw meat
	Pregnant women should wear gloves when gardening where an animal may defecate

Roundworms
(Ascarids)

Who gets them?	Dogs and cats
	Note: Young children (especially under age four) may become infected with the larvae (a rare disease, called *visceral larva migrans*), which can move to the eye, liver, lungs, or brain, causing blindness, pneumonia, or other problems
What do they look like?	White, round worms, coiled into disks that may grow three to four inches long
	They may appear in the stool or in vomit
How are they spread?	The worm eggs are introduced by licking infected ground or eating infected insects or mice
	Puppies can be infected by larvae passed in the mother's milk
What is their life cycle?	The larvae migrate through the liver, lungs, and trachea on their way to the small intestine
	About a month after being swallowed, they reach sexual maturity and start reproducing
Are there any signs to look for?	Potbelly
	Thinness
	Dry hair coat

Are there any signs to look for? (cont.)	Vomiting
	Diarrhea
	Coughing (as the larvae migrate through the lungs and breathing tubes)
	Note: Adult animals can develop an immunity and show no signs of infection
How are they diagnosed?	Check successive stool samples
What is the treatment?	Medication is necessary
	Note: Medication kills only the adults in the intestine, not the larvae migrating through the body, so two or more wormings may be necessary to kill all the parasites
Can they be prevented?	Keep environment sanitary
	Remove feces from your yard
	Wash concrete runs often
	Control mice and cockroaches
	Have your veterinarian check at least two or three successive stool samples of a new pet and worm your pet, if necessary

Strongyloides

Who gets them?	Dogs and cats
	Note: This parasite can penetrate the skin of humans and cause intestinal problems
What do they look like?	They are too small to be seen with the naked eye
How are they spread?	The free-living parasites burrow through the skin
What is their life cycle?	They migrate through the internal organs on their way to the small intestine
	Strongyloides attach to the wall of the small intestine and when sexually mature, shed larvae in the feces
Are there any signs to look for?	Loss of appetite
	Pneumonia
	Bloody diarrhea
	Weight loss
	Weakness
	Skin infections can also occur from skin invasion
	Note: Younger pets have the more serious signs

How are they diagnosed?	Check successive stool samples for the larvae
	Note: When getting a stool sample, be sure not to include any soil, which has free-living worms that look like strongyloides but don't cause disease
What is the treatment?	A drug called *thiabendazole* is effective
Can they be prevented?	Keep environment sanitary
	Remove feces from your yard
	Wash concrete runs often, with salt or sodium borate (borax), if possible, which may be helpful in killing the eggs and larvae
	Note: These chemicals can damage or kill grass and other vegetation

Tapeworms

Who gets them?	Dogs and cats
	Note: There have been a few reported cases of children getting tapeworms from swallowing infected fleas
What do they look like?	Live tapeworm segments are off-white and flat and move in a back-and-forth motion
	They may be seen attached to the hair around the anus, in the stool, or on bedding
	The dried-out segments look like rice granules or sesame seeds
How are they spread?	The larvae are introduced by eating infected insects (fleas) or mammals (rats and mice, rabbits, or raw fish, beef, or pork)
What is their life cycle?	The tapeworm matures in the intestine
	When sexually mature, the segments, loaded with eggs, detach and pass out the anus
Are there any signs to look for?	Weight loss
	Occasional diarrhea
How are they diagnosed?	Check successive stool samples
	Note: Examination of a segment can reveal the *source* of infection
Can they be prevented?	Control flea infestation
	Keep your dog away from rodents
	Do not feed your pet raw meat or fish

Whipworms

Who gets them?	Dogs
What do they look like?	They are very thin and threadlike, less than an inch long, and shaped like a whip
	They are hard to detect with the naked eye
How are they spread?	The eggs are introduced by licking infected ground
What is their life cycle?	The baby whipworms emerge en route to the intestine
	When mature, they attach themselves to the lower intestinal tract and begin to reproduce
Are there any signs to look for?	Severe, bloody diarrhea, streaked with mucus
	Weakness
	Anemia
	Weight loss
How are they diagnosed?	Check successive stool samples
What is the treatment?	Medication is necessary
	Two or more wormings are usually required to kill all the worms
Can they be prevented?	Keep kennel area dry
	Keep environment sanitary
	Remove feces from your yard
	Wash concrete runs often, with salt or sodium borate (borax), if possible, which may be helpful in killing the eggs and larvae
	Note: These chemicals can damage or kill grass and other vegetation

BASIC TRAINING

Keeping your dog healthy starts with proper training—of both you *and* your dog. You need to be trained in order to make your dog a good citizen and to lessen the chances of seeing your veterinarian for traumatic encounters (auto accidents, fights), foreign body obstructions, poisonings, or obesity. Proper training can help you avoid many of these problems.

Seven to twelve weeks of age is a critical time in a puppy's mental and social development with humans. This is the time when the strongest bond between dogs and humans is formed. Before seven weeks of age, the pup was in the world of its mother and littermates, where it received food, warmth, and consolation. The pup learned the ways of the dog world through play and interaction with its brothers and sisters.

After seven weeks of age, the pup will depend on you to meet its needs. Give your pup a lot of affection and demonstrate that you want it to share your life. Let adults and children hold it and play with it and your puppy will become well-adjusted to people.

A puppy has an overwhelming desire to please and to gain your approval. There is no dishonesty in a puppy's heart. You should give the puppy no less of yourself. This is the time to begin teaching your pup its name and simple commands, such as "No," "Sit," "Stay," and "Come" (see the specifics later on in this section). Only one family member should be the teacher, and this person should be someone who will be spending a lot of time with the dog and who is patient and affectionate. The other family members should not be present during the training sessions. The lessons from seven to twelve weeks should be playful, with no discipline involved, since the pup is still very young and easily frightened and confused. You need to develop "animal sense," to put yourself in the puppy's place. Besides, you want your pup to like "school" and to learn out of a desire to please.

Try to "feel" the communication with your puppy through eye contact, and watch its body motions. Dogs "talk" with their eyes, facial expressions, and tails. Any subtle changes are important to learn, and not for training alone: they may also be the first sign that your dog is not feeling well. Observe your pup closely and you'll be speaking dog language in just a few weeks.

Your pup learns by the repetition of simple words—or more accurately, their sounds. The tone of your voice and your body motions should *always* be consistent. When you say "Come, Sheba" and "Good girl!" use a pleasant tone of voice and give lots of affection and approval if your dog responds appropriately. Repeat this often until it has become second nature. The lessons should last only about ten minutes. Remember, most of the time is just playing with the pup.

At twelve weeks of age discipline begins. By now, your pup should feel comfortable with you and its new home and will do almost anything to please you. Like a two- or three-year old child, your pup will now also start to test you to see what it can get away with. A firm "No" should correct any bad behavior, such as chewing furniture or clothes, which usually accompanies the teething stage (four to eight months of age). However, some physical punishment may be necessary to rein-force the word. In this case, a firm spank on the rear or a shake of the scruff of the neck works well. It is best to not let your pup see the hand that hits it. Three impor-tant points:

1. Do *not* hit your pup around the head unless you want to raise a hand-shy dog.
2. Do *not* call your pup by name and then discipline it. Always walk over to the pup for discipline. Calling the pup's name should only be for good things. Therefore, your hand and the pup's name are pleasant associations.
3. Stop the physical punishment as soon as the word "No" is effective or you will have a severely neurotic dog.

Housebreaking

This is, naturally, one of the first things you'll want to teach your pet. Two watch-words for this period are patience and praise. Patience will get you through the al-most-inevitable accidents (remember, your puppy's just a baby); praise, given at the right times, may help avoid the inevitable. I've found it easier to housebreak in two stages: training the puppy to paper, which generally takes a few weeks, and then moving it outside, which will take about a month. However, you can skip the first stage and take your puppy straight to the outdoors, if you'd like.

Paper training

This will be easier if the puppy is limited to one room and if the room has an easy-to-clean floor—a kitchen is great. Place several layers of newspaper over the entire surface of the floor in this room. When your puppy soils it (and how can it miss?) give some praise. Remove *only* the top, soiled layers of the newspaper—the paper underneath retains the scent to remind your puppy where to go next time (that's why several layers are needed).

Gradually limit your papering to smaller and smaller areas of the floor. If you catch your puppy in the act away from the paper, scold it ("No!") and put it back on the paper. *Note:* Don't bother disciplining your pet for accidents you don't witness; the discipline is effective only when the "crime" is still in progress.

Moving outside

While still in the paper stage, start taking your puppy outside on a leash. Do it first thing in the morning, after naps and meals, and last thing at night. Go to the same place every time. Take along some soiled newspaper to give your puppy the right idea. If nothing happens, have patience; if something does, praise is definitely in order.

For this stage, it's important to know your puppy's signals. Look for floor scratching, walking in circles, crying, or sniffing—they usually mean a trip outside is needed.

"Sit!"

This is the next thing to be taught and it's pretty simple. All you do is gently push your puppy's rear end down toward the floor while saying the command "Sit!"

Keep repeating this procedure, using the same tone of voice. When your puppy sits, lavish it with praise. Don't scold if your pet doesn't catch on quickly. Keep everything light and lots of fun.

"Stay!" and "Come!"

Once your dog has mastered the art of sitting, you can start with harder commands. For these two, a six-foot leash with a choke collar will come in handy. Attach the collar and leash and make your dog sit at your left side. Now raise your palm to the dog and say "Stay!" Holding the leash, walk *slowly* away, turning often to raise your palm and repeat the command. If your dog starts to follow you, say "No!" and make it sit again.

When your dog obeys the command for the distance of the leash, it's time to teach the second half: Squat down, tug on the leash, and say "Come!" Praising your dog's performance will reinforce the lesson. Practice the "Come!" command off the leash, as well.

"Heel!"

Again, use a six-foot leash with a choke collar. Attach the collar, but shorten the leash so that there is just a little play in it between your hand and the collar. Have your dog stand beside you on your left—not slightly forward or behind—and step off with your left foot. At the same time, give a slight jerk to the shortened leash and say "Heel!" Walk slowly and your dog will learn faster. And don't forget the praise when the training session is over.

There are several good books on training dogs. I especially recommend the following:

1. *City Dog*, by Richard A. Wolters (New York: E. P. Dutton, 1975)
2. *The Pearsall Guide to Successful Dog Training*, by Margaret and Milo Pearsall (New York: Howell Books, 1973)

GROOMING

Regular grooming of your dog consists of hair treatment, bathing, nail trimming, ear cleaning, and dental care.

Hair Treatment

Different coats need different strokes: The combing or brushing needs vary according to the length and coat type. In general, comb short-haired dogs once or twice a week with a grooming glove. Longer coats need bristle, wire, or card brushes, and pet combs with rounded teeth that avoid irritating the skin. Comb out long-haired dogs before you bathe them.

Long-haired dogs often have matted hair (from infrequent brushing and combing) behind their ears and under their legs. This should be pulled gently apart and combed out.

Many breeds of dogs need regular clipping and stripping. You can learn to do it at home or find a professional groomer, who should be gentle and have a clean and odorless establishment. Ask your neighbors and friends for recommendations.

Start the brushing and combing early (about twelve weeks of age) and keep gentle and patient, and this will be an enjoyable and healthy experience for you and your pet.

Bathing

Dogs need baths just as humans do, because tongues are *not* adequate cleansing tools. Since the oils come back in the hair and skin within twenty-four hours, bathing could be done as often as necessary, but once every month or two is adequate.

Start bathing your puppy at fourteen weeks of age (sooner if it gets very dirty—just avoid chilling it) so that it will be accustomed to regular baths. The *best* way to bathe is to make your pet comfortable and to make it a game. No noise and slow motions will ease your job. Before placing your pet in the sink or bathtub, fill it with a small amount of warm water (running water will only scare your pet). In warm weather, bathe your dog outside using a garden hose. While talking quietly and stroking and petting your pup, place it in the warm water. Continue the petting motion and wet your pet with a soft spray hose attached to the faucet or use the water in the tub. The same petting and stroking can be used to lather the shampoo (preferably a good pet shampoo or "no tear" baby shampoo) into the hair coat. It is a good idea to first protect the eyes with a few drops of cod-liver oil or ophthalmic ointment and the ears with a small wad of cotton. Rinse with a soft spray hose attached to the faucet, still stroking, petting and talking to your pet. Rinse thoroughly since dried soap can irritate the skin. A creme rinse or hair conditioner can then be used to make the hair softer and more manageable for combing out. Don't forget to remove the cotton from the ears!

Towel dry your pet and continue all the ploys you used for the bath. The noise of a hair blow-dryer disturbs most animals, but you can try it later—*after* your pet is accustomed to baths. Make the whole experience pleasant and playful. A dog treat would definitely be in order after a successful bath.

Nail Trimming

Start trimming the nails at twelve weeks of age to accustom your pet to this important grooming practice. Dogs that exercise on a hard surface, such as a concrete run, usually keep their nails worn down so that they don't touch the ground. Long nails can get caught in carpeting, grow into the footpad, or cause your pet to stand improperly. The dewclaw (equivalent to the thumb) does not touch the ground and needs more frequent trimming.

You can trim your dog's claws with a "Resco" or a "White" nail clipper. Trim just in front of the pink area, or *dermis*, which contains nerves and blood vessels. If the nail is dark and the pink area cannot be seen easily, shine a bright penlight through the nail to see where the dermis begins. Otherwise, just trim the nail as it curves down.

A nail trimmed too short will bleed. A styptic pencil or direct pressure with gauze or a clean cloth will stop the bleeding.

Pink area

Resco nail clipper

Ear Cleaning

Many owners neglect proper ear care and are made aware of its importance only when their dog "smells funny." Then they look in the ear and discover an infection (see Ear Discharges, page 190).

The wax in the ears should be cleaned once a month (more often if your dog has a history of ear problems). Clean only that part of the ear canal that you can see; otherwise, you may damage the eardrum. Use a cotton swab soaked in mineral oil or alcohol. Wax protects the ear canal, so a small amount left behind is beneficial.

The hair in the ears should not be plucked unless there is so much hair that it impedes air circulation. If your doctor feels this is necessary, use your fingers to remove only the hairs that come out easily. Plucking can expose the hair follicle to bacteria, so be careful. Some doctors recommend an antibiotic ointment after plucking to prevent infection.

TRAVELING WITH YOUR DOG

Dogs travel well if you plan ahead. If you start them traveling while they are still puppies, they'll grow into well-adjusted adult travelers. Start with frequent short trips in the car. Soothing talk, loving strokes, and gentle playing will help give your pet confidence that nothing terrible will happen.

Be sure your dog always has an identification tag on its collar or harness when traveling. For extra assurance, your pet can also be safely tattooed with identification marks. In addition, your dog should be in good health, with all vaccinations up to date.

One more general rule: Try to make reservations at hotels or motels that allow pets.

By Car

Do *not* feed your dog for six hours before the trip, and if carsickness is usually a problem, remove access to drinking water two hours before departure. (If needed, *Bonine*® or a medication prescribed by your veterinarian can be used to counter motion sickness.) Always let your pet urinate and move its bowels before you start out. On long trips, plan for regularly scheduled exercise and water breaks. Feeding should be done at the final stop.

Take your dog's favorite food and bedding along. If feasible, take water from home as well, since the different mineral contents of water in new locations can give your pet diarrhea.

Note: Do *not* keep a leash on your pet in the car. The leash can get caught on door handles and other projections and cause serious injury. If you leave your dog in the car in hot weather, be sure that at least one window is open for good ventilation (*see* Heatstroke, page 124).

By Plane

When traveling by air, prior coordination with the airline will smooth things considerably. Each company has different procedures, so call in advance to find out what you need to do. In any case, follow the feeding, water, and motion sickness guidelines listed for travel by car. If traveling to a foreign country, contact the nation's nearest consular office to get any further instructions.

Generally, the airline will request (a) to see a health certificate for your dog; (b) that the dog travel in an approved carrier (available from the airline or from a pet store); (c) that both animal and carrier have proper identification tags, showing your name, address, and telephone number and your dog's name; and (d) that you check in at least one hour before departure. Some airlines will allow the carrier to travel with the passengers, under your seat.

BOARDING YOUR DOG

A good boarding kennel should be clean, relatively quiet, and well ventilated. The staff should treat boarders gently. Your veterinarian will be able to recommend a good place, if he or she does not have boarding facilities.

In general, you should call for reservations at least one or two weeks in advance (allow more time around holidays). Your dog must be healthy—all vaccinations up to date—and it should have an identification tag or tattoo. The staff should also ask for your veterinarian's name and telephone number and for a way to reach you in case of emergency.

If, on your return, you find that your dog has diarrhea, you might request that the kennel feed its regular, at-home diet the next time you board there. Also, a mild tranquilizer might be helpful—but first discuss this with your veterinarian.

Chapter 4

Going to the Veterinarian

Throughout your dog's life, veterinary attention—from vaccinations to laboratory tests, from radiology (X rays) to surgery—will be needed. In this chapter, I will discuss some of the encounters that your pet will have with the veterinarian. Guidelines will be provided to help you choose a veterinarian to meet your dog's needs.

THE "G.P." AND SPECIALISTS

A local professional will probably be able to handle all your dog's health needs throughout its lifetime. This person will be your dog's family doctor or general practitioner, although sometimes he or she will have an advanced degree in a veterinary specialty, such as internal medicine. It takes four years of premedical or preveterinary education and four years of veterinary school for a person to become a veterinarian. Recently, internships and advanced degrees in over twenty specialties have become available to the twenty-two veterinary schools in the United States.

Solo Practice

The typical local veterinarian works very hard and is usually available when needed—like the physician in "the good old days"—although of course he or she takes time off for personal activities and to attend veterinary meetings. However, if

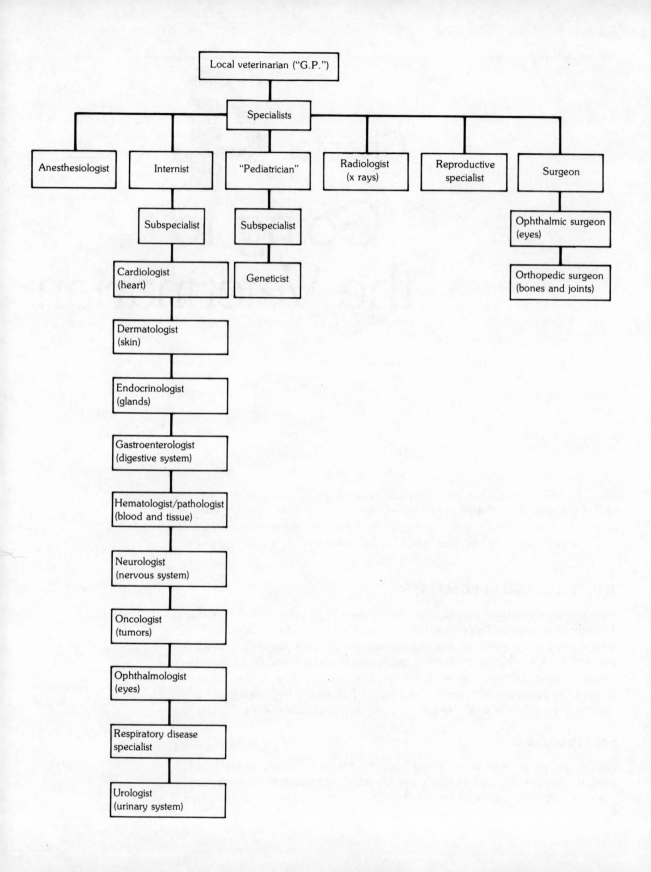

your local veterinarian is a "solo practitioner"—a veterinarian without partners —you may not always be able to see him. Upon reaching your veterinarian's answering service, you may be referred to another professional who is "on call" for the emergency group.

Group Practice

Veterinary group practice—a few doctors practicing in one building, or a central hospital with satellite out-patient clinics—has become a popular arrangement for veterinary care in the last few years. The sharing of night calls and weekend coverage, the reduction of office costs by shared expense, the availability of consultation, and a more medically stimulating environment for the veterinarian all contribute to its increased popularity. The larger group practices may have a few specialists associated with them.

Referrals

Veterinary medicine is just like human medical care: Sometimes the local doctor needs a specialist's expert help. If your local veterinarian feels that your dog has an especially serious or puzzling medical or surgical problem, you and your dog will be referred to a specialist in the area. Most specialists are found in group referral practices—for example, a cardiologist, an orthopedic surgeon, and a neurologist working together—or at veterinary schools. Most specialists complete three or more years of training after graduation from basic veterinary school. If your dog needs to see a specialist, your veterinarian will write a letter of introduction for you and provide a copy of your dog's complete medical and surgical history.

The types of veterinarians available for your dog's care can be grouped as shown on the opposite page.

EVALUATING THE VETERINARIAN

Selecting a veterinarian deserves the same consideration as choosing your own family physician. Ask your neighbors, friends, local dog breeders and groomers, or even your own general practitioner for a recommendation.

The most important factor in the selection is your confidence in that person. To help you select and evaluate your veterinarian, consider the following points:

1. **Is the office clean and well equipped?**
2. **Is the doctor on an appointment system?**

This reduces your waiting time considerably, makes the reception area less crowded, and makes your doctor less rushed.

3. **Can you take a tour of the clinic at a convenient time for the doctor or the staff?**

Most veterinarians will be proud to show you their facilities.

4. Does the veterinarian take an appropriate medical history?

All veterinarians have been trained to organize background information in a logical, concise, and accurate way. This is called "taking the medical history," and it is extremely important to good veterinary care. A history is divided into the major problem(s), the present illness, a review of the systems, and the past medical history. Emergencies (such as injuries), simple problems, and well-pet exams (vaccinations) may not require many questions by the doctor.

The Major Medical Problem(s)   Before your visit, write down all the problems that your dog is having so that you won't leave out an important detail. The major medical problem should be expressed as the *title* of your story:

"Ralph has been urinating more than usual and drinking a lot more water."

Identify each problem without unnecessary details and let the doctor pick up from there.

The Present Illness   Your veterinarian will want to establish the progression of the present illness. This means that you must observe your pet very carefully at home so that you can provide all the relevant information. Again, organize your thoughts so that all the important facts are given:

"Three days ago, Ralph began drinking a lot more water. In fact, I had to fill up a 100 oz. bowl three times during the day. Now Ralph [yes, I *do* see female pets with "male" names] is drinking six bowls of water daily. Her appetite is unsatisfied, though, and she keeps begging for food. She asks to go out to urinate every half an hour, even during the night. She also began wetting on the kitchen floor. I didn't see any blood in the urine. I took her temperature when all this started, and it was normal."

Other information that may be useful is any medication that your pet took before and during the present illness. Bring the medications (or their names) with you. If X rays or laboratory tests had been performed for past illnesses or for the present illness at another veterinarian's office, have the results phoned or sent to your present veterinarian. If your dog is allergic to any medication, make sure the doctor knows this.

The Review of Systems   Your veterinarian will ask you specific questions related to the skin, heart, lungs, stomach, intestines, urinary system, muscles, bones, nervous system, eyes, ears, nose, and throat. These questions will help your doctor determine which systems are involved in the present illness.

The Past Medical History   In many cases, previous illnesses, injuries, surgical procedures, or medications are related to the present illness. Be sure that you keep *complete* records. "She had little blue pills," does not tell your doctor anything, so be sure all medications are *named* when dispensed, and write the name in your pet's home health record. Dates of illnesses (both those treated and those not requiring a visit), dates of and reasons for hospitalization (with a *complete* list of all lab tests, X rays, and drugs administered), and surgical procedures (including the anesthesia used) should be recorded. You would be surprised how many times this information is relevant to the present illness. (See the sample home health chart, Your Dog's Records, on page ii.)

5. Does your veterinarian do a complete physical examination?

Your pet deserves a *complete* physical examination even during well-pet visits, such as for vaccinations. Many early problems can be picked up at these semiannual or annual visits. A thorough medical history and physical examination will probably suggest the diagnosis to most competent veterinarians.

Each doctor has his or her own order in the physical exam. Some start by taking the temperature; others may examine the head or hair coat. A good physical exam can be very rewarding. Please do not talk to your doctor at this time unless a question is asked of you, since complete concentration is required.

The veterinarian will follow the same basic physical outlined in Chapter 2. Palpation will determine pain, size, shape, or consistency of the tissues and organs. Your dog's prostate gland and the general health of the entire rectal area will be examined. Sharp taps with the fingers on the abdomen or chest wall will tell your doctor the hollowness or solidity of the body part examined. For example, an area that should sound hollow but sounds solid may indicate a mass that does not belong there. Using a stethoscope for *auscultation* allows the sounds of body functions (heartbeats, and lung and intestinal sounds) to be amplified. A visual inspection of your pet's gait, posture, hair coat, gum color, and other visible parts is also a feature of a complete physical. An *otoscope* will be used to look in your pet's ear canal; an *ophthalmoscope* will magnify the eye and its inner structure. An examination of your pet's retina (the back of the inner eye) is part of a thorough physical exam because the presence of certain systemic or local diseases can be discovered by checking the retina.

Certain diseases of the skin, mouth, ears, or internal organs have characteristic odors (for example, a sweet breath may indicate diabetes), so your veterinarian's sense of smell will also be brought into play.

6. Does your veterinarian encourage you to ask questions?

All your questions should be answered in a clear, concise way and in language that you understand—not in medical jargon. Diagrams or simple line drawings are helpful, too.

7. Is your veterinarian gentle with your pet?

Sometimes a little calm talk or a few strokes is all that is needed to make the exam easier.

8. Does your veterinarian have any pets of his own?

9. Is your veterinarian careful with a biting or scratching pet?

Your veterinarian should explain that your pet will be gently but firmly restrained so that nobody gets hurt. Most doctors will use a veterinary assistant or a muzzle.

10. If you are a new pet owner, does the veterinarian give you literature on good health maintenance and training, or does he or she explain it to you?

11. Will your doctor refer you to a veterinary specialist if needed?

A good veterinarian knows his limitations.

12. Is your veterinarian a member of an emergency group, or is there another doctor on call when your veterinarian is not available?

13. Are all rates and fees explained to you?

If your doctor does not take the initiative, be sure to ask what the fees will be for vaccinations, lab tests, radiographs, surgery, hospitalization, and treatment. Sometimes it is impossible to give you an exact figure, but high and low estimates are feasible, unless your pet's condition is so unpredictable that the treatment may change. If your pet will be hospitalized for a few days, you could ask your doctor to keep you informed daily of your pet's accumulated tab. Many veterinary hospitals are nearly as well equipped as human hospitals, and the care is also equivalent—sometimes even better! At the moment there is no national pet care insurance to take the sting out of paying those bills, but knowing the daily financial picture as well as the health picture can be comforting.

14. Does your veterinarian use laboratory tests and radiographs (X rays) discriminately, to confirm a diagnosis?

Your doctor should explain to you in simple language why each test or series of radiographs is being done:

"I'm going to *catheterize* Ralph—that is, place a sterile tube into the bladder. She'll be tranquilized so it won't be uncomfortable. The urine collected will be checked to see if she has a bladder infection. A *culture* will be taken to isolate, identify, and count the bacteria. The appropriate antibiotic for killing the bacteria will be determined by exposing the bacteria to various antibiotics in an antibiotic *sensitivity test*. I'll take radiographs of the bladder to rule out bladder stones or bladder tumors."

15. Does your veterinarian hospitalize only for serious problems?

Many pets' problems don't need hospitalization, and in fact, pets seem to fare better in the home environment. Being treated by their owners, in close cooperation with the veterinarian, is a very comfortable situation. Most treatment and lab tests can be done on an outpatient basis. Besides, hospitalization can be expensive.

16. Is your veterinarian's hospital well equipped?

This may be difficult for you to evaluate, but up-to-date veterinary hospitals do have modern radiograph equipment, surgical facilities, and laboratories.

If your answers are positive, you have a wonderful veterinarian. Congratulations! If you cannot give a positive answer to most of these questions, or if you are not comfortable with your veterinarian's diagnosis or treatment, seek another doctor or another opinion.

A happy veterinarian-owner relationship also requires a cooperative, aware, and concerned owner. You can have the best veterinarian in the whole world but if you do not follow instructions, or do not understand the instructions, your relationship—and your pet's health—can deteriorate rapidly. Because you live intimately with your pet and know its habits and routine, you can often pick up very early and subtle changes that may go unnoticed by your doctor. The concerned and aware owner will use this book to best advantage by checking the Decision Charts and other chapters whenever necessary.

When a visit is necessary, bring paper and pen and write down (or have your veterinarian write down) *all* important instructions. Trying to remember everything is usually a waste of your time and money and may cause your pet's medical problem to persist, return, or get worse. In many cases, this situation leads to the denouncement "That vet is no good!" If you do not understand why a medication was prescribed, its side effects, or how long it should be given, or the importance, expectations, or limitations of a treatment or surgical procedure, ask your veterinarian to *make* it understandable. Lack of communication, not poor professional care, is the most frequent problem in the veterinarian-owner relationship.

For example, do *not* "double-up" on the medication at night if you were too rushed in the morning to give your dog its medicine. Excess doses can be worse than none at all. Let your doctor demonstrate the best method to administer the medicine if you feel that you will have problems. And do *not* stop the medication just because Ralph seems better. Follow your doctor's instructions. Stopping medication too early can cause an even more serious problem. If your pet experiences side effects from the medication, phone your veterinarian. A change in dosage or in the interval between doses—or a new drug altogether—may be recommended. If your doctor wants a follow-up exam, follow up!

One final word: Thank your doctor when he or she does a good job and is interested in your pet's health. Everyone, including your veterinarian, likes to be appreciated.

LABORATORY TESTS

Tests are often needed to confirm a diagnosis or to determine the best mode or the effectiveness of treatment. Some of the most common tests that may be requested are stool sample, skin scrapings (for skin parasites or fungus), complete blood count, blood chemistry, urinalysis, bacteriology, and tissue biopsy.

Stool Sample

Since dogs like to examine their surroundings by licking both the ground and their peers' private areas, and since they walk bare-footed and eat things they shouldn't, a stool sample should be checked once or twice a year. Most doctors will recommend that you bring it with you at vaccination time. A little is all that is needed. If you are gathering an outdoor sample, try not to include any soil, since it contains some worms (harmless "soil" strongyloides) that may confuse the examiner.

Skin Scrapings

If your doctor suspects *demodex* or *sarcoptes mange,* a few of the infected skin areas will be gently scraped with a scalpel blade in order to find the mite. The skin scraping is stirred into a drop of mineral oil, which is transferred to a glass slide. Microscopic examination will then reveal the mites—if luck is on your side. If your doctor comes back for another scraping, don't fret. This whole process can be equated to fishing: You know where the fish are, and you cast the line to that spot, but nothing bites. So you try another spot. The same thing happens with skin scraping. The skin lesions may look like typical mange lesions, but several scrapings may be needed to confirm the diagnosis.

Confirming a fungus infection (see Ringworm, page 178) involves transferring a skin scraping of the lesion to a container that contains "fungus food." Confirmation may take one to two weeks. As the fungus grows and uses the "food," the media in the container changes color—from yellow to red. If there is a suspicion of a fungus infection, treatment will begin at the time of scraping.

Complete Blood Count

If firemen are in a smoking building, you assume that there is a fire and that it will soon be under control. If there are smoke and flames and no firemen, the building may burn to the ground. Your dog's body has a remarkable "fire department" that consists of specialized cells, floating through miles and miles of blood vessels. Some carry oxygen (red blood cells), giving the blood its red color. Others can be mobilized to defend areas of tissue injury (from bacteria, trauma, chemicals, or heat, for instance) and inflammation by "eating up" the particles that invaded your pet's body (white blood cells). These "firemen" consist of *erythrocytes* (red) and *leukocytes* (white). The white blood cells are divided into *neutrophils, lymphocytes, monocytes, eosinophils,* and *basophils.* The bone marrow produces all red blood cells and the neutrophils, eosinophils, and basophils. Lymphocytes and monocytes are produced in the lymph nodes, the spleen, the tonsils, and the lymphoid cells of the intestine. The number and type of these "firemen" may help your doctor determine the type of disease present. Parasites that attack the red blood cells, such as *babesia,* can be identified by staining a blood smear and then looking for the parasite in the cells.

The neck (*jugular*) and front leg (*cephalic*) veins are the two most common sites for *venipuncture* (literally, puncturing the vein) to obtain blood for tests. Gentle restraint and a sterile needle and syringe are used, and most pets tolerate the procedure very well. However, fat or hyperactive dogs and those with rolling or unusual veins (such as dachshunds) may make it difficult to get a blood sample on the first try. Every veterinarian and technician has dealt with "problem veins." Reactions from the owner such as, "You mean you have to stick poor Ralph *again?*" will just add more stress to the job—so quiet, please!

Blood Chemistry

The health of your dog's body depends on the health of all its parts, and an unhealthy organ will eventually affect the other organs. In order to confirm a diagnosis or to monitor your pet's return to health or its setbacks, various enzymes and products of metabolism found in the blood should be measured. An increase or decrease in their levels can identify and monitor the organ (or organs) that is sick and the proper treatment can begin. A blood test alone is *not* a substitute for a physical examination, but veterinary recognition of the importance of blood chemistries has made this commonplace for good veterinary care.

Most veterinarians are taking advantage of a new development in the field —using a reliable commercial laboratory that provides accurate results at a fair price. However, veterinarians may perform certain tests, such as kidney function or blood sugar, in their own clinics, since the results from commercial labs may not be available for twenty-four to forty-eight hours. Pets that are very ill also need immediate results. Even so, the tests require time. In fact, your veterinarian may have to institute basic treatment before the final analysis is known. (In serious cases, life support care, such as antibiotics, fluids, oxygen, and any other treatment thought necessary, *will* be started before all the test results have come back.) If you call the office the day after your dog has been examined to find out what exactly is wrong, your doctor still may not be sure of the complete picture.

The commercial laboratories may run as many as fifteen or twenty different tests on your dog's blood sample. This is called a *biochemical profile*. A few of the most common blood chemistries and other tests in a profile are briefly explained in the next section.

Biochemical profile

Blood Sugar (glucose)   Your doctor will run this test if diabetes is suspected (*see* pages 146, 148, and 152).

Blood Urea Nitrogen (BUN) and Creatinine   Urea and creatinine are end-products of metabolism that are normally eliminated by the kidney in the urine. If the kidneys are not functioning properly, these products will be increased in the blood. This will not tell your doctor the *cause* of the kidney problem, just that the kidneys are involved. Special radiographs, urinalysis, and even a biopsy may be needed to define the disease process.

Amylase and Lipase   More cases of acute *pancreatitis* (inflammation of the pancreas) are being diagnosed and treated properly, thanks to the availability of these tests. If your pet has abdominal pain and sudden and severe vomiting and is very weak and depressed, these tests may be beneficial. The cells of an inflamed pancreas release the amylase and lipase enzymes into the bloodstream, so their number is markedly elevated.

Liver Profile Tests   The liver has so many functions that to see how it is functioning overall, a liver profile has to be done. The blood tests include *bilirubin*, *protein*, *SGPT*, *SGOT*, *cholesterol*, and *alkaline phosphatase*. Sometimes this still is not enough to tell your doctor the *cause* of the liver problem, so other tests, such as a liver biopsy, may be necessary.

Heartworm Test   A blood sample is drawn in the same manner as for the complete blood count. Your doctor will check the blood directly under the microscope for the microfilariae, or he may first concentrate the blood by spinning it in a *centrifuge* or by passing it through a filter. The filter technique seems to be the best method for finding the microfilariae.

Urinalysis   This is an extremely helpful test for diagnosing diseases of the urinary tract and other problems, such as *diabetes mellitus* and liver disease. Your doctor will check to see if your pet is concentrating its urine (specific gravity) and will study the chemical analysis for such abnormalities as sugar in the urine, which may indicate diabetes or a kidney defect. Microscopic examination of the urine can spot cells that may indicate inflammation, infection, or degeneration anywhere along the urinary tract.

Bacteriology   Bacterial infections are very common in bite-wounds (*abscesses*) and in problems involving the ear, eye, and urinary tract. Your doctor may suggest culture and sensitivity tests, which involve transferring a small amount of the infected material to a container filled with "food" in which the bacteria can flourish. Small paper disks, each containing a different antibiotic, are placed in the container at even intervals. The antibiotics that are effective against the bacteria will produce *zones of inhibition*—areas around the disks where no bacteria will be growing. The bacteria will also be identified by its growth pattern and microscopic features. Using a good general antibiotic may cure your dog's infection, but performing culture and sensitivity tests—especially in infections that won't clear up—is better practice and may be cheaper in the long run.

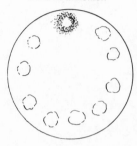

Zone of inhibition

Tissue Biopsy

Removing a tissue section for microscopic examination is often an excellent way for your veterinarian to make a proper diagnosis, to determine if the disease process can be reversed, and to suggest the best therapy for your dog.

Of course, biopsy of the internal organs is more difficult and has more risks than biopsy of the skin, but in skilled hands and with the proper instruments, tissue can be studied from the kidney, intestine, prostate, bone marrow, liver, or any other organ. Often, a local anesthetic and the appropriate biopsy instrument are all that is needed to obtain the sample. Biopsy is a good tool that your veterinarian may need to determine the chance for your dog's complete recovery from a disease and the type and cost of the best therapy.

Radiographs (X rays)

Radiographs have become another important tool for diagnosis. The radiographic equipment in many veterinary hospitals is equivalent to that in human hospitals—and just as expensive. Modern X-ray equipment provides excellent "pictures" of the bones and internal organs and the spaces between them. The procedure of taking radiographs is painless and relatively harmless, but your pet may be sedated because any movement may cause a blurry image. Two or more views are needed to get a three-dimensional "picture" of the area under investigation.

To get the "picture," X rays are released and directed through your dog's body. They travel very rapidly and then penetrate a plate containing the film. X rays pass through air easily, but solid masses, such as internal organs and bones, will stop some of them. Those that hit the film turn it black when it is developed. The areas on the film not touched by the X rays remain white. So a chest radiograph will have white areas (such as the heart, backbones, and ribs) and black areas (lung tissue, containing air). Your doctor will study the radiographs under a bright light, looking for changes in the normal shape, size, and density of the organs.

Electrocardiogram

An electrocardiogram (ECG) is a graphic measure of the electrical activity produced by the heart muscle. Electrocardiography is an inexpensive, safe, and painless technique to help your veterinarian determine whether your pet has heart disease. It is also helpful for diagnosing and monitoring treatments of illnesses not originating in the heart, such as urinary obstructions and Addison's disease. To obtain the ECG, your pet is placed on its right side and "leads" are attached to its legs and body using clips. Dogs rarely need to be sedated for this procedure. The various leads are recorded and the heart rate and rhythm and changes in the heart size are evaluated.

Chapter **5**

Your Dog's
Home Pharmacy

Home medical care of your dog's minor illnesses and injuries may require medication—*sometimes. Sometimes,* because many of your pet's medical problems, such as a minor abrasion, a sprain, or occasional vomiting or diarrhea, resolve themselves without medication. Canine bodies have a remarkable capability for healing themselves, but we are a drug-oriented society: We feel that an injection of this or a tablet of that will do the job. In reality, a little time and knowledge are often all that are needed, and they may well be the most effective (and the cheapest!) treatment. This should not be abused, however. If the Decision Charts recommend seeing a veterinarian or trying drug or non-drug treatments, such as cleaning and soaking a wound or encouraging fluid intake, follow the instructions.

Veterinarians are occasionally confronted with an injury or minor illness that has healed itself even when the owner did not use the medication or follow the instructions. The owner calls a week later to say that the ear infection is completely healed or the diarrhea has disappeared. This does *not* mean that you should not follow your doctor's instructions!

BASIC NECESSITIES

Below is a list of medications that are good to have on hand, as well as the ailments they treat. Items in bold print are essentials; the other preparations are not so vital. *Remember:* Keep all medicines out of the reach of children. The when and why of using medications, including dosage and side effects, are discussed afterward.

Medication	Ailment
*Antihistamines	Allergy
*Milk of magnesia Bulk laxatives Mineral oil Fleet® enema	Constipation
Guaifenesin (Glyceryl guaiacolate)	Coughs
Kaopectate®	Diarrhea
Antibiotic ophthalmic ointments	Eye irritations
Tinactin®	Fungus
*Bonine®	Motion sickness
*Aspirin	Pain and fever
Hydrogen peroxide (3 percent) **Activated charcoal** Milk of magnesia	Poisoning • to induce vomiting • to absorb poison • to speed passage through the digestive tract
A and D Ointment® **Antibiotic ointment** Betadine® Domeboro® solution **Hydrogen peroxide (3 percent)**	Skin irritations
Tomato juice Cranberry juice Vitamin C	Urinary infections
Kaopectate®, *Maalox® *Mylanta® **Pepto Bismol®**	Vomiting and stomach upsets

*Do *not* give to puppies without your veterinarian's approval.

Allergy

Antihistamine compounds, such as *diphenhydramine* (Benadryl®) and *chlorpheniramine (Chlortrimeton®)*, are helpful for some allergies. These drugs seem to reduce the itching and to have a beneficial sedative effect that prevents your dog from scratching itself raw. But they should only be used at home for short-term therapy. Antihistamines may produce drowsiness, and since allergies are not all caused by histamine release, antihistamines are not always effective. *Note:* Do *not* give antihistamines to pups or pregnant dogs without your veterinarian's approval.

Benadryl®

Dosage For dogs weighing twenty-five pounds, give 12.5 mg. once daily; for dogs heavier than fifty pounds, give 25 mg. once daily.

Chlortrimeton®

Dosage For dogs heavier than twenty-five pounds, give 8 mg. every twelve hours.

Constipation

Laxatives should *not* be used on a regular basis unless recommended by your veterinarian. Safe laxatives are made from *psyllium* (see below). Alternative laxatives are milk of magnesia or mineral oil. If an enema is needed, use warm water (best) or a Fleet® enema.

Bulk laxatives

Products such as Metamucil® and Mucilose® are refined from the psyllium seed. It is not absorbed by the digestive tract; it only passes through. Thus, it is a natural product and one with essentially no contraindications and no side effects. It provides bulk by drawing water into the stool. *Note:* If you think your dog has an intestinal obstruction or impacted feces, do *not* use a laxative.

Dosage ½ to 1 teaspoon mixed in the food once or twice daily. Be sure to mix water into the food and supply drinking water at all times.

Milk of magnesia

The active ingredient, *magnesium,* causes fluid to be retained within the bowel and in the feces. It is also helpful in speeding passage of any poisons through the digestive tract.

Dosage 2 teaspoons per ten pounds of body weight once daily, but dogs weighing over sixty pounds need only 6 teaspoons, maximum. One dose should do the job.

Side Effects Milk of magnesia is nonabsorbable but it does contain magnesium and some salt and should *not* be used if your pet has kidney or heart disease.

Mineral oil

This is the cheapest and most effective laxative, but it can be dangerous if administered improperly or given for a long period of time. Mineral oil should *never* be given directly in the mouth because it is bland and may enter the breathing tubes and lungs before your pet can cough. Mineral oil in the lungs will cause a severe pneumonia. Instead, mix it in the food. If mineral oil is given for a long period of time, it can cause deficiencies of the fat soluble vitamins A, D, E, and K.

Dosage   1 teaspoon per ten pounds of body weight mixed in the food once daily, but dogs weighing over eighty pounds need only 8 teaspoons maximum.

Side Effects   Pneumonia or vitamin deficiency if administered improperly.

Fleet® enema
If your pet has *obstipation* (impacted or hard feces in the lower intestine and rectum), you should see your doctor. If you must give the enema, use the Fleet® pediatric enema. This may lubricate and soften the hard feces.

Dosage   The lubricated nozzle is inserted into the rectum and one ounce of the solution is gently administered. Another enema can be given half an hour later, if necessary.

Side Effects   *Note:* Severe complications can result if used when fever, nausea, vomiting, or abdominal pain is present. Do *not* use in dogs that are dehydrated or have known kidney disease.

Coughs

The only safe cough medicine I recommend for use without veterinary consultation is an expectorant. The expectorant liquefies the secretions and allows the body's defenses to get rid of the bad material. Cough suppressants should *not* be used without your doctor's advice, because they contain such narcotics as codeine. Over-the-counter cough suppressants may contain dextromethorphan, a close chemical relative.

Glyceryl guaiacolate (Guaifenesin)
If your dog has a dry, hacking cough, a lubricant soothes the inflamed area. If your pet has a cough with mucus, glyceryl guaiacolate liquefies the mucus secretions so that they may be coughed free. It does not suppress the cough reflex, but encourages the natural defense mechanisms of the body.

Read the label: Do *not* use Robitussin® or 2-G® with the additives PE (for the decongestant *phenylephrine*), CF or DM (for the cough suppressant *dextromethorphan*), or AC (for codeine). Use only Robitussin® or 2-G® with only glyceryl guaiacolate (guaifenesin) in 3.5 percent alcohol.

Dosage   ½ to 1 teaspoon every four hours.

Side Effects   No serious side effects, but check with your doctor if the cough persists or the Decision Chart so indicates.

Diarrhea

Kaopectate® is a very safe medication for dogs, but if it does not control the diarrhea, a stronger medication containing paregoric may be used. See your veterinarian if diarrhea persists or if the Decision Chart so indicates.

Kaopectate®

Kaopectate contains *kaolin* and pectin, which coat the intestinal tract and help to form a solid stool.

Dosage   2 teaspoons per ten pounds of body weight every four hours.

Paregoric preparations

Paregoric is a derivative of opium, a narcotic that decreases the activity of the digestive tract and thus slows down the diarrhea. The kaolin and pectin of Parepectolin® coat the intestinal tract and help to form a solid stool. *Note:* This should only be used if a change in diet and kaopectate have not controlled the diarrhea. Paregoric compounds, such as Parepectolin®, are available without a prescription in most states, although you must sign for them at the time of purchase.

Dosage   ½ teaspoon per ten pounds of body weight every six hours, but dogs weighing over twenty pounds need only 1 teaspoon every six hours.

Side Effects   The narcotic may make your dog drowsy; if so, decrease or stop the medication. Sometimes paregoric may work so well that your dog will go without a bowel movement for three or four days, even after you stop the medication. As long as your dog remains alert and active and eats well, don't worry.

Eye Irritations

For short-term use, apply an ophthalmic ointment such as Neosporin® or Neopolycin® to your dog's eye three or four times daily. These ointments contain three antibiotics: *polymyxin, bacitracin,* and *neomycin.*

Fungus

Tinactin®

If your pet has only one ringworm lesion, you can use this cream. It is available over the counter in drugstores.

Dosage   Apply the cream to the skin lesion with a Q-tip® twice daily. *Note:* Do *not* touch the lesion with your finger.

Side Effects   If the skin becomes more irritated, stop the medication and see your veterinarian. *Note:* Do *not* get the medication in the eye.

Motion Sickness

First, try all the preparations for preventing motion sickness given on page 60.

Bonine®

If you are unsuccessful, an antihistamine called Bonine® (*meclizine hydrochloride*) can be used. It is effective against the apprehension, salivation, and vomiting or diarrhea that some pets experience when traveling. If Bonine® is not successful in eliminating the motion sickness, your veterinarian can provide you with tranquilizers or antihistamines that are effective.

Dosage   For dogs under twenty-five pounds, give 12.5 mg.; for dogs between twenty-five and fifty pounds, give 25 mg.; for dogs heavier than fifty pounds, give 50 mg.

Side Effects   Your pet may experience drowsiness. *Note:* Do *not* give Bonine® to a pregnant dog—it may cause birth defects.

Pain and Fever

Aspirin, one of the oldest and safest human medications, controls fever and reduces pain and inflammation. In other words, aspirin treats the signs; it does *not* cure the problem. Be sure to check the appropriate Decision Charts before using it. Buffered aspirin is preferable; it irritates the stomach less and therefore decreases the chances of vomiting. *Note:* Do *not* give aspirin to puppies without your veterinarian's recommendation, because puppies have problems detoxifying and excreting the aspirin.

Dosage   For dogs under ten pounds give 1 grain every six hours ("baby aspirin" is useful); for dogs under twenty pounds, give 2.5 grains every six hours; for dogs over thirty-five pounds, give 5 grains every six hours.

Side Effects   Aspirin can upset your dog's stomach. To avoid this, try giving the aspirin a half hour after feeding, when the food in the stomach will act as a buffer. Coated aspirin, such as Ecotrin®, should not upset the stomach, but some dogs may not digest the coated aspirin and may not receive the full benefit of the aspirin. *Note:* If given improperly, aspirin has the potential to cause hemorrhage in the digestive tract. Do *not* use aspirin that has additional ingredients, such as caffeine and phenacetin.

Poisoning

To induce vomiting: hydrogen peroxide
If your dog swallows a poison that can be expelled by vomiting, hydrogen peroxide 3 percent works very well. Do *not* induce vomiting if the poison swallowed is a petroleum-based compound or a strong acid or strong alkali (see Swallowed Poisons, page 126). Be sure that the hydrogen peroxide purchased is not a higher strength (such as for bleaching hair).

Dosage   1 or 2 teaspoons every ten minutes until your dog vomits. Repeat this two or three times if necessary. If this treatment is unsuccessful, 1 or 2 teaspoons of salt or a mustard and warm water solution put on the back of the tongue should induce vomiting.

To absorb poison: activated charcoal
After vomiting, a few teaspoons of activated charcoal mixed in milk or water can be given to absorb the poison if the specific antidote is not known. Activated charcoal can be purchased in drugstores.

To speed passage through the digestive tract: milk of magnesia
Dosage   1 teaspoon per five pounds of body weight once daily.

Skin Irritations

Sterilizing agents and antiseptics
Soap and water is the best way to clean a wound. Hydrogen peroxide (3 percent strength) foams and cleanses wounds very well, and is inexpensive. Betadine®, a nonstinging iodine preparation, kills germs and is a good agent to use on the skin, but it is expensive. To soothe the skin temporarily, calamine lotion can be applied, but it loses its effectiveness when it dries out. It must be washed off and reapplied frequently. *Note:* Do *not* get it in the eyes.

Dosage Cleanse the wounds three times daily. Trim the hair around the wound, if necessary.

Domeboro® solution
This is a soothing wet dressing for relief of skin inflammation. It has antiseptic properties and reduces itching.

Dosage Dissolve one teaspoon or tablet in a pint of warm water. Bathe or apply wet dressings of the solution to the affected skin for fifteen minutes. You can repeat this three or four times daily.

Ointments
A and D Ointment® soothes irritated skin and can be applied three or four times daily to affected areas. The ointments containing antibiotics (Neosporin®, Neopolycin®, and Mycitracin®) can be applied to affected skin three times daily.

Urinary Infections

Acidifiers help control bacterial infections of the lower urinary tract and help prevent a recurrence of crystal or stone formation in the tract.

Vitamin C and cranberry juice
Tomato juice or cranberry juice are excellent urinary acidifiers—if your pet will drink them. You can measure their effectiveness by testing urine with litmus paper. If blue litmus paper turns red, the urine is acidic.

Dosage ¼ to 1 cup of cranberry juice or tomato juice per day should be adequate. 250 to 500 mg. of vitamin C three times daily.

Vomiting and Stomach Upsets

Kaopectate®, Maalox®, Mylanta®, Pepto Bismol®
All of these products soothe the stomach lining.

Dosage 2 teaspoons of Kaopectate® per ten pounds of body weight every four hours. ½ teaspoon of Maalox® or Mylanta® per ten pounds of body weight every eight hours. ½ teaspoon of Pepto-Bismol® per ten pounds of body weight every four hours.

Side Effects Maalox® and Mylanta® may loosen the stools a little. If your pet has a history of heart or kidney disease, consult your veterinarian before using either of these.

THE FIRST AID KIT

This is a *must*. Keep the kit in a convenient location but out of the reach of small children. A fishing tackle box works very well, by the way.

Adhesive tape, 1 inch wide

Gauze bandages, 1-inch rolls

Absorbent cotton

Sterile gauze pads, 3 × 3 inches

Cotton-tipped swabs (Q-tips®)

Rubbing alcohol

Rectal thermometer

Teaspoon

Tweezers

Sharp scissors with rounded ends

Medications (those in bold print on page 76 are the basic requirements)

GIVING LIQUIDS TO YOUR DOG

- Hold your dog's head at a 45° angle.
- Make a pouch in the corner of the lip fold by pulling the cheek outward.
- Using a spoon or eye dropper, slowly pour the liquid into the pouch.
- If your dog does not swallow the liquid automatically, jiggle the pouch slightly or tap on the nose with your finger; this will cause it to swallow. Be sure to keep the head at a 45° angle until the liquid is swallowed.

Note: Placing your dog in the bathtub will help avoid mess.

GIVING PILLS TO YOUR DOG

Caution: Giving pills to dogs with neck pain or to vicious dogs can be dangerous.

- Place the palm of your hand over your dog's muzzle. With the thumb on one side and your fingers on the other, press hard against and under the upper teeth.
- Tilt the head up slightly. This usually causes the lower jaw to relax and drop a little.
- Using the middle finger of your other hand, push the lower jaw open.
- With your thumb and index finger, place the pill in the center of the tongue near its base.
- Close the mouth quickly and tap your pet's nose with your finger. This will cause the dog to lick and then swallow.

A plastic pill gun (purchased from your veterinarian or pet shop) is very handy and can save your fingers from getting hung up on your dog's teeth. A flexible tip holds the tablet or capsule within the barrel until deposited in your dog's mouth. A sharp push on the barrel delivers the pill to the back of the throat.

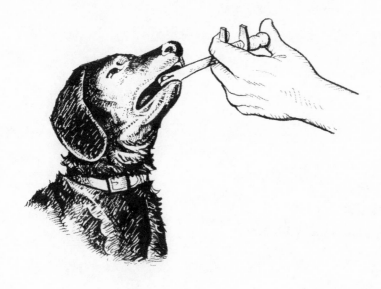

Part **II**

Caring For Your Dog

HOW TO USE THIS SECTION

This section describes most of the common problems of dogs, many of which can be treated at home, without visiting your veterinarian. The system of Decision Charts should help you become confident in diagnosing the problem and using the right treatment for happy results. Prevention is also discussed. Remember the old adage: "An ounce of prevention is worth a pound of cure."

Finding the Right Decision Chart

If you suspect an illness, determine the chief sign—for example, coughing—and look it up in the contents or in the index. Then turn to the correct page. If your dog has more than one problem simultaneously, you may have to use more than one Decision Chart. For instance, if your pet has a cough and runny eyes, check the chart for each problem. If one recommends home treatment and the other advises a visit to your veterinarian, *see your doctor.*

Using the Decision Chart

It is very important to first read all the general information on the particular problem. In many cases, the chart may advise you to see the doctor immediately, but emergency treatment may also be needed before you get to the doctor's office. After reading the information, start at the top of the Decision Chart (do *not* skip around) and answer each question.

If home treatment is indicated, follow all instructions exactly, or the treatment will not be effective. If your dog is not improving, even with good care, *see your veterinarian.*

If the chart indicates veterinary consultation, it does not necessarily mean that the illness is serious. It may mean that more vigorous treatment or further examination and lab tests are needed. "See veterinarian NOW" means *immediate attention is needed.* "See veterinarian within 24 hours" is self-explanatory. "Make appointment with veterinarian" means a visit should be made in the next few days.

The procedures discussed on the next few pages will give you step-by-step guidance on how to handle any emergency. Read the entire section and practice the procedures to become familiar with them *before* you have to use them. Your veterinarian will be happy to help you with any you don't fully understand. I hope you'll never have to use these procedures, but your doctor will be very proud of you for being a prepared and helpful partner if an emergency does occur.

This chapter and Chapter 7, Accidents and Injuries, will help you to recognize an emergency situation. Your job is to preserve your dog's life and to prevent further injury until veterinary care is available. *Note:* There are some other emergencies listed in Chapter 8, Common Problems and Diseases, so scan that chapter as well and become familiar with those situations. In addition, certain problems require emergency treatment from you before going to the doctor's office, so read the descriptive sections carefully *before* an emergency develops.

Chapter **6**

Emergency Procedures

Approaching an Injured Dog

The friendliest animal, if injured, may try to bite because of fear and pain, so approach the dog slowly, talking in a quiet and reassuring voice. Call the dog by name, if it is known. Stop your approach when you are about a foot from the animal. Bend down slowly to the pet's level, still talking calmly. Gradually extend your closed hand, knuckles upward, toward the dog. If no aggression is seen, pet it first with your closed hand. If the animal displays aggression, try reassuring talk for a minute longer. If this is not successful, use restraint (next page).

Next, you should check for vital signs. Be sure the airway is clear and the dog is breathing. If not, give artificial respiration (page 90). Check the heartbeat and pulse (page 22), control any bleeding (page 100), look for signs of poisoning (page 126), treat for shock (page 93), and check for fractures (page 108).

Restraining an Injured Dog

The gentlest and least restraint is best. Applying a *muzzle* is a safe step for the dog and for you. It tends to calm most animals and, of course, protects you from getting bitten by a frightened pet or a pet in pain. Don't muzzle for long periods of time, however, because your dog needs to pant in order to perspire.

Note: Do *not* muzzle an animal whose breathing is labored.

Using a piece of rope, a necktie, a cloth belt, or a gauze roll, form a loop around the dog's nose and mouth and tighten it over the nose. Bring the ends of whatever you're using under the jaw and tighten another loop. Pass the ends beneath the ears and tie them behind the head.

Note: If the dog tries to vomit, remove the muzzle *immediately.*

Dogs with short noses are difficult to muzzle. Instead, wrap a coat or blanket over the head for protection. The covering shields noise and light and therefore calms your pet.

Leashes made from rope, cloth, or even a belt can also be used for gentle handling. If your small dog is unwilling to be held, tighten the leash so that it cannot turn its head suddenly. With the leash held tight, pass your other hand and arm around and under its body to lift it. Keep the leash just tight enough so that your dog can't turn around and bite.

Giving Artificial Respiration

If there are signs of a breathing problem, such as blue gums, labored breathing, or a staring expression, or if the dog has collapsed, you will need to administer artificial respiration. Before beginning, however, check the pulse (page 22). If you cannot feel it, apply cardiopulmonary resuscitation (next page).

Place the dog on its belly or side. If there is no back or neck injury, extend the head and open the pet's mouth to look for obstructions. Clean the mouth of any blood or mucus with your fingers, then close it. Recheck the pulse.

Now: Inhale; put your mouth over the dog's muzzle, forming an airtight seal; exhale. Remove your mouth and allow the dog's chest to deflate. Repeat this process ten to fifteen times per minute, and continue it until you arrive at the veterinarian's office or veterinary hospital. Be sure to recheck the pulse often while performing artificial respiration. Treat also for shock (page 93).

Giving Cardiopulmonary Resuscitation

If your dog is not breathing and has no heartbeat and pulse, you have an immediate life-threatening situation. If brain tissue is deprived of oxygen for more than four or five minutes, permanent damage or death will occur. Administering cardiopulmonary resuscitation (CPR) may keep the brain tissue from dying. A combination of heart massage and artificial respiration, CPR forces blood out of the heart by simulating the heart's pumping action. To be effective, it must be done rhythmically and in combination with artificial respiration. Veterinary aid is needed quickly as well, so send someone for help while you begin the treatment.

In human medicine, heart attacks (*myocardial infarctions,*) choking, and strokes are common CPR emergencies. These are rare in veterinary medicine, however, so there are only a few instances where CPR is needed. Electrocution, near-drowning, and collapse from congestive heart failure may require CPR. If your dog is unconscious, has no pulse or heartbeat, or is gasping for breath, or if its pupils are dilating, you need to administer CPR. *Note:* If there is massive external or internal bleeding, CPR will *not* be effective because there is not enough fluid in the blood vessels to carry the oxygen.

Respiration
Place your pet on its side. Clean the mouth of blood and mucus. Inhale air, put your mouth over the dog's muzzle, forming an airtight seal, and exhale. Give your pet a new breath every three seconds (twenty per minute), while massaging the heart.

Massage
Place the heel of one hand over the dog's chest, just in back of its elbow, and your other palm on top of that hand. Pump firmly and quickly, doing it once every second (sixty per minute). Hold each thrust for a count of two and release for a count of one. Be careful not be break any ribs or to further injure any rib fractures. Have someone else feel for a femoral pulse (see page 22) as you massage. Discontinue the massage when the heartbeat is restored, but continue the artificial respiration until your dog breathes on its own.

Applying a Tourniquet

Seek veterinary aid immediately. A tourniquet should be used only if direct pressure is unsuccessful in stopping the bleeding. *Never* place a tourniquet over a fracture or a joint.

You can use a handkerchief, a cloth belt, or a piece of cloth as a tourniquet. Adjust it about one inch above the wound by tying a loose loop around the limb. Place a short, strong stick in the loop and twist the tourniquet until the blood stops flowing.

Loosen the tourniquet every ten minutes to allow some circulation. *Note:* Do *not* loosen it in the case of a snakebite (see page 132). Treat the animal for shock (next page) as well.

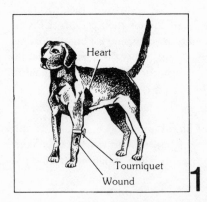

Heart

Tourniquet

Wound

1

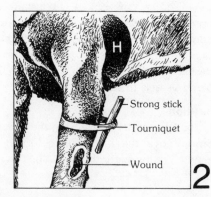

Strong stick

Tourniquet

Wound

2

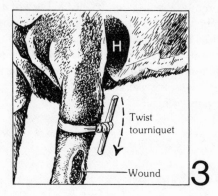

Twist tourniquet

Wound

3

Treating Shock

Shock is caused by severe insult to your dog's body—heavy bleeding, trauma, fluid loss (from vomiting, diarrhea, or burns), infection, heart failure, or breathing problems. It is a syndrome in which the heart and blood vessels are unable to deliver the nutrients and oxygen to the cells and are equally unable to remove the cells' toxic waste products. If not treated promptly, the shock process may be impossible to reverse and your dog can die.

The major signs of shock are:

1. Pale or muddy gums
2. A weak and rapid pulse (see page 22)
3. Capillary refilling takes longer than two seconds (see page 21)
5. Rapid breathing (over forty breaths per minute)
6. A low rectal temperature (below 100°F), with skin and legs cool to the touch

Shock requires prompt veterinary attention. For immediate aid you should be sure the dog's airway is clear so it can breathe. If not, administer artificial respiration (page 90), check the heartbeat and pulse (page 22), and control any bleeding (page 100). If necessary, apply CPR (page 91).

Maintain body heat (with a blanket or coat) and very gently transport the dog to the veterinary hospital. If your pet is unconscious, keep its head lower than the rest of the body. If possible, phone the hospital so that they can prepare for your animal.

Large quantities of intravenous fluids, *corticosteroids,* * and oxygen given in time can save your pet's life. In shock, the capillaries are like a dry riverbed. The intravenous fluids flood the capillaries and renew the vigorous blood flow that nourishes the dried-out cells.

Do *not* change the injured pet's position rapidly. A fast lift or rotation can cause shock to move into the irreversible stage.

If the dog is in electrical shock from chewing on wires, there is an added precaution: Do *not* touch the dog if it is still in contact with the current! Unplug the electrical cord from the outlet and then check the dog's pulse and heartbeat and continue treating as for shock. You may also need to treat for burns in the mouth (page 120).

---

*Corticosteroids are hormones produced by the adrenal gland that have many functions, including the ability to help cells fight destructive agents. They are also produced synthetically by pharmaceutical companies, for use in human as well as veterinary medicine.

Water Rescue

Most dogs are excellent swimmers, but even the strongest swimmer can drown if it becomes exhausted or falls through thin ice. If your dog begins to drown in a lake or pool, the first thing you should do is send for help. Then try to reach your dog from land with your hand. If you must swim out, try to take a float with you. Grab your pet by the tail or the back of the neck, or let it grab the float with its front legs. Hold on to the dog and swim to shore.

Once you are both safely ashore, hold your dog upside down by the hind legs (hold at the hocks) and give a few sharp shakes to drain excess water from the lungs. Remove any weeds or other hindrances from the mouth. Lay the dog on its side and give artificial respiration (page 90). Check for pulse (page 22). If there is no pulse or heartbeat, apply CPR (page 91).

You can help to revive the dog by holding spirits of ammonia under its nose. When the dog becomes conscious, wrap it in a blanket or coat to keep it warm. If you rescued it from ice water, treat for frostbite and hypothermia (page 118).

Applying a Splint

If you suspect that your dog has fractured its leg, a temporary splint is needed to prevent jagged bone edges from injuring the neighboring blood vessels, tissues, and nerves. *Note:* For stability, a splint should include the joints immediately above and below the fracture. An improperly applied splint is worse than no splint at all.

Place a clean cloth around the limb for padding. Fasten a rolled (U-shaped) magazine, newspaper, or cardboard to the leg with tape.

Many times, the shape of a dog's leg and its resistance to handling when injured will make it impossible to apply a temporary splint. In this case, gently support the limb with a towel, blanket, or board on the trip to your veterinarian's office.

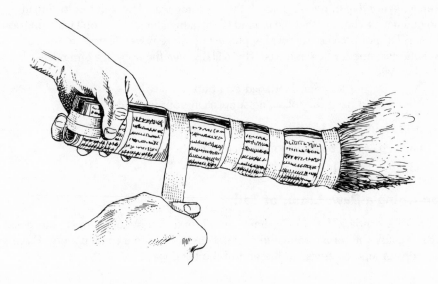

Bandaging

Bandages are used to stop bleeding, to keep dirt and bacteria out of the wound, to keep the edges of the cut together, to support the injured area, and to keep your dog from scratching or excessively licking the wound. Bandages should not be so tight that circulation or breathing is compromised. *Caution:* If the wound isn't clean when you cover it with a bandage, you may hide a developing infection from early discovery, so get the cut clean and keep it clean.

A pressure bandage is any bandage applied with pressure. You can hold the bandage firmly with your hand or tie it in place. A Band-Aid® is another pressure bandage, but it is limited to fairly small cuts and wounds.

Some dog owners leave bandages on too long. They should be changed frequently, every day or two and also if they become wet. The skin has to "breathe," and you have to be sure that the wound is not getting infected—don't wait until you can smell it. For painless removal apply nail polish remover liberally to the back of the adhesive tape for five minutes. This will dissolve the adhesive and release both skin and hair.

Note: Do *not* let your bandaged dog outside.

You should have the following supplies in your first aid kit:

gauze bandages, 1″ wide

padding, either a cotton roll or a clean cloth

adhesive tape, 1″ wide

Bandaging a Paw, Limb, or Tail

To make a bandage for a paw, limb, or tail, wrap the wound firmly with gauze pads, a gauze roll, or a clean cloth or handkerchief, using a spiral pattern. Place a few strips of tape crosswise at the end of the bandage.

Bandaging

Starting at the toes (or tip of tail), wrap the adhesive tape in overlapping bands securely over the first layer. Be sure to include hair on both sides so the bandage will not slip. To avoid having the lower leg, paw, or tail end swell, the bandage must include all of the extremity.

Bandaging the Chest or Abdomen

Place a gauze pad or clean cloth over the wound. A *many-tailed bandage* is made by tearing the narrow ends of a large, rectangular piece of clean cloth lengthwise into 1-inch wide strips—but only one-third of the way down—so that it will fit amply around the chest or abdomen. The strips are then tied over your dog's back.

Transporting an Injured Dog

You can carry a small or medium-sized dog by supporting its rear end with your inner right arm. Support its chest with your inner left arm. Large dogs or giant breeds, of course, are carried much easier by two people—one supporting the chest, the other supporting the rear and abdomen.

If your dog is seriously ill or injured, it is very important not to make the situation worse. If your pet is in shock (see page 93), a fast lift or rotation can cause irreversible harm. Injuries to the spinal cord, chest, abdomen, or limbs can be made worse by inconsiderate handling. A blanket, coat, air mattress, or even a window screen can be used to transport the seriously injured or ill dog.

If your dog has paralysis of both hind legs or stiffness or paralysis of the front legs, and pinching the paw does not seem to produce any pain, a spinal injury should be suspected. In this case, gently slide your dog onto a blanket or board, check its respiration, and stop any bleeding. But be very careful: Even a slight movement of the spine could be damaging.

Chapter **7**

Accidents and Injuries

Cuts and Wounds

Bleeding—even small amounts—frightens many pet owners, but the blood's remarkable clotting mechanism stops most bleeding in five minutes. When a small blood vessel is injured, it *constricts* (narrows) to allow less blood to escape. *Platelets,* which are blood cells, arrive at the scene to plug the hole, and chemicals released by the platelets combine with factors in the blood to produce fiberlike strands called *fibrin,* which complete the blood clot and stop the bleeding.

 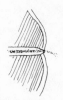  

| Skin wound (bleeding from blood vessel) | Constriction (narrowing) of blood vessel | Mobilization of platelets in blood vessel | Fibrin combines with platelets to complete the blood clot |

Sometimes the injury to the blood vessel is too large for the clotting mechanism to be effective. Apply direct pressure to the wound for five or ten minutes and allow the clotting mechanism to work; that's usually all that is needed. Use the cleanest material available—gauze pads, sheets, towels, or clothing. A *pressure bandage* (page 96) can be applied for sustained pressure. If these measures are unsuccessful, a tourniquet (page 92) is needed.

Cut Footpad

The footpad has a lot of blood vessels and can therefore bleed profusely when cut. Since your pet walks barefoot, carelessly discarded beer can pop-tops, jagged broken bottles, and other modern conveniences are constant hazards. Generally, dogs are very good about sidestepping such things, so this should be a rare injury. However, it's good to be prepared.

Home Treatment

Clean the wound with soap and water after the bleeding stops. Hydrogen peroxide (3 percent) can also be used. Do *not* rub the wound hard or the clot may loosen and the bleeding will recur. Gently remove any hair, dirt, or other foreign material from the area.

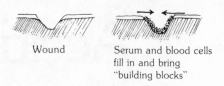

Wound   Serum and blood cells fill in and bring "building blocks"

Wound contraction

Wounds heal by skin contraction and by the presence of serum and blood cells at the site. Even gaping wounds will heal in time by this process if kept clean. There probably is some truth to the statement that dogs lick their wounds to keep them clean and to enhance healing.

Direct pressure with a gauze pad or clean cloth should stop the bleeding of a cut footpad. If you cannot get to a veterinarian, check the wound for dirt or other debris and then bandage firmly. If it starts bleeding again, flush it gently with 3 percent hydrogen peroxide and rebandage.

Shallow footpad wounds do not have to be sutured. Your pet may have a sore paw and a limp for a few weeks, but nightly flushings with clean water and hydrogen peroxide will help heal the wound. If the wound becomes infected, go see your doctor.

What to Expect at the Veterinarian's Office

You should see your doctor if the wound is very deep, very large (longer than one-half inch), very dirty, or has become infected. In these cases, your veterinarian will probably recommend surgery. A narcotic or tranquilizer and a local anesthetic (or general anesthesia) will be used so that your pet will not feel any pain. The

Cuts and Wounds

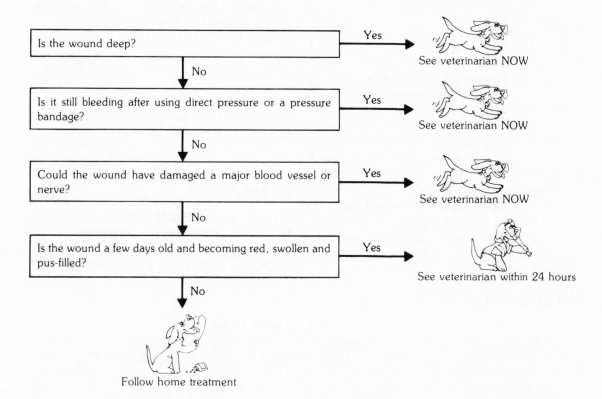

Is the wound deep? — **Yes** → See veterinarian NOW

No

Is it still bleeding after using direct pressure or a pressure bandage? — **Yes** → See veterinarian NOW

No

Could the wound have damaged a major blood vessel or nerve? — **Yes** → See veterinarian NOW

No

Is the wound a few days old and becoming red, swollen and pus-filled? — **Yes** → See veterinarian within 24 hours

No

Follow home treatment

wound will be explored for hair, dirt, and other foreign particles and flushed with sterile water mixed with antibiotics to prevent or eliminate infection. It will be sutured to decrease the healing time and to prevent dirt from reentering. If your dog chews its wounds, or if it is overactive, tranquilizers and/or a special protective collar may be prescribed during the healing period. Your veterinarian will also determine whether antibiotics are necessary.

Deep footpad wounds need to be sutured. Your doctor may also suggest antibiotics if the wound was extremely dirty. Dogs are quite resistant to tetanus, but if the wound occurred around stables, your veterinarian may recommend a tetanus shot.

Removing Stitches. Your veterinarian will tell you when the stitches are to be removed. Unless your doctor wants to recheck your pet, you can do the job yourself. Gently grasp a loose end of the knot with tweezers. Using a pair of small, sharp scissors, cut the stitch as close to the skin as possible and pull it out. Cutting close to the skin reduces the chance of contamination and infection.

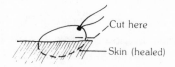

Cut here

Skin (healed)

Punctures and Animal Bites

One of the saddest things to see is a helpless dog admitted to our hospital after being shot or knifed. Puncture wounds can cause severe bleeding and injury to the internal organs. Veterinary aid is needed immediately.

If your pet was bitten by another animal, that animal should be quarantined for ten days to be sure it does not have rabies (page 144). If you know the owner and can ascertain that the animal has a current rabies vaccination, the quarantine can be done at home. If the owner is not known or if the animal is wild, such as a bat, fox, raccoon, or skunk, quarantine is maintained at a veterinary hospital, a public health facility, or a local pound.

Broken Nail

If a dog's nails are allowed to overgrow, they may break. This can be quite painful, and lameness may be seen. To correct the problem, restrain the dog (and muzzle it, if necessary) and pull off the nail quickly with a pair of pliers. Apply an antiseptic to the nail remnant. Bleeding is usually not excessive, but direct pressure or a pressure bandage may be helpful. Remove the pressure bandage the next day. The nail will regrow in a month. Be sure to check the other nails, including the dewclaw. If they are long, trim them (see page 59).

If you are having a problem removing the nail, your doctor will spray the area with a local anesthetic and quickly pull it off. Antibiotics are needed only if an infection develops, which is rare.

To prevent this problem, keep your dog's nails trimmed, and don't forget the dewclaw— the area where the thumb would be (see page 30).

Embedded Fishhook

Dogs really are curious, even about things that may hurt them, such as fishhooks. All too often, a dog sniffing around a fishing camp or a cluttered garbage can will get a fishhook caught in its lip or nose. Restraining the dog (page 89) is necessary if you are going to remove the hook at home. Remember, just as a fish cannot escape a fishhook once it is embedded, neither can a dog. Therefore, the barb must be pushed through the skin and cut with pliers. The rest of the fishhook can then be removed.

Amputated Tail

If your dog's tail is caught in a slammed car or house door or run over by a car, arrange to see the veterinarian immediately after you apply emergency measures (see Home Treatment).

Home Treatment

EMERGENCY   Check the entry and exit areas of puncture wounds. If necessary, give artificial respiration (page 90). Check the heartbeat and pulse (page 22) and control any bleeding (page 100). An amputated tail may require a tourniquet (page 92). Treat also for shock (page 93). Bullet and knife wounds can fracture bones, so a temporary splint (page 95) may be necessary.

The most common result of animal bites is not rabies but simple bacterial infections. The skin is normally a strong barrier against bacteria, but if penetrated, bacteria, hair, and dirt can enter and cause a serious infection or an abscess (page 182) days later.

Clip the hair around the wound with scissors; then clean the wound with soap and water and alcohol and remove any debris. Cover it with a gauze bandage or clean cloth. If the origin of the bite is unknown, quarantine may be necessary. Check with your doctor.

Punctures and Animal Bites

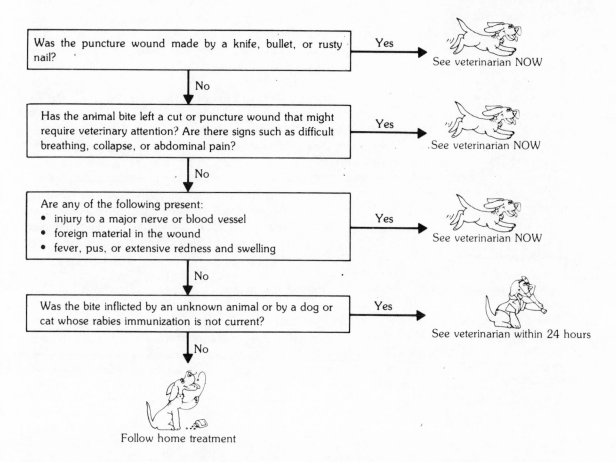

Was the puncture wound made by a knife, bullet, or rusty nail?

Yes → See veterinarian NOW

No ↓

Has the animal bite left a cut or puncture wound that might require veterinary attention? Are there signs such as difficult breathing, collapse, or abdominal pain?

Yes → See veterinarian NOW

No ↓

Are any of the following present:
- injury to a major nerve or blood vessel
- foreign material in the wound
- fever, pus, or extensive redness and swelling

Yes → See veterinarian NOW

No ↓

Was the bite inflicted by an unknown animal or by a dog or cat whose rabies immunization is not current?

Yes → See veterinarian within 24 hours

No ↓

Follow home treatment

What to Expect at the Veterinarian's Office
Your veterinarian will be concerned about three things: (1) controlling the bleeding (if this hasn't been done); (2) cleaning the wound and possibly suturing it to avoid infection; and, in the case of an animal bite, (3) identifying and confining the other animal.

Your pet may have to be given a tranquilizer and a local or general anesthetic in order to be cleaned and sutured. Antibiotics may be given to avoid infection, especially for dirty fishhook punctures. A rabies vaccination will be given if it is overdue.

If there is dislocation of a tail bone but your dog can move its tail, your veterinarian will probably suggest that no treatment is necessary. However, large gaping wounds with no dislocation will require suturing. Sometimes the nerves, tissue, and bones are damaged beyond repair. Complete amputation of the tail will be recommended in this case.

Insect Bites and Stings

Some insect bites will cause a local reaction, but a serious systemic reaction occurs only rarely. Bites from poisonous spiders are also rare, but they are life-threatening and need immediate attention.

Dogs, since their paws (and often their noses) are always on the ground, can easily be stung by an angry wasp, hornet, or yellow jacket. Swelling and pain of the muzzle or paw may occur; *hives* (bumps that appear suddenly all over the body) may also be seen. A dog will usually cry out when bitten, and if bitten on the muzzle will continuously rub its face on the ground.

Home Treatment
For bee stings, remove the stinger with tweezers, if you can see it, and apply a paste of baking soda and water to the swollen area to stop the burning and itching. The swelling will subside within twenty-four hours. Most dogs do not go into shock from bee stings, but if your pet collapses, administer artificial respiration (page 90) and treat for shock (page 93). See your veterinarian immediately.

If your pet is bitten by a black widow spider or a brown recluse (a brown spider with a white violin-shaped pattern on its back), apply ice packs immediately to the bitten area. The cold constricts the blood vessels there and decreases the local reaction. A tourniquet (page 92) will stop the poison from traveling throughout the body. After applying emergency measures, see your veterinarian.

What to Expect at the Veterinarian's Office
Your veterinarian will need to know what sort of insect or spider bit your dog. If a severe local or systemic reaction has occurred, your doctor will give injections of steroids and antihistamines to counteract the swelling and inflammation. Pain relievers may also be given. Your veterinarian may want to hospitalize and observe your pet for twenty-four hours. If breathing is impaired (this is rarely seen), oxygen will have to be given at the hospital.

Prevention
Watch your dog carefully around wood piles, where spiders like to hide. If your pet generally has severe allergic reactions to insect bites, ask your veterinarian to give you or to prescribe an emergency kit of injectable steroids and antihistamines to keep on hand at home, along with instructions on its proper use.

Insect Bites and Stings

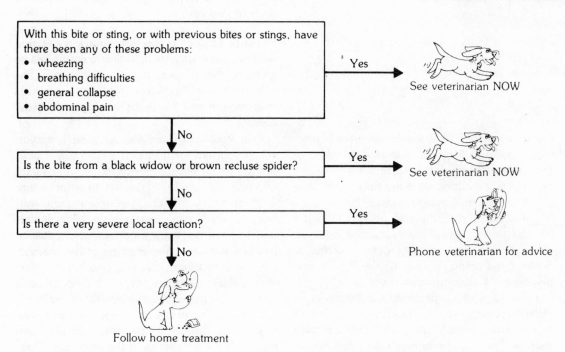

With this bite or sting, or with previous bites or stings, have there been any of these problems:
- wheezing
- breathing difficulties
- general collapse
- abdominal pain

Yes → See veterinarian NOW

No

Is the bite from a black widow or brown recluse spider?

Yes → See veterinarian NOW

No

Is there a very severe local reaction?

Yes → Phone veterinarian for advice

No

Follow home treatment

Convulsions and Seizures

Convulsions are temporary disturbances of electrical activity in the brain that lead to a loss of control of all the dog's skeletal muscles. A severe or lengthy convulsion does not necessarily indicate a serious underlying disease.

The *aura,* or preseizure period, may last from a few seconds to hours. Common signs are staring, lip licking, twitching, getting restless or nervous, salivating, hiding, wandering, or displaying more affection toward you.

The signs of a generalized seizure are an inability to stand, a loss of consciousness, a loss of bowel and/or urine control, and violent muscle spasms. The dog's body may stiffen and twitch, a frothy saliva may appear, and the eyes may jerk back and forth. After a seizure, the dog will be confused and appear blind and unresponsive, while at the same time salivating heavily and pacing back and forth.

Home Treatment

EMERGENCY Try to hold the dog down gently with a blanket. If you can't do so, clear the area of objects that may injure your pet. Stay calm —watching a seizure can be a frightening experience, but most seizures are not life-threatening. Your pet may have a few seizures in a row. If there is a high fever—greater than 106°F—an ice water bath will help lower the fever. Ice packs placed in the inner thighs and under the front legs are also helpful. See Fever, page 140, for other suggestions.

After the convulsion, calmly and quietly pet your dog and reassure it with your presence. Keep lights and noise to a minimum, since the brain is very sensitive. Seek veterinary aid as soon as you can.

What to Expect at the Veterinarian's Office

Intravenous injections of anticonvulsants will be given if the seizures have not stopped. The veterinarian will perform a complete physical examination and will probably suggest hospitalization.

In veterinary medicine, a good history is very important for diagnosis—especially if your pet has had a seizure. For example, at less than one year old, any breed can get distemper (page 142) or heavy intestinal parasitism (page 47), both of which can cause seizures. Toy breeds and hunting dogs are especially susceptible to low blood sugar, another cause of convulsions. From one to three years old, poodles, beagles, Irish setters, German shepherds, dachshunds and St. Bernards are susceptible to epilepsy; over five years old, some dogs have a predispositon to tumors in the brain (boxers and Boston bulls) or tumors in the pancreas. Dogs may also get low blood calcium, which can occur during pregnancy and the nursing period and cause convulsions.

Many household chemicals, if ingested, will cause seizures (see Swallowed Poisons, page 126), and any head injuries accompanied by unconsciousness occurring within the last two years could also be a factor. Since there are so many possible causes, tests are necessary for diagnosis. Your veterinarian may recommend:

- complete blood count (infection, lead poisoning)
- BUN (kidney disease)
- urinalysis (kidney, liver disease)
- blood sugar test
- blood calcium test
- liver function blood tests

Convulsions and Seizures

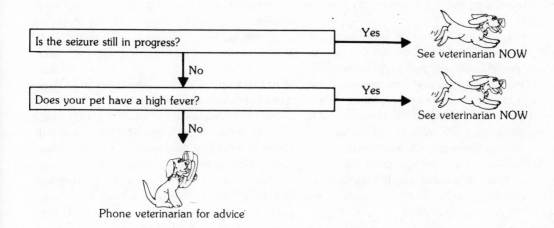

Is the seizure still in progress?	**Yes** → See veterinarian NOW

No ↓

Does your pet have a high fever?	**Yes** → See veterinarian NOW

No ↓

Phone veterinarian for advice

If spinal taps, specialized X rays, and electroencephalograms are required, they are usually done at universities or referral hospitals.

Medication can control convulsions, but you must be patient: It may be necessary to try various doses and combinations of drugs. No medication is needed if your dog has only one seizure and the cause is not determined. Occasionally, it may not be possible to regulate your dog. If so, you should be referred to a veterinary neurologist.

Bone Fractures

If your dog (1) is not bearing weight on a limb, (2) has a crooked limb, or (3) has limb pain and swelling, you should suspect a break. *Crepitus,* the sound or feel of bone rubbing on bone, is even stronger evidence of a fracture. If a piece of bone is protruding through the skin, there is no doubt.

In a *compound fracture,* a bone fragment penetrates the surface, and severe damage to the skin, muscle, nerves, and blood vessels can result. Delayed healing and infections can be serious problems in compound fractures. Since bone is not very resistant to infection, cover a compound fracture immediately with gauze or a clean cloth and get veterinary assistance.

Limb fractures are not life-threatening, but they should be temporarily splinted so that the jagged bone edges do not injure any neighboring tissues and nerves. Remember: A splint should include the joints immediately above and below the fracture.

Fractures of the spine from trauma are extreme emergencies, especially if your dog is hit by a car. You may see a paralysis of the hind legs and a stiffness (outstretching) of the front legs after trauma.

Home Treatment
EMERGENCY Gently restrain your dog (page 89) and muzzle it if it is breathing normally. Apply ice packs to decrease the swelling and inflammation. Splint the limb (page 95), but do *not* try to reset it. If the break is in the tail, immobilize it with a slender piece of wood or a tongue depresser. If the break is in the dog's spine, pelvis, or hindlegs, you will need to transport it by stretcher. See also Lameness, page 158.

What to Expect at the Veterinarian's Office
Your veterinarian will check all other systems to be sure that they were not injured. A radiograph (X ray) is needed to verify the fracture and to determine the best method of repair. Some fractures will heal with external stabilization (splints or casts) alone, while others need internal fixation (metal pins, plates, or wires). Discuss the chances of healing and the cost of each technique with your veterinarian. Today, no dog has to be put to sleep because it has a fracture—a three-legged dog is still more agile than a two-legged person!

Bone Fractures

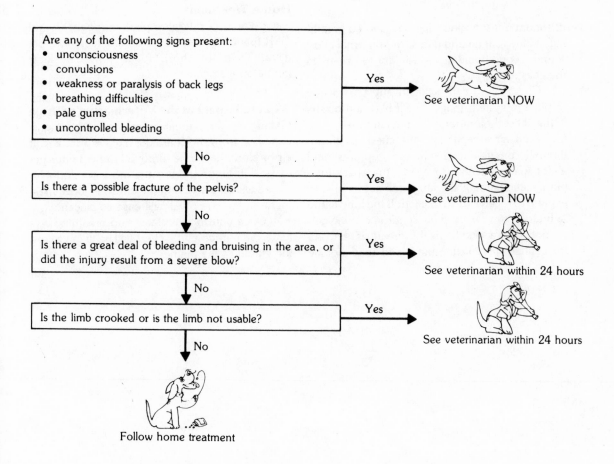

Are any of the following signs present:
- unconsciousness
- convulsions
- weakness or paralysis of back legs
- breathing difficulties
- pale gums
- uncontrolled bleeding

Yes → See veterinarian NOW

No

Is there a possible fracture of the pelvis?

Yes → See veterinarian NOW

No

Is there a great deal of bleeding and bruising in the area, or did the injury result from a severe blow?

Yes → See veterinarian within 24 hours

No

Is the limb crooked or is the limb not usable?

Yes → See veterinarian within 24 hours

No

Follow home treatment

Chest Injuries

If, for any reason, your dog has labored breathing, a blue tongue and gums, or abnormal chest sounds, you should suspect injury to organs in the chest.

Chest injury can occur in any part of the respiratory system (page 23). If bleeding occurs in the chest (hemothorax), if the lung tissue ruptures and air escapes into the chest (pneumothorax), or if the diaphragm ruptures and abdominal contents move into the chest (diaphragmatic hernia), the lungs will not be able to expand to receive fresh oxygen. If the lung tissue is bruised (*traumatic lung syndrome*), oxygen cannot be received. If the heart is bruised (*myocardial irritability*), the blood may not be pumped efficiently. Thus, you can see that *all* chest injuries are potentially life-threatening.

Home Treatment
EMERGENCY   Artificial respiration (page 90) and CPR (page 91) may be needed to keep your pet alive. Treat for shock (page 93). Transport gently on a stretcher.

What to Expect at the Veterinarian's Office
Getting oxygen into its system and stabilizing its condition from shock are the highest priorities. If air or blood has to be removed to help your pet expand its lungs and breathe more comfortably, a tube will be inserted in the chest. A local anesthesia in the chest wall will ease its placement.

Once your dog is stable and breathing better, a radiograph of the chest will be taken to see the extent of the injuries.

Chest Injuries

Are any of the following signs present:
- labored breathing
- blue tongue and gums
- abnormal chest sounds

Yes →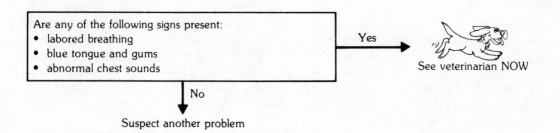

See veterinarian NOW

No

Suspect another problem

Head Injuries

All head injuries are potentially life-threatening, even if there is no outward sign of injury. The skull is a bony casing, and the brain bounces against the skull when there is a blow on the head. This can cause bleeding to occur within and around the brain, and the accumulation of blood can compress the brain.

If your pet is or becomes unconscious, immediate veterinary attention is necessary. Other signs that the brain has been affected are:

1. uneven pupil size (caused by pressure on the brain from bleeding)

2. pale gums

3. a slow pulse (less than 60)

4. limb paralysis or stiffness

5. convulsions

If your dog is unconscious, extend its head and neck and pull the tongue forward. Clean the blood and fluids from the mouth, and transport the animal on a flat, hard surface to the veterinarian or veterinary hospital.

The most frequent cause of serious head injury is being hit by a car. Puppies will also occasionally sustain head injury from being hit by falling objects. Adult dogs are fortunate in having large muscles that cover their skulls and cushion some blows to the head. In serious accidents, do *not* overlook possible chest, abdomen, or limb injury, as well.

Home Treatment

EMERGENCY   Observe your dog very carefully: Check the pupils, pulse, and gums frequently, and treat for shock. Control any bleeding with direct pressure, using a clean cloth. Remove all blood, mucus, and debris from the mouth and give artificial respiration (page 90), if necessary. If the skull is fractured (see Bone Fractures, page 108), transport your dog on a flat, hard surface to the doctor's office.

If your pet appears normal but has convulsions in four to six months after the injury, check with your doctor. This condition is occasionally seen and requires no medication; the convulsions usually disappear in a few months. This is thought to be a temporary abnormal electrical brain discharge, provoked by the injury, which resolves itself. Of course, if the seizures get worse, further tests will be needed.

What to Expect at the Veterinarian's Office

Your veterinarian will need a good history of the accident that happened. Your pet's head, eyes, ears, nose, throat, and neck will be examined. The back of the eyes will be examined with an ophthalmoscope to check for pressure on the brain and for evidence of hemorrhage. A complete neurological exam, including checking the reflexes, will be done. The chest and abdomen will be examined for injury or internal bleeding. The limbs and pelvis will be checked for fractures or dislocations.

Since bleeding within the skull can be suspected from a thorough physical examination and not by X rays in general practice, skull X rays are helpful only if a fracture is present.

Oxygen and medication (steroids) may be used to reduce brain swelling, but your veterinarian will not give tranquilizers or other medication that may obscure the observation of your pet's improving or deteriorating brain injury. If your dog was unconscious at any time, ask your veterinarian to make sure someone competent will be monitoring your pet through the night; an increasing number of hospitals are equipped for *intensive* twenty-four care. (If not, ask if you could monitor the dog at home.) Registration in a university veterinary hospital or an emergency hospital may be requested if one is nearby and if your doctor feels that it would be helpful.

Prevention

Of course, dogs that are on a leash or in a fenced yard don't get the opportunity to tangle with

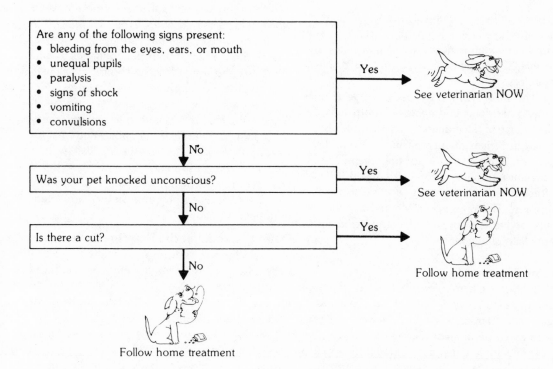

Are any of the following signs present:
- bleeding from the eyes, ears, or mouth
- unequal pupils
- paralysis
- signs of shock
- vomiting
- convulsions

Yes → See veterinarian NOW

No ↓

Was your pet knocked unconscious?

Yes → See veterinarian NOW

No ↓

Is there a cut?

Yes → Follow home treatment

No ↓

Follow home treatment

cars. Keep your dog in a fenced yard and walk it on a leash to prevent trauma from dog fights and other injuries—especially if your dog is a fighter.

I'm all for exercising dogs in wide open spaces that are *not* near roads. *Never* allow your dog to walk unleashed near a street. I've seen too many "trained" dogs who spotted another dog across the street, ran across, and bango!! —got hit by a car. When crossing at a corner with your leashed dog, be sure that you shorten the leash so that your dog is at your side—not in front of you—or you may end up holding a leash with an injured dog at the other end.

Another point: When you're traveling, put a leash on your dog before getting out of the car. Many dogs have dashed out from excitement only to be hit by a passing car.

Eye Injuries

All eye injuries are potentially serious. Whenever an eye or eyelid is injured, an examination by your veterinarian is necessary. Minor injuries to the eye, if not treated properly, can result in vision loss.

The most common causes of eye injuries are auto accidents and fights. These usually result in eyelid lacerations, lacerations of the cornea (the clear membrane in the front of the eye), or internal injury to the eyeball itself. Sometimes the injury is so severe that the eyeball is forced out of the socket, a condition called *proptosis*. The presence of chemicals, such as acids or lye, or foreign objects also requires immediate attention.

Home Treatment

EMERGENCY Chemicals splashed in the eye need to be *immediately* flushed out, using lots of clean water. This must be done as soon as possible to avoid permanent damage to the cornea. Flush five to ten minutes; afterward, apply a clean cloth or gauze bandage to protect the eye from further injury. See your doctor immediately.

Eyelid lacerations can bleed profusely. Applying direct pressure with a gauze or clean cloth to the lid for five minutes should control the bleeding. If the laceration is on the eyeball, cover it with gauze or clean cloth, but do *not* apply pressure.

If a foreign object is under one of the eyelids, your pet will paw at the eye and squint. Of course, these signs are also seen in other conditions, but take a look under the lid—you may see a piece of sand or a loose eyelash. Use a bright light when looking for a foreign body in the eye. Pull the lower lid down with your thumb

and inspect the pink conjunctiva that lines the eye and the inner surface of the eyelids; do the same to the upper lid. A cotton-tipped applicator moistened with water and *gently* moved across the conjunctiva can remove the object. You can also flush the inner lid surfaces with clean water while holding the lid open. *Note:* Do *not* try to inspect or swab behind the third eyelid; you may scratch the cornea. If your pet continues to paw at the eye and squint for a few hours, check with your doctor. The cornea may be injured.

Proptosis is an obvious surgical emergency. Since the cause is a severe head injury, check the breathing, heartbeat, and pulse and treat for shock (page 93). Protect the eyeball with a cold, moist gauze sponge or clean cloth so that it will not dry out or be further injured. Control any bleeding with direct pressure. Immediate veterinary help is needed.

What to Expect at the Veterinarian's Office

Your doctor will perform a complete physical if generalized injury from an auto accident has occurred. An ophthalmoscope will be used to inspect all the structures within the eyeball, including under the lids.

A local anesthetic will make it easier to check behind the third eyelid if a foreign body is suspected. If a foreign body is found, a moistened cotton swab or eyewash solution will remove it. An antibiotic ointment is sometimes applied.

A harmless fluorescent dye will be administered and the eye then examined with an ultraviolet light. Whenever the cornea is injured, the dye will confirm the extent of the damage. This procedure is painless. If there is damage to the cornea, antibiotic drops or ointment will be used to protect this delicate membrane from infection. If an *iritis* (an irritation of the colored part of the eye) is present, drops to dilate the pupil are needed. Steroids are used to decrease the inflammation in minor injuries to the cornea (*corneal abrasions*).

Eye Injuries

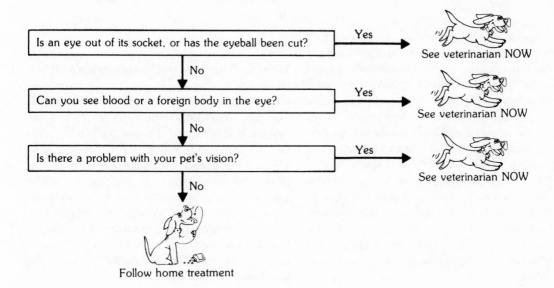

Is an eye out of its socket, or has the eyeball been cut? — Yes → See veterinarian NOW

No

Can you see blood or a foreign body in the eye? — Yes → See veterinarian NOW

No

Is there a problem with your pet's vision? — Yes → See veterinarian NOW

No

Follow home treatment

In a case of proptosis, your doctor will recommend replacement of the eyeball in the socket, *if* the accident just occurred and the globe is not severely damaged. If the vessels and nerves were not injured, vision may be saved.

Severe injury to the eyeball may necessitate removing the eye, or *enucleation*. Dogs with one eye or no vision get around remarkably well and are very happy. So do not suggest "putting my dog to sleep" if an eye has to be removed.

Prevention

Keep your dog away when you are working with corrosive materials.

Internal Bleeding

Massive internal bleeding reduces the amount of fluid carrying oxygen and nutrients through the body. If the organs do not get enough oxygen, they die. Immediate veterinary help is needed if profuse bleeding is noted from any body orifice or if your dog shows the following signs: weakness, pale gums, abdominal pain, breathing difficulty, weak pulse. If your dog was injured by an automobile, assume that there is some internal bleeding. Internal bleeding of the stomach is usually indicated by a bright or dark red color to the dog's vomit. If its excrement is dark and tarry or bright red, the intestines may be bleeding. If a red foamy material is coughed up, the lungs may be affected. Some poisons can also cause internal bleeding.

Home Treatment
Lay the dog down and cover it lightly. *Note:* Do *not* struggle with it. Transport the animal gently, since its body's ability to carry oxygen is decreased.

What to Expect at the Veterinarian's Office
EMERGENCY If possible, call your veterinarian so that he or she can prepare for your arrival. The first, most important steps are to provide oxygen and to replace the lost fluids with intravenous fluids and/or blood. Antibiotics to prevent infection and corticosteroids to maintain cellular health will also be given. Your pet will be kept warm with a heating pad or blankets. Its urine output and blood will be monitored to measure progress or deterioration of the condition. If these measures are not sufficient, surgical intervention may be necessary to stop the bleeding.

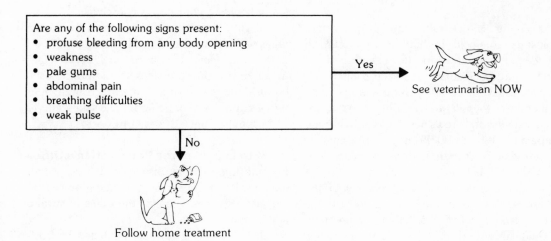

Are any of the following signs present:
- profuse bleeding from any body opening
- weakness
- pale gums
- abdominal pain
- breathing difficulties
- weak pulse

Yes → See veterinarian NOW

No ↓

Follow home treatment

Hypothermia and Frostbite

A dog's fur is generally enough protection against extreme cold, but any long exposure to low temperatures and wind (for example, if the dog is injured and unable to reach shelter) can produce a severe lowering of your dog's body temperature (*hypothermia*). Shivering, stumbling, exhaustion, drowsiness, and a low body temperature (80° to 90°F) may be present.

Frostbite is also rare in dogs; however your dog's ear tips, tail, and scrotum may be frozen on very cold days. Their position on your pet predispose them to the full fury of chilly winds and icy temperatures. Frostbitten ear tips may appear leathery and stiff, and the hair on the tips may turn white. The scrotum may become red and scaly.

Home Treatment
EMERGENCY   For hypothermia, place the dog in a warm room. Warm water baths, hot water bottles, and an electric heating blanket (carefully used) will increase the body temperature. (Be patient; it increases slowly.) You can measure progress by rectal temperature (page 34) and by the dog's response (it will be more alert). Give warm liquids if your dog is conscious.

If your dog is frostbitten, warm the frozen areas with your hands or with moist, warm (*not* hot) towels. *Note:* Do *not* rub or squeeze. Ointments or pressure dressings should *not* be used because this may further injure the tissue. If your pet has discomfort or pain, or if the skin seems to be becoming infected, see your doctor.

What to Expect at the Veterinarian's Office
If home treatment is unsuccessful, your veterinarian will treat for shock, continue the rewarming methods, and monitor the dog's heart and kidney function.

If any tissue is severely damaged by frostbite, antibiotics will be needed to avoid infection. Pain relievers may be suggested as well. Hasty surgery to repair or amputate the damaged tissue is usually not necessary. If the tissue is kept clean and antibiotics are given, healing usually is seen in a week.

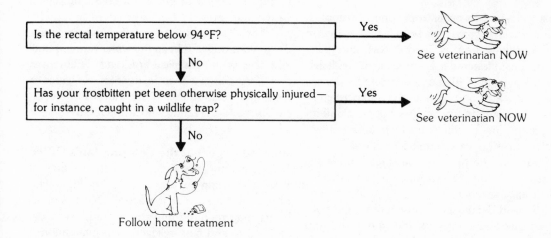

Is the rectal temperature below 94°F?   Yes → See veterinarian NOW

No

Has your frostbitten pet been otherwise physically injured— for instance, caught in a wildlife trap?   Yes → See veterinarian NOW

No

Follow home treatment

Burns

Most burns in dogs occur from coming in contact with hot water, grease, or tar, from chewing on electrical wires, from licking hot barbecue grills, or from being trapped in burning buildings. If less than 15 percent of the body is affected, chances of recovery are good. If more than 50 percent of the body is burned, recovery is not anticipated.

Burns are classified by their depth. First-degree burns are very superficial. The skin is red and painful. The hair may be singed but is still attached. Veterinary assistance is not needed, and healing is rapid.

Second-degree burns are more extensive: Severe swelling is present; the skin is red and painful and will slough; healing is slower. In addition, there may be a significant fluid loss from the burn. See your veterinarian.

Third-degree burns are very serious and need emergency veterinary care. The hair falls out, and the skin may be either black or pearly white. Since the entire skin layer has been destroyed, infection and fluid loss are great dangers. The burn is painless, however, because the nerves in the area have been destroyed. Healing is very slow unless a skin graft is performed.

Home Treatment

EMERGENCY   Clip hair away from a first-degree burn with scissors, then flush the area with cold water. Gently dry it with clean or sterile gauze. You can also apply cold compresses. *Note:* Do *not* use ointments. Deeper second-or third-degree burns should be seen by your veterinarian immediately. Simply cover the affected area with a clean cloth (*not* cotton), treat for shock (page 93), and go to your doctor. *Note:* Do *not* apply water, antiseptics, or ointments.

Dogs that are burned by chewing on electric cords should be seen by your veterinarian, also. There will be burns on the lips, tongue, and gums but the threat to life is that the heart may stop or that fluid may get in the lungs (*pulmonary edema*). Feel the chest for the heartbeat and feel for the femoral pulse. If there is no heartbeat, and your pet is not breathing, begin CPR (page 91).

For chemical burns, run a shower or hose down your dog and keep the water running until all traces of the chemical are gone. Then cover the affected area with a clean, cold, wet gauze or cloth and treat the animal for shock. For electrical burns, see Treating Shock, page 93.

What to Expect at the Veterinarian's Office

Your veterinarian will determine the severity of the burns. Clipping, cleaning, and giving antibiotics may be all that is needed. More serious burns may require intravenous fluids, steroids, antibiotics, and pain relievers. Hospitalization is also necessary for these cases since close nursing care is required to save your pet's life. If the burns are extensive and your dog survives, skin grafts may be necessary.

A puppy that has bitten through an electric cord may have burns just in the mouth that require antibiotics to prevent infection and anti-inflammatory drugs to reduce swelling. If the current has injured the heart or lungs, intensive treatment for shock, including oxygen, may be needed to save its life.

Prevention

Don't allow your dog to lie below the stove when cooking, since a pot of boiling water or oil can easily be tipped over. If your pet insists on lying near the stove because it can't resist the wonderful smells, use the back burners whenever possible.

At the dinner table, never pass hot food over your pet's head. Many hot foods have been spilled on a pet waiting for a free handout.

Whenever a puppy in the teething stage (three to eight months) is left in a room unobserved for a long period of time, unplug the electric appliances that are not being used.

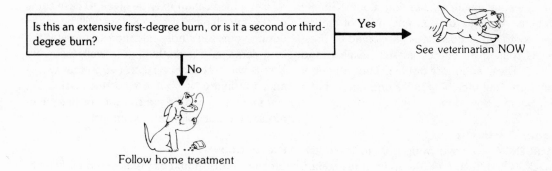

Is this an extensive first-degree burn, or is it a second or third-degree burn?

Yes → See veterinarian NOW

No ↓

Follow home treatment

Smoke Inhalation

Fire does not injure by burning alone: Smoke contains very little oxygen and a lot of carbon monoxide. Other poisonous gases may be present as well, from burned plastic, textiles, and rubber. These add more trouble. Thus a fire not only burns the breathing tubes and lungs, but it also poisons your dog.

Home Treatment
EMERGENCY Remove your dog to fresh air. Check its breathing and use artificial respiration (page 90). Treat your dog for shock (page 93), then seek veterinary aid.

What to Expect at the Veterinarian's Office
If your dog is conscious, and there is no blood-tinged sputum being coughed up and no fluid in the lungs, humidified oxygen and steroids may be given to try to prevent such problems as severe pneumonia from developing during the critical period—the next forty-eight hours. Pain-relieving medication may be given to ease some of the breathing distress. X rays will be taken during your dog's hospitalization to monitor the lung damage. If everything goes well, follow-up X rays will probably be taken two to four weeks after the injury. If your dog is unconscious, is coughing up blood-tinged sputum, or has pneumonia, the outlook is more serious.

Prevention
Smoke alarms should be installed, and any other fire prevention measures should be taken. Your local humane shelter or fire department can provide you with a decal for your door that will notify the fire department of the number of pets to look for and their usual location in your home in case of fire.

Smoke Inhalation

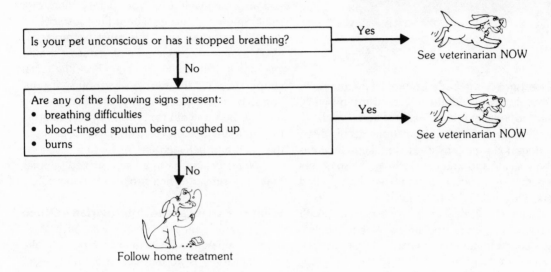

Is your pet unconscious or has it stopped breathing? — **Yes** → See veterinarian NOW

No

Are any of the following signs present:
- breathing difficulties
- blood-tinged sputum being coughed up
- burns

— **Yes** → See veterinarian NOW

No

Follow home treatment

Heatstroke

In heatstroke, the body is completely unable to lower its fever. All the mechanisms normally used to regulate body temperature, such as panting, are ineffectual. Heatstroke occurs often in dogs that, on hot days, are kept in areas where shade and water are lacking. It also occurs in pets that are left in unventilated, hot, parked cars. Dogs with short noses (boxers, bulldogs, Pekingese), old, or fat pets are especially prone to heatstroke, since they are less able to regulate their body temperature in warm or hot environments.

The signs of heatstroke are dramatic and include a rectal temperature of over 106°F, extreme panting, a fast-pounding pulse, weakness, a staring expression, and collapse.

Home Treatment

EMERGENCY A high body temperature must be lowered rapidly to avoid brain damage or death. As in the treatment for fever, a cold water bath or shower must be given immediately. Ice applied to the head and between the thighs is beneficial. Being in an air-conditioned room also helps bring down the fever. If the body temperature has not dropped to 103°F in ten minutes, a cold water enema may be necessary. See the section on fever, page 140, for instructions on giving a cold water enema. *Note:* After a cold water enema, improvement *cannot* be measured by rectal temperature.

If your dog stops panting, seems more relaxed, and responds normally to your voice, you are doing well. Give your pet ice cubes or a small amount of water. Great fluid loss occurs during heatstroke, and this must be replaced. Once your pet seems improved, a doctor should examine it. If this is impossible, check the rectal temperature for the next twelve hours. If your dog's condition gets worse, seek veterinary aid quickly. Be sure your car is well ventilated during the trip to the doctor. Keep applying ice cubes to the head and between the thighs.

Note: Eclampsia in a bitch nursing puppies may look similar to heatstroke (see page 238).

What to Expect at the Veterinarian's Office

If your emergency treatment was successful, your veterinarian will examine your pet to make sure that there is no permanent brain or organ damage. If emergency treatment at home was not successful, it will be necessary to replace lost water and treat for shock (intravenous fluids and steroids). Cold water baths and enemas will be continued. Oxygen will be given if needed, and your dog will be hospitalized so that it can be observed closely for twenty-four hours.

Prevention

Adequate ventilation, shade, and free access to water are necessary. If you have to leave your dog in the car on a warm day, be sure that you park in the shade and keep the window open for ventilation. Carry water in the car for your pet. Check car-bound dogs frequently; remember, the sun changes direction. *Note:* If your pet is short-nosed, old, or fat, these precautions may not be enough. Try keeping them in a cool room with an adequate water supply.

Heatstroke

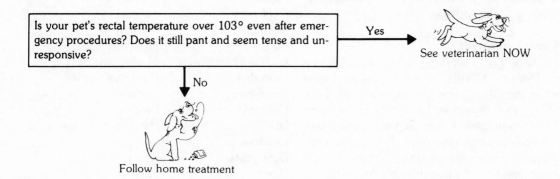

Is your pet's rectal temperature over 103° even after emergency procedures? Does it still pant and seem tense and unresponsive?

Yes → See veterinarian NOW

No → Follow home treatment

Swallowed Poisons

Dogs, when curious, can get into a lot of trouble by swallowing products that are around the house or in the garbage.

Home Treatment

EMERGENCY   If your dog swallows a poison (see the Decision Chart), call your poison control center immediately and get veterinary aid. Take the poison container and a sample of the vomit to the veterinarian. If your dog stops breathing, give artificial respiration (page 90). If you cannot reach your veterinarian or poison control center, check for the poison on the following lists and give the prescribed treatment. If the poison cannot be identified, force your dog to swallow egg whites, milk of magnesia, and/or milk (see Giving Liquids to Your Dog, page 82).

List A: Petroleum Products, Acids, and Alkalies

Dishwasher granules	Oven cleaner
Drain cleaner	Paint remover
Floor polish	Paint thinner
Furniture polish	Shoe polish
Gasoline	Toilet bowl cleaner
Kerosene	Wax (floor or
Lye	furniture)
	Wood preservative

Signs of poisoning by these products are bloody vomit, diarrhea, shock, depression, coma, convulsions (sometimes), coughing, abdominal pain, and redness around the mouth. *Note:* Do *not* induce vomiting! Make your dog swallow milk, egg whites, or olive oil to prevent absorption of the poison into your dog's system. Treat also for shock (page 93).

Acids and alkalies can also burn the mouth and skin, so flush these areas with large amounts of water. Apply a sodium bicarbonate paste to acid burns. Apply vinegar to neutralize alkali burns.

List B: Other Known Poisons

Acetone	Insecticides
Alcohol	Linoleum (lead salts)
Algae toxins	Matches
Amphetamines	(*Note:* Safety
Aspirin	matches are non-
Antifreeze	toxic)
Arsenic	Medicines
Bleach	Moth balls
Carbon tetrachloride	Mushrooms, wild
Chlordane	Paint, lead-based
Cosmetics	Perfume
Crayons	Pine oil
DDT	Rat or mouse poison
Deodorants	Red squill
Detergents	Roach poison
Fabric softener	Shellac
Fireworks	Sleeping pills
Fluoroacetates	Snail bait
Garbage toxins	Strychnine
Hair dye	Suntan lotions
Hexachlorophene	Thallium
(in certain soaps)	Warfarin
Indelible markers	Weed killer

Signs of poisoning by these products include severe vomiting, diarrhea, delirium, collapse, coma, and convulsions. If your dog is conscious, induce vomiting: Mix equal amounts of hydrogen peroxide (3 percent strength) and water and administer one tablespoon of this fluid. A mustard and water solution also works well. Another way to induce vomiting is to put a few tablespoons of salt on the back of the dog's tongue; repeat this until vomiting occurs. Then treat for shock (page 93).

What to Expect at the Veterinarian's Office

If your dog is unconscious, oxygen and intravenous fluids will be given. Other life-preserving procedures, such as stomach pumping, may be necessary. Hospitalization will be required.

If your dog is conscious, treatment will depend upon the particular poison swallowed and whether an antidote is known.

Swallowed Poisons

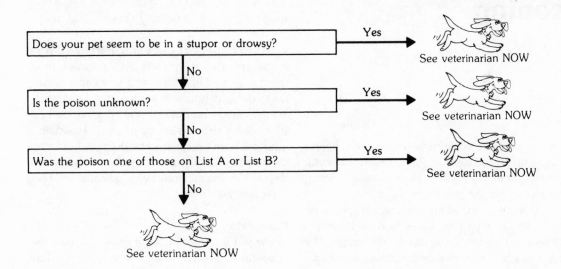

Does your pet seem to be in a stupor or drowsy? — Yes → See veterinarian NOW

No ↓

Is the poison unknown? — Yes → See veterinarian NOW

No ↓

Was the poison one of those on List A or List B? — Yes → See veterinarian NOW

No ↓

See veterinarian NOW

Carbon Monoxide Poisoning

Exhaust fumes contain carbon monoxide. If your dog is put in the trunk of the car with the motor running or in a car with a poor exhaust system, carbon monoxide poisoning can occur.

Carbon monoxide blocks the transportation of life-giving oxygen to the body cells. If oxygen cannot get to the cells, death will occur. The signs of carbon monoxide poisoning are weakness, cherry-red gums, twitching muscles, and an elevated temperature (see also page 122).

Home Treatment
EMERGENCY Get your dog into fresh air. If breathing has stopped, give artificial respiration (page 90). Seek veterinary assistance at once.

What to Expect at the Veterinarian's Office
If you provided immediate aid, no further treatment may be necessary, and you can probably take your dog home. If not, oxygen (to counteract the carbon monoxide) and intravenous fluids (to treat for shock) may be needed, especially if your pet hasn't recovered by the time you reach the veterinarian's office. Observation for a few days in the hospital may be suggested if your dog is recovering slowly.

Prevention
Never put your dog in a car trunk. Be sure that your car's exhaust system is in good working order. If camping, do *not* use propane gas stoves or heaters in an unventilated tent.

Carbon Monoxide Poisoning

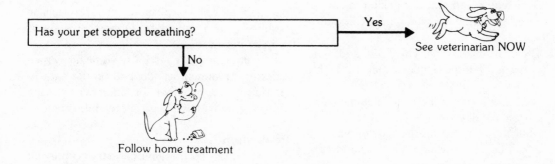

Has your pet stopped breathing? — Yes → See veterinarian NOW

No ↓

Follow home treatment

Poisonous Plants

Dogs may be curious and chew up your house plants. Following are some common house-plants that are dangerous to your dog:

Christmas cherry: The berry is poisonous.
Dieffenbachia, also called Dumb cane: The leaves can cause vomiting, diarrhea, swelling of the tongue, and even suffocation.
Dried arrangements: The seed pods and beans of tropical plants may be highly toxic.
Ivy: The leaves can cause breathing and stomach illness.
Mistletoe: The berries are highly toxic and can cause vomiting, diarrhea, and convulsions.

The following outdoor plants can also be hazardous if chewed and/or swallowed:

Castor bean	Lobelia
Daphne	Mistletoe
Foxglove	Monkshood
Horse chestnut	Nightshade
Jimson weed	Poison Hemlock
Larkspur	Water Hemlock
Laurels	Yew
Lily-of-the-valley	

Home Treatment

EMERGENCY If you discover that your dog has dined on a houseplant, call your poison control center immediately and get veterinary aid. If you don't know the name of the plant, take it along to the veterinarian's office. Give artificial respiration (page 90), if necessary. If you cannot reach a poison control center or your veterinarian, see Swallowed Poisons, page 126, and follow the treatment.

What to Expect at the Veterinarian's Office

If your dog is unconscious, oxygen and intravenous fluids will be given. The stomach may be pumped, as well. Hospitalization will probably be required, since other life support procedures may be necessary.

If your dog is conscious, vomiting will be induced. Treatment will depend on the particular poison and whether the attempts to make your dog vomit have been successful.

Prevention

There is one step that you can take to prevent poisoning from houseplants: Do *not* keep known poisonous plants in the house! If you just can't do without that beautiful plant that is potentially hazardous, the following may prevent its ingestion:

1. Be sure your puppy gets a lot of outdoor exercise during the teething stage (three to eight months). A tired pup chews less.

2. Hard rubber toys, such as rawhide bones or Nylabones®, will also keep your puppy busy.

3. Keep the hazardous plants high up or in an area where the puppy can't get to them.

4. If you must give your dog a real bone, please see page 40 for an appropriate guideline to follow.

Poisonous Plants

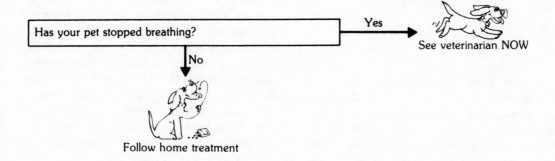

Has your pet stopped breathing? — Yes → See veterinarian NOW

No ↓

Follow home treatment

Snakebites

Dogs are not bitten by snakes very often because they are "street smart" and usually stay away from poisonous snakes. Snake venom attacks the blood cells and/or nervous system and can cause immediate pain, severe swelling, weakness, vomiting, diarrhea, bleeding from the nose and anus, paralysis, convulsions, and coma.

Home Treatment
EMERGENCY   Identify the snake by checking the fang marks. A poisonous snake usually leaves

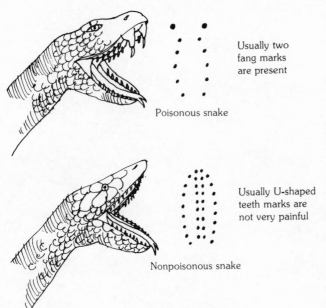

Usually two fang marks are present

Poisonous snake

Usually U-shaped teeth marks are not very painful

Nonpoisonous snake

just two marks (fangs) in the skin. A non-poisonous snake usually leaves U-shaped teeth marks, and the bite is not very painful.

If the snake was poisonous, apply a tourniquet (page 92) between the bite and the heart. You should be able to get one finger under the tourniquet, so that the wound can ooze slightly. Leave the tourniquet on for one to two hours maximum. Keep your dog quiet and lying down. Clip the hair over the wound with scissors. Apply alcohol to the wound and make a shallow linear (not X-shaped) cut over the fang marks using a flame-sterilized knife or razor. Use a suction cup to suck out the venom. You can use your mouth also—but only if there are no open sores. Spit out the venom—do *not* swallow it. Repeat for fifteen minutes. Leaving the tourniquet on, wash the wound with soap and water and apply cold compresses. Clean the wound with alcohol.

If your dog is struggling too much, just apply a tourniquet and see the veterinarian as quickly as possible.

If the snake was nonpoisonous, apply cold compresses and clean the wound with soap, water, and alcohol.

What to Expect at the Veterinarian's Office
Hospitalization will be necessary. Additional suction of the wound will be done. Ice packs will be applied to decrease pain and tissue damage. *Antivenin,* if available, will be given to neutralize the venom. Shock treatment, antibiotics, fluids, steroids, and possibly oxygen may be needed.

Prevention
Keep your pet away from known snake-infested areas. Keep an antivenin kit handy.

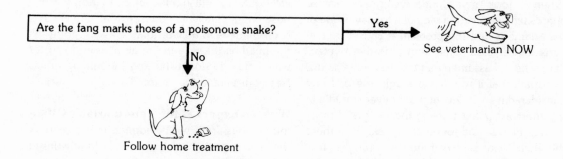

Are the fang marks those of a poisonous snake? —— Yes ——▶ See veterinarian NOW

No

Follow home treatment

Toad Poisoning

When I took my Florida veterinary license boards ten years ago, a slide of a toad was one of the "name it and the problem it causes" questions. Since I had come from a northern veterinary school, I assumed that this was either so unimportant that it was never taught me or I had considered it so irrelevant that I never stored it in my memory. After passing the boards, I practiced in Florida and found out quickly that there the Bufo toad is as common as oranges. It is found in other areas, too, but the Florida variety seems to be much more deadly.

Bufo toads are slow-moving creatures, and a dog may pick one up in its mouth. The wartlike salivary glands on the back of the toad's neck release a poison that, after being rapidly absorbed through the dog's mouth and stomach lining, causes heart irregularities. Within minutes, the dog will shake its head, salivate profusely, and become uncoordinated. The breathing and heart rates become rapid. Collapse, convulsions, and death can occur within fifteen minutes.

Home Treatment

EMERGENCY   Wash out your dog's mouth with a hose immediately if you see that contact has been made with a Bufo toad. Be sure not to tilt the head all the way in the air as you do so, or water may go down the dog's breathing tubes. See your veterinarian immediately.

What to Expect at the Veterinarian's Office

Intravenous drugs will be administered to correct the heart irregularities. If you have already rinsed out the dog's mouth yourself and have managed to get the dog to the veterinarian quickly, your dog has the best chance for survival.

Prevention

Leash-walk your dog at night, which is when the toads like to be out. When I lived in Florida, my dog ran after a few toads, but fortunately he was even slower than they were.

Toad Poisoning

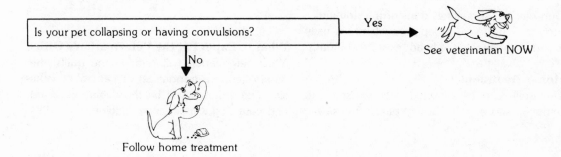

Is your pet collapsing or having convulsions? —— Yes ——→ See veterinarian NOW

No

Follow home treatment

Porcupine Quills

Curiosity can sometimes transform a dog into a furry pin cushion. Porcupine quills are usually found embedded in the head, nose, and mouth.

Home Treatment
The quills can be softened with vinegar and removed more easily using pliers, by slowly twisting out each quill. This is *extremely* painful, and it may be difficult to restrain your dog without sedation. If you get the quills out, be sure to cleanse the puncture wounds with an antiseptic, since quill wounds can get infected very easily.

What to Expect at the Veterinarian's Office
Your veterinarian will remove the quills after administering a tranquilizer or general anesthesia. The wounds will be thoroughly cleansed, and your dog will be given antibiotics.

Porcupine Quills

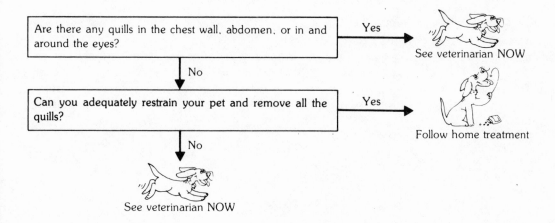

Are there any quills in the chest wall, abdomen, or in and around the eyes? → **Yes** → See veterinarian NOW

↓ **No**

Can you adequately restrain your pet and remove all the quills? → **Yes** → Follow home treatment

↓ **No**

See veterinarian NOW

Chapter **8**
Common Problems and Diseases

Fever

In dogs, a body temperature above 103°F is a fever, but an elevated temperature is not necessarily a sign of illness. Many healthy pets will have a variation in temperature of one or two degrees depending on the time of day, their emotional state and amount of activity, or the environment, such as riding in a hot automobile. Muscle activity and food digestion are the most important ways dogs produce heat to maintain body temperature. Some healthy animals that are nervous will shake so much (i.e., increase their muscle activity) at the doctor's office that a 104°F temperature may be recorded.

The most common causes for persistent fevers in dogs are viral and bacterial infections. Examples are distemper and hepatitis (viral), skin abscesses and pyometra (bacterial), and respiratory infections (viral and/or bacterial). Other causes are heat stroke (environmental), *eclampsia* (low blood calcium), and cancer (lymphosarcoma or leukemia).

The hair coat of most dogs insulates against heat loss or heat gain. If it is a hot day, the only way they can lower their body temperature is by panting, since they do not have sweat glands (except on the footpads). If they are in a closed, unventilated car on a hot day, the panting mechanism will not be able to lower the body temperature enough, and heatstroke will result.

Bacteria, viruses, and probably cancer cells cause fever by stimulating certain white blood cells to produce chemical substances called *pyrogens*. Pyrogens can be helpful in combating unwanted invaders. Therefore, fever is not always a bad sign—it may mean that your pet's body is responding to the challenge and fighting the infection.

There are a number of signs that will tell you when your dog has a true fever. Depression, a sad expression, and lack of appetite are common signs. Some dogs seem cold and shiver; others feel hot and pant or seek cool places. You may also notice an increase in both the heart and and respiratory rates.

Home Treatment

Take your dog's temperature as you did during the home physical, using a rectal thermometer, which has a rounded tip. Shake down the thermometer and apply vaseline or mineral oil to the bulb. If necessary, restrain your dog (page 89), lift its tail, and gently slide the thermometer into the anus. Leave it in for three minutes. It is advisable to hold the back end of your pet with one hand and the tail and the thermometer with the other, so that your pet cannot move and break the thermometer. Remove the thermometer and read the mercury level as you normally do.

If the fever is over 105°F, see Heatstroke (page 124). A cold water bath or shower must be given immediately to lower the body temperature before brain damage or death results. Ice applied to the head and inner thighs is also beneficial. If the body temperature has not dropped to 103°F in ten minutes, a cold water enema may be necessary. Fill an enema bag with cold water and ice cubes. Lubricate the tip and insert it gently into the anus. Hold the bag high until your dog shows signs of discomfort, then let the water drain out. *Note:* After a cold water enema, improvement *cannot* be measured by rectal temperature.

Fever in dogs can be controlled by aspirin. Buffered aspirin is preferable; it tends to irritate the stomach less and thus decreases the chance of your dog vomiting from the medication (see Your Dog's Home Pharmacy, page 75).

If your pet has a fever and is not vomiting, be sure that it eats and drinks. The caloric (energy) requirements increase when heat increases because energy is used faster and must be replaced. There is also an increased need for fluids in the feverish body. If your pet will not drink voluntarily, see Giving Liquids to Your Dog, page 82. *Note:* Water should *not* be given if your pet is vomiting. If that is the case, let it lick ice cubes.

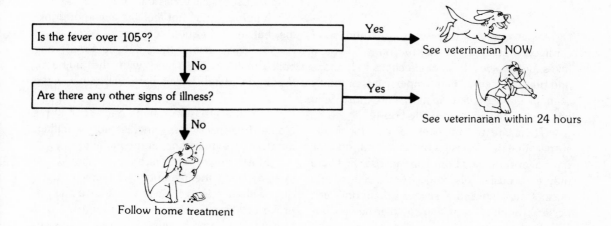

Is the fever over 105°? → **Yes** → See veterinarian NOW

↓ **No**

Are there any other signs of illness? → **Yes** → See veterinarian within 24 hours

↓ **No**

Follow home treatment

Dogs that will not eat or drink and cannot be nursed by you should be seen by your doctor as soon as possible, especially if your pet's condition deteriorates.

What to Expect at the Veterinarian's Office
Again, a fever may be a *sign* of illness. If your pet has a fever along with other signs and is getting worse, do not hesitate to see your veterinarian.

Your doctor will do a complete physical examination. Blood tests, urinalysis, and X rays may be necessary to find the cause of the fever.

If an infection is suspected, antibiotics will be given. Fluids may be administered intravenously or subcutaneously if your pet has not been able to take in enough fluids to meet the body's daily needs. Fluid therapy is very important for pets that will not eat or drink.

Canine Distemper

Distemper is a viral disease of dogs and other carnivores, such as skunks, raccoons, coyotes, foxes, and wolves. It is not infectious to humans and does not cause "bad temper." It is primarily seen in *unvaccinated* animals and those who have not received their yearly booster shots.

There are several signs to look for if you suspect that this disease is present: Your dog will have a fever ranging from 103° to 105°F. There may be a puslike discharge from the eyes and nose. Coughing and a severe pneumonia can occur. In addition, vomiting and diarrhea are frequently seen.

The distemper virus can also damage the brain. Your dog may have convulsions or a rhythmic twitching of a body part (face, leg, or neck), called *chorea*. Some dogs may continuously circle or pace or undergo personality changes. Other signs are a loss of appetite, weakness, and thickened footpads. *Note:* These signs are seen with many other diseases besides distemper, so a visit to your veterinarian is needed for a correct diagnosis. Distemper is quite contagious to unvaccinated dogs of all ages, through airborne transmission or by direct contact with infected animals.

Home Treatment

Your doctor may ask you to be an active partner in helping your dog get well. Good nursing care is as important to recovery as the antibiotics and fluids that your veterinarian will administer. The important things are to provide nutrition, to maintain body condition and fight the infection; fluids, to prevent dehydration; and antibiotics. The distemper virus damages body cells and suppresses the immune response, thus allowing bacteria to do further damage. The antibiotics kill the bacteria, giving the body time to overwhelm the virus and repair the damage. There is no drug that specifically kills the virus.

Your dog may not feel like eating or drinking, but small, frequent feedings of egg yolks or cooked eggs, milk, strained baby foods, and boiled chicken will help with the nutrition. Water, milk, and chicken broth will help with the fluids.

See the Decision Charts and Your Dog's Home Pharmacy for remedies for vomiting, diarrhea, eye infections, and coughing.

Most dogs with distemper should be treated, since the majority will recover. Even dogs with muscle twitchings can survive and improve in a few weeks or a few months. Good nursing care, good veterinary care, patience, and understanding can be very rewarding.

What to Expect at the Veterinarian's Office

Since the signs of distemper can look similar to those of other diseases, blood tests and examination of the eye with an ophthalmoscope (since the virus can damage this organ) may be helpful in diagnosis. Of course, a complete physical examination will be done to determine the extent of the digestive, respiratory, and nervous system involvement. Your doctor may suggest home care and possibly frequent veterinary visits as the best treatment plan. Antibiotics, fluids, antidiarrheals, cough medicine, vitamins, and sometimes anticonvulsants and oxygen therapy are needed to help your dog recover.

Prevention

The puppy series should begin at seven to eight weeks of age, with the last one given at twelve to sixteen weeks. Yearly boosters are needed to keep up the antibody level and to keep the body's "memory system" on guard.

Canine Distemper

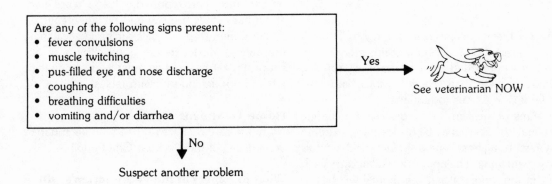

Are any of the following signs present:
* fever convulsions
* muscle twitching
* pus-filled eye and nose discharge
* coughing
* breathing difficulties
* vomiting and/or diarrhea

Yes → See veterinarian NOW

No

Suspect another problem

Rabies

The word rabies evokes fear, and rightfully so. A viral disease that attacks the brain, it is seen in many warm-blooded animals, especially skunks, raccoons, foxes, bats, coyotes, dogs, and cats. *Note:* It *is* infectious to humans.

One of the signs of the disease is a change of behavior. There may be restlessness, extreme shyness, or aggressiveness. In fact, wild animals may seem tame. Their pupils are dilated, as well.

In the *furious stage,* the animal will bite at anything in its way. Loud noises or bright lights can stimulate the biting attacks. The animal also becomes uncoordinated. In this stage, the animal may die during convulsions or it may go on to the *dumb stage.*

In the dumb stage, the paralysis of the throat causes voice changes, salivating, and an inability to eat or drink. The lower jaw will be paralyzed and unable to close, and the tongue and lower jaw will hang loose. Generalized paralysis, coma, and death follow.

The virus is spread by the bite of a rabid animal—the virus-laden saliva enters the wound. Airborne transmission in caves inhabited by bats has been reported. (Just a word here about bats—they are shy and helpful creatures. At dusk, many types of bats can be seen catching mosquitos. Most bats are good citizens of our spaceship earth—leading quiet lives, doing their job and not getting sick with rabies).

Home Treatment
No home care is effective. See your veterinarian *immediately* if the Decision Chart applies.

What to Expect at the Veterinarian's Office
An animal suspected of being rabid will be quarantined and public health officials will be notified.

Prevention
Keep your dog's rabies vaccination up to date. The first vaccination is given between three and six months of age. A booster is given at one year and then annually thereafter.

Rabies

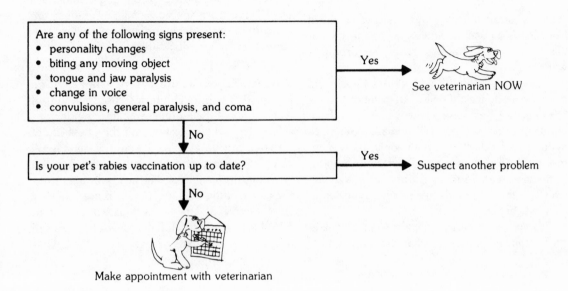

Are any of the following signs present:
- personality changes
- biting any moving object
- tongue and jaw paralysis
- change in voice
- convulsions, general paralysis, and coma

Yes → See veterinarian NOW

No ↓

Is your pet's rabies vaccination up to date? — Yes → Suspect another problem

No ↓

Make appointment with veterinarian

Increased Water Intake

Water is essential for life and your pet obtains it from foods as well as liquids, since the metabolism of food (especially fats) also produces water.

Dogs need about 25 ml. (¾ oz.) water per pound of body weight daily, but lactation, fever, hot weather, exercise, and water loss from vomiting and diarrhea will increase your pet's need. Dry foods that contain only 10 percent moisture will also increase water consumption. In addition, certain medications, such as antibiotics and corticosteroids, may cause your dog to become very thirsty.

However, excessive thirst is seen as well in such serious illnesses as diabetes and kidney disease. Therefore, veterinary attention may be necessary.

Home Treatment
An increased water intake in an alert and active pet is of no concern. Keep your dog's water bowl filled. If there are any signs of illness or if you are concerned about the amount of water consumed, see your veterinarian.

What to Expect at the Veterinarian's Office
If your dog is drinking an increased amount of water, bring a fresh urine sample to the doctor's office. The urinary system and the possibility of diabetes can be evaluated from this sample. A complete history and physical examination will be done. If vomiting or diarrhea is thought to be the cause of the fluid loss and increased thirst, a stool sample and bowel X rays will be taken. Blood tests may be needed to check the status of all the internal organs.

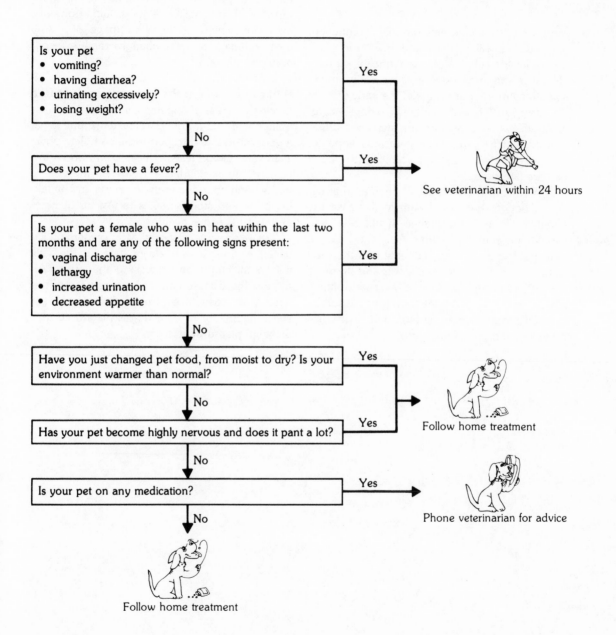

Is your pet
- vomiting?
- having diarrhea?
- urinating excessively?
- losing weight?

Yes

Does your pet have a fever?

Yes

See veterinarian within 24 hours

No

Is your pet a female who was in heat within the last two months and are any of the following signs present:
- vaginal discharge
- lethargy
- increased urination
- decreased appetite

Yes

No

Have you just changed pet food, from moist to dry? Is your environment warmer than normal?

Yes

No

Has your pet become highly nervous and does it pant a lot?

Yes

Follow home treatment

No

Is your pet on any medication?

Yes

Phone veterinarian for advice

No

Follow home treatment

Increased Appetite

More exercise, a cold environment, pregnancy, and nursing will increase the need for food, especially for calories of good quality protein. However, an increased appetite could mean something more. For example, the early signs of diabetes, which is seen frequently in dogs, are an increased water consumption, increased urination, weight loss despite a voracious appetite, and possibly depression and vomiting (these last two are late signs).

Worms may also cause an increased appetite, although they could equally decrease the appetite or cause no change at all. Still, you should not rule out worms (see page 47). If your pet has a voracious appetite, but the food just passes out as unformed stools and dramatic weight loss occurs, pancreatic, liver, and intestinal problems (in which the food is not absorbed or used properly) may be indicated. These require veterinary attention, also.

Home Treatment

If you suspect that more exercise, a cold environment, pregnancy, or nursing may have increased your dog's caloric and protein requirements, no professional treatment will be necessary, in all probability. You should, however, read the section on nutrition (page 36). Any other dramatic appetite changes require veterinary consultation.

What to Expect at the Veterinarian's Office

Since an increased appetite can be caused by so many things, your doctor will take the time to get a good history and to perform a complete physical exam. Blood tests, a fecal exam, and a urinalysis may be needed. Prepare for the visit by not feeding your dog in the morning and by taking urine and stool samples to test for diabetes and worms, respectively.

A word about diabetes: Most owners of diabetic pets do a remarkable job in giving the daily insulin injections and checking the urine. Although the disease cannot be cured (as of this writing, at least), a controlled diabetic can still live a happy life. If your dog is diagnosed as a diabetic, please treat it.

Increased Appetite

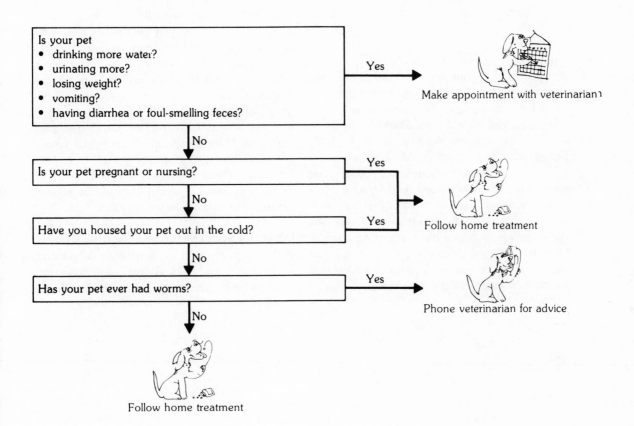

Is your pet
- drinking more water?
- urinating more?
- losing weight?
- vomiting?
- having diarrhea or foul-smelling feces?

Yes → Make appointment with veterinarian

No

Is your pet pregnant or nursing?

Yes →

No

Have you housed your pet out in the cold?

Yes → Follow home treatment

No

Has your pet ever had worms?

Yes → Phone veterinarian for advice

No → Follow home treatment

Decreased Appetite

Dogs—just like people—have their good days and bad days. If your pet is alert and active and shows no signs of illness but has not eaten any or all its food for a day or two, don't worry. Dogs who roam free are sometimes fed by neighbors, or else they feed on available garbage. While this is not advisable, it could obviously affect your dog's appetite at home, and begging on your hands and knees won't help if your pet has eaten elsewhere. And remember the effect that environment has. Both humans and animals consume less food and have less of an appetite in warm weather. However, loss of appetite (*anorexia*) is also seen with many dog illnesses, so see your veterinarian if the Decision Chart so indicates.

Home Treatment

Try adding some Brewer's yeast or garlic salt to the food. They add "zing" and may coax the problem eater out of its problem.

If the problem is serious and you cannot see your veterinarian immediately, force feeding may be necessary to provide the calories, nutrients, and water necessary for survival. Strained baby foods, soft boiled eggs, raw egg yolks, whole milk, and boiled chicken are good sources of calories and protein. You can also try feeding your pet's regular food by hand: Place a small amount of food on the roof of your dog's mouth with your finger, a spoon, or a tongue depressor. See also Giving Liquids to Your Dog, page 82. *Note:* Force feeding is *not* to be used instead of a veterinary visit. It should be used in coordination with professional care.

What to Expect at the Veterinarian's Office

A thorough physical examination will be done. Sometimes blood tests, X rays, a urinalysis, and stool samples will be necessary to identify the problem and determine the best treatment.

Decreased Appetite

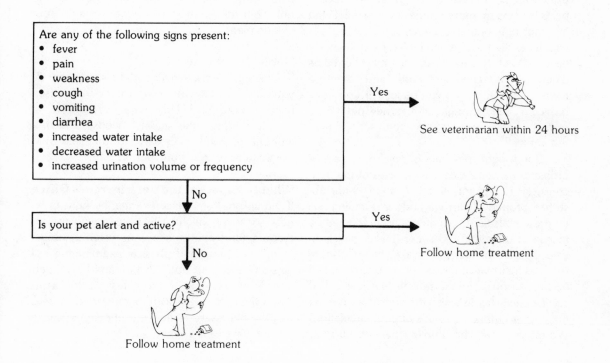

Are any of the following signs present:
- fever
- pain
- weakness
- cough
- vomiting
- diarrhea
- increased water intake
- decreased water intake
- increased urination volume or frequency

Yes → See veterinarian within 24 hours

No ↓

Is your pet alert and active?

Yes → Follow home treatment

No ↓

Follow home treatment

Underweight

Dogs that are underweight or have lost weight usually are not receiving enough calories. If your pet is burning up more calories than usual (living in a hot environment, exercising more, or becoming excited over a nearby female in heat will all do it), eating a new food that may not be as digestible, or eating less food (and therefore fewer calories), weight can be lost. If you have moved recently, brought another new pet home, or had a baby, your dog may be upset and may not eat well.

But weight loss can occur from medical problems as well. In certain diseases of the pancreas, liver, and intestines the food is not absorbed properly (diarrhea and/or vomiting will be present also). A weight loss accompanied by increased urination and water intake may indicate diabetes or kidney disease. Heart disease (such as heart valve disease or problems caused by heartworms) can cause a weight loss called *cardiac cachexia*, in which the body does not get the proper nutrition because of poor circulation. Worms can steal the nutrition needed by your dog's body. The list of medical problems that can cause weight loss is endless, so an examination by your veterinarian is essential.

There is nothing really wrong with being just a little underweight, however. Healthy pets that are on the lean side seem to have less joint, heart, lung, and pancreatic problems. To find out your dog's proper weight, consult your veterinarian.

Home Treatment

If your dog is alert, active, and does not seem ill, you could try increasing the caloric intake (see Feeding Your Adult Dog, page 40). Check the weight desired, the caloric needs, and the amount of food necessary to maintain that weight, and weigh your pet weekly.

What to Expect at the Veterinarian's Office

If the weight loss is accompanied by signs of illness, or if no weight gain is seen with the increased food intake, see your veterinarian. A complete history and physical examination will be done and your dog's dietary and bowel patterns will be scrutinized. Blood tests, a stool sample, urinalysis, electrocardiogram, and X rays may be necessary to find the underlying cause for the weight loss.

Underweight

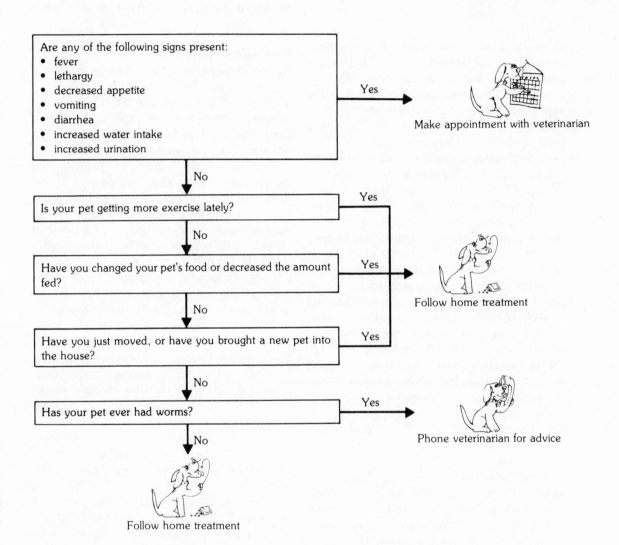

Are any of the following signs present:
- fever
- lethargy
- decreased appetite
- vomiting
- diarrhea
- increased water intake
- increased urination

Yes → Make appointment with veterinarian

No

Is your pet getting more exercise lately? Yes

No

Have you changed your pet's food or decreased the amount fed? Yes

No

Have you just moved, or have you brought a new pet into the house? Yes → Follow home treatment

No

Has your pet ever had worms? Yes → Phone veterinarian for advice

No → Follow home treatment

Overweight

Obesity in dogs, in most cases, is from too many calories and not enough exercise. Fat people seem to have fat pets. I'm convinced that this is caused by an eating pattern ("just a little bit more won't hurt") shared between owner and pet. If fat people don't exercise enough, why should their pets have a different life-style?

Weight gain can be very insidious until one day you say "What happened!" As a pet matures or gets old, its metabolism and activity change, and its caloric intake should be reduced accordingly. People have the same problem keeping off that extra weight after the "middle years" arrive. If there is an increase in caloric intake, a slow-down in metabolism (due to body-age changes), or a decrease in exercise (due to action on your part or to a lazy or aging pet), a weight gain will be seen. *Hypothyroidism* (a lack of thyroid hormones) is *not* an uncommon cause of obesity or related signs in dogs. Although any breed (including mutts) can have an underactive thyroid gland, Dobermans, Irish setters, spaniels, dachshunds, and golden retrievers have a high incidence. Signs include a dull, dry hair coat, laziness, hair loss (especially on the neck, back, and chest), a gain in weight, and being a "heat seeker"—i.e., they chill easily.

But sometimes owners misinterpret a weight gain or "large belly" as a fat problem when in reality a heart, liver, or kidney problem (with fluid accumulation in the abdomen) or a hormone imbalance is the cause. Overweight dogs can have more pancreatic (diabetes and inflammation of the pancreas), heart, lung, and joint problems because these parts are continually being overstressed by the excess fat and weight. Surgery and healing can also be extremely difficult in an overweight dog.

Your veterinarian is *also* overstressed by obese pets. It makes the physical examination more difficult because it's harder to hear the heartbeat and lung sounds and to feel the internal organs. Trying to find a vein for blood tests or intravenous fluids in a fat pet can be a major undertaking.

Home Treatment

Before starting a weight reduction program, it is a good idea to have your veterinarian perform a physical and, if necessary, blood tests to rule out related health or hormone problems. The program itself involves finding the desired weight (see Feeding Your Adult Dog, page 40) and the number of calories needed to maintain that weight. Feed your dog just 60 percent of that daily total until you reach the desired weight.

For instance, if your dog weighs twenty pounds, and fifteen pounds is the desired weight, 600 calories × 60% = 360 calories should be fed daily until your dog weighs fifteen pounds. Be patient, it may take three or four months. Once the goal is reached, you can slowly increase the calories to the calorie maintenance level (600 calories for fifteen pounds).

The dog's normal food or special prescription diets can be used for the weight reduction program, but all family members must cooperate. No table food or treats are allowed because these add considerable calories. Keep a weekly record of your dog's weight. If there is not a steady weight loss, contact your veterinarian. *Note:* If your pet roams free and is fed by neighbors or gets into trash, forget about weight reduction.

Take a "before" and an "after" picture of your dog. Your veterinarian will be proud of you and your pet's accomplishment. A sincere owner who practices good preventive medicine for his pet is deeply respected by veterinarians. I want to share with you a postcard I received this summer from Smokey Meisner, on vacation in the Poconos:

Dear Doctor Sheldon,
I am feeling fine, eating well, running, and feeling full of pep. My sugar color chart is

Overweight

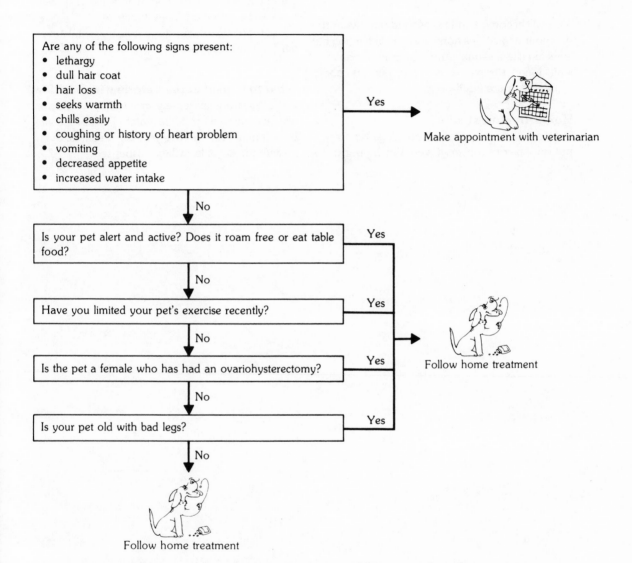

Are any of the following signs present:
- lethargy
- dull hair coat
- hair loss
- seeks warmth
- chills easily
- coughing or history of heart problem
- vomiting
- decreased appetite
- increased water intake

Yes → Make appointment with veterinarian

No ↓

Is your pet alert and active? Does it roam free or eat table food?

Yes →

No ↓

Have you limited your pet's exercise recently?

Yes →

No ↓

Is the pet a female who has had an ovariohysterectomy?

Yes → Follow home treatment

No ↓

Is your pet old with bad legs?

Yes →

No ↓

Follow home treatment

staying between blue negative and +1. My owners are happy and enjoying their vacation because of how you help me. They appreciate you, and I love you.

Lick, lick, lick!
Smokey Meisner

Smokey had been terribly overweight but went on a diet and lost it all. The Meisners brought me "before" and "after" pictures, and the difference is truly amazing. Smokey, I am sad to say, became a diabetic (a high risk with obesity) but is otherwise happy.

Skunk Encounters

You will become a truly seasoned pet owner the day your dog comes home looking like a dog but smelling like a skunk. And you may not have to wait long: Puppies are more curious about skunks than are adult dogs.

Home Treatment
Before you begin to make your dog "de-scent," put on a pair of rubber gloves. Wash your dog's eyes with warm water, and bathe its entire body with soap and water. Towel dry and soak your dog with tomato juice (you can add a little diluted lemon juice). This whole process may have to be repeated a few times.

Throw away your dog's collar—you'll never get the smell out of it.

What to Expect at the Veterinarian's Office
If the eyes are extremely irritated, your doctor will flush them with sterile water. The cornea will be examined for damage. An eye antibiotic (with or without steroids) will be dispensed.

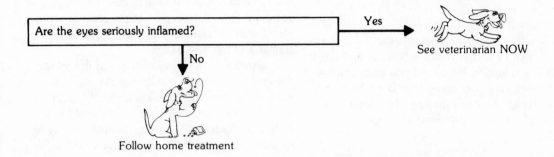

Are the eyes seriously inflamed?   **Yes** → See veterinarian NOW

No

Follow home treatment

Lameness

Neither an owner nor a veterinarian can always tell by eye or feel whether a bone is broken. If your dog is limping badly and you suspect a fracture, have an X ray taken (see Bone Fractures, page 108). The chart on page 161 gives a rundown of common problems and how to check for them.

Three common problems that can cause a weakness of your dog's hindlegs are pelvic fractures, disc prolapse of the back, and instability of the neck bones (the cervical vertebrae). Pelvic fractures are common injuries from being hit by cars. Disc prolapse and spinal injury are discussed on page 162. Instability of the cervical vertebrae is seen especially in young (one to two years of age) Doberman pinschers and Great Danes. A wobbly gait develops in the rear legs, and the spinal cord becomes compressed by the unstable neck bones.

Besides these three major causes, there are other reasons for lameness. Tar, paint, and thorns can stick to your dog's footpad and between the digits. When your dog trys to chew off these substances, its paws can get irritated. The irritation, in turn, makes your pet tender on the paw and then lame. Pimples and "hot spots" between the footpads or the toes are another potential cause. See also page 102.

Tissues that connect the bones of a joint and give it stability during movement are called *ligaments*. Sometimes these are strained (stretched), sprained (slightly torn), or completely torn. The most common ligament sprain or complete tear is seen in the knee of the dog. The *anterior cruciate ligament* prevents the knee bones from rubbing together, so a partial or complete tear will cause severe pain. Your doctor will be able to determine the degree of tearing.

Something else that should be mentioned here is *paper bone disease (osteoporosis)*, which can be seen in growing puppies that are fed a diet with the wrong balance of calcium and phosphorus (an all-meat diet such as beef heart or liver) and not enough vitamin D-3. In this case the calcium is lost from the bones. The puppy is reluctant to walk, has pain in the legs, and may stand with its paws turned inward. Its bones are fragile and fracture easily.

Osteoarthritis (bony changes in the joint) is the end result of joint instabilities that were not or cannot be corrected satisfactorily, of joint injuries, or of the aging process (one old fellow called it "older-itis"). After sleeping or lying down, your pet is stiff and feels pain that seems to get better as your dog moves around during the day.

Dislocation of the Hip or Knee

Dislocations of the hip joint are occasionally seen in dogs that have been hit by cars. The hip joint is a snug "ball and socket" arrangement. Trauma can tear the muscles and tendons over the hip and pop the ball out of the socket, causing a dislocation, or a *luxation*, of the hip joint. If the hip is dislocated, the dog may not be able to place the leg on the ground. Fractures of the pelvis may accompany traumatic injury to the hips.

Home Treatment
Time and activity restriction (home confinement) can be tried for a few days, if the chart so indicates. Dogs can be given aspirin to decrease the pain and inflammation.

If tar or paint is the problem, soak the paw in mineral or vegetable oil for twelve to twenty-four hours. Wash the paw with soap and water after removing the bandage. Thorns or other foreign objects can be removed from the paw with your fingers or tweezers.

Any lameness that get worse or lasts longer than three days should be checked by your veterinarian.

What to Expect at the Veterinarian's Office
If the fragments are in adequate alignment, pelvic fractures need only confinement for four to six weeks for good healing. If the fragments are

158

Lameness

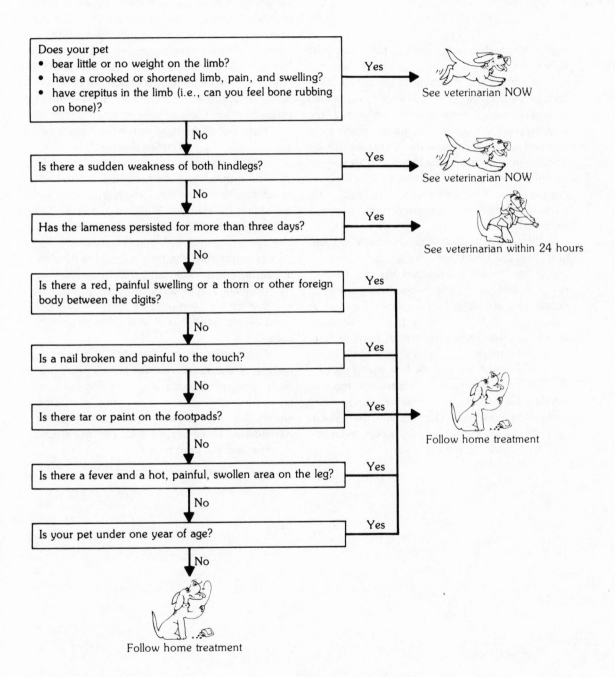

Does your pet
- bear little or no weight on the limb?
- have a crooked or shortened limb, pain, and swelling?
- have crepitus in the limb (i.e., can you feel bone rubbing on bone)?

Yes → See veterinarian NOW

No ↓

Is there a sudden weakness of both hindlegs?

Yes → See veterinarian NOW

No ↓

Has the lameness persisted for more than three days?

Yes → See veterinarian within 24 hours

No ↓

Is there a red, painful swelling or a thorn or other foreign body between the digits?

Yes →

No ↓

Is a nail broken and painful to the touch?

Yes →

No ↓

Is there tar or paint on the footpads?

Yes → Follow home treatment

No ↓

Is there a fever and a hot, painful, swollen area on the leg?

Yes →

No ↓

Is your pet under one year of age?

Yes →

No ↓

Follow home treatment

Lameness

(cont.)

not in good alignment, pins or plates may be necessary.

Surgery is the treatment of choice for instability of the cervical vertebrae, since its results are generally good. If surgery is not performed, the dog may get progressively weaker in the back legs and lose its ability to walk. X rays are usually needed to confirm the diagnosis and to see the extent of the disease. Mild cases of *osteochondritis* are treated with rest and buffered aspirin for a month. If there is no improvement, surgery is indicated.

Elbow dysplasia is also correctible by surgery, and the results are very good.

If you suspect a dislocated hip, see a veterinarian within twenty-four hours, since recent hip dislocations are easier to replace in the socket. A radiograph (X ray) will confirm the dislocation and may reveal other hip injury, such as fractures of the pelvis. A general anesthesia is given to relax the muscles and, by firm manipulation, the hip bone is replaced. A bandage may be needed for ten days to prevent unnecessary movement in the joint. Occasionally, the dislocation can be corrected only by *open reduction* (surgically entering the hip area).

Hip dysplasia is best treated with buffered aspirin to relieve the intermittent pain. Keeping your pet in warm, dry areas and keeping its weight normal will lessen the amount of bony changes (osteoarthritis) in the joint. *Note:* Do *not* over-exercise or force a dog with hip dysplasia to jump or walk on slippery surfaces. There are a few surgical procedures that may alleviate the pain associated with hip dysplasia, but most dysplastic dogs can lead a near-normal life. Euthanasia is not necessary in most cases.

Removal of the head of the hip bone is very successful for *Legg-Perthes disease.*

Chronic *patellar luxation* and rupture of the anterior cruciate are best treated by surgery, which stabilizes the joint. However, some cases are simply treated medically; the dog leads a relatively normal life with intermittent lameness. Discuss the options with your veterinarian.

In *panosteitis,* the pain in one leg may disappear in a few weeks and shift to another leg. Diagnosed by X rays and blood tests, this disease resolves itself in a month or two. Usually buffered aspirin is all that is needed to relieve the pain.

Osteosarcoma, bone cancer, is primarily a disease of young (six months to two years old), large, and giant breed dogs. Radiographs are needed for diagnosis. If a leg bone is affected, amputation of the leg may prolong the dog's life. Remember: Three-legged dogs can get around just fine and are very happy.

	Problem	Seen in	Check for pain by
Shoulder	Osteochondritis (degeneration of the shoulder bone)	Large dogs 4 to 12 months old	Flex and extend the shoulder joint
Elbow	Elbow dysplasia	Large dogs (especially German shepherds) 6 to 12 months old	Press in the elbow joint
Hip	Hip dysplasia (degeneration, instability, and malformation of the hip joint)	Large dogs 6 months to 2 years old	Press in the hip joint or move the leg
	Legg-Perthes disease (erosion of the hip bone)	Small dogs under 1 year old	Press in the hip joint or move the leg
Knee	Patellar luxation* (loose kneecap)	Toy and miniature breeds (especially poodles and Yorkshire terriers) of any age	Press in the knee area to see if the knee-cap is out of position
	Tear or rupture of the anterior cruciate ligament *	Adults and older dogs	Place one hand above the knee and one below; move the joint back and forth
The long bones	Panosteitis (inflammation along the length of the bone)	Large dogs (especially German shepherds) 5 to 12 months old	Press on the long bone
	Osteosarcoma (bone cancer)	Large dogs 6 months to 2 years old	Look for pain and swelling over affected bone

*It is best to muzzle your dog before checking the kneecap. This injury can cause severe pain.

Neck or Back Pain

The most common cause of acute neck or back pain is protrusion of disc material into the space occupied by the spinal cord. The pressure on the nerve roots and spinal cord produces severe pain. Disc prolapse in the neck may produce pain down one or both front legs, since the nerves for sensation and movement for the front legs originate in the neck area. Occasionally, a weakness in the front legs will be seen. A disc prolapse in the back can produce pain, weakness, or paralysis of the back legs and loss of bowel and urine control. Beagles, Pekingese, dachshunds, French bulldogs, miniature poodles, and cocker spaniels have a high incidence of disc disease.

Disc Prolapse

The normal disc material is jellylike and acts as a shock absorber for the spinal cord. It is located between the back bones of the neck and back. A layer of fibers called the *annulus fibrosis* lies above the disc material. Degenerative processes cause the disc material to "pop-up" and press on the spinal cord. In turn, the spinal cord, which is housed in the bony cavity of the backbones, swells from this insult, causing pain signals to radiate around the involved area (in cervical disc prolapse, for example, that would be the neck and front legs).

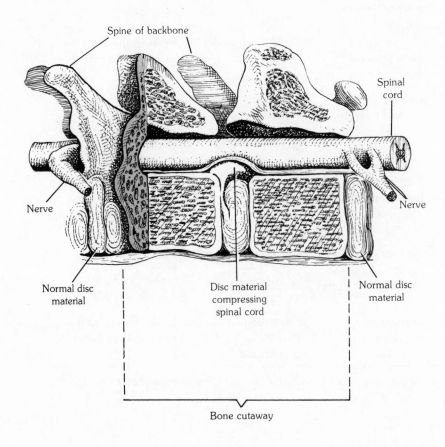

Spine of backbone

Spinal cord

Nerve

Nerve

Normal disc material

Disc material compressing spinal cord

Normal disc material

Bone cutaway

Neck or Back Pain

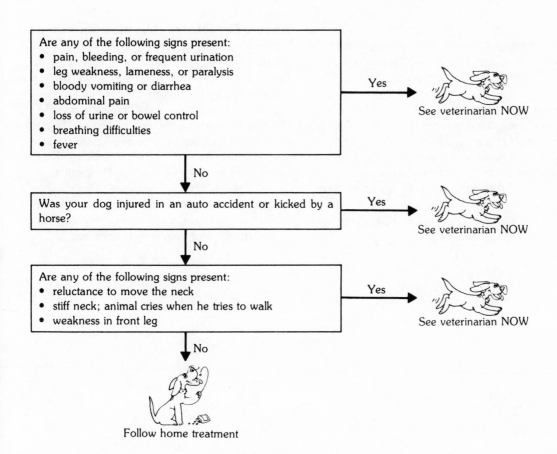

Are any of the following signs present:
- pain, bleeding, or frequent urination
- leg weakness, lameness, or paralysis
- bloody vomiting or diarrhea
- abdominal pain
- loss of urine or bowel control
- breathing difficulties
- fever

Yes → See veterinarian NOW

No

Was your dog injured in an auto accident or kicked by a horse?

Yes → See veterinarian NOW

No

Are any of the following signs present:
- reluctance to move the neck
- stiff neck; animal cries when he tries to walk
- weakness in front leg

Yes → See veterinarian NOW

No

Follow home treatment

Neck or Back Pain

(cont.)

If the pressure on the spinal cord is severe and prolonged, permanent damage, such as limb weakness, paralysis, and the loss of bladder and/or bowel control, can result.

Home Treatment
Restrict your dog's movement. Confine it to one room and keep it away from furniture. Do *not* let it go up or down stairs; instead, carry it outside when it needs to move its bowels or urinate. You can also put newspapers in the room so that a trip outdoors is not necessary. Give aspirin for the pain (see Your Dog's Home Pharmacy, page 75).

Recovery from a mild attack may take several weeks. Be prepared for recurrences since the underlying disease process has not been corrected.

What to Expect at the Veterinarian's Office
If a weakness develops in any of the legs, or if the pain persists, you should *not* treat at home. Full or near-full recovery is seen when there is quick action by both owner and veterinarian.

Your veterinarian will conduct a complete physical exam with emphasis on the neurological system. High doses of anti-inflammatory drugs will be given to relieve the inflammation and spinal cord swelling. X rays will be taken to locate the site of the disc prolapse. Cage rest or surgery will be suggested to decrease further spinal cord injury and to monitor improvement or deterioration of your dog's condition.

SKIN PROBLEM CHART

Problem	Itching	Color	Skin appearance	Major location	Breed predilection	Age seen	Duration	Other signs
Allergic inhalant dermatitis	Severe	Red to yellow, with pus	Crusty areas if infected	Generalized	Setters, retrievers, poodles, Dalmatians, terriers	Begins at 1 to 3 years of age	Usually seasonal, unless house is dusty	Bites paw, rubs face, sometimes sneezes
Flea bite dermatitis	Moderate to severe	Red to yellow, with pus; moist	Some hair loss; crusty areas if infected	Base of tail, lower back, inner thighs, neck	None	Over 6 months	Warm weather, unless fleas are in house	
Contact dermatitis	Sudden and severe	Red or yellow, with pus; flat	Raised if infected	Neck (around flea collar), armpits, abdomen, between digits	None	Any age	Until controlled, unless plants are abundant (seasonal)	
Mange	None	Red to gray	Crusty areas, hair loss, redness	Around eyes, mouth corners, front legs	None	Begins at 3 months to 1 year	Most heal after 1 year old	
Scabies*	Severe	Red to gray	Hair loss; crusty areas	Ear margins, elbows	None	Any	Until controlled	
Ticks	Moderate	Yellow to red	Scabs; yellow to red moist areas if infected	Ear flaps, between toes, head, neck, shoulders	None	Any age	Until controlled	
Ringworm*	Occasional	Red	Hair loss; round, scaly, inflamed areas	Face, front legs, paws		Usually young	Until controlled	
Nodule	None	Gray	Hair loss; thickened and wrinkled	Elbow, outside of hock	None; large and fat dogs seem susceptible	Any	Until lies on soft areas	
Lick granuloma	None	Red to gray	Firm, raised, hairless	Top of front paw, outside of back paw	Large breeds	Any age	Until controlled	
Abscess	None	Red	Swollen, soft, hot areas; scabs	Anywhere— face, legs, tail base		Any age	Until controlled	Usually fever, appetite loss, lethargy, lameness if on leg

*Infectious to humans

Allergies

Your dog's body has a remarkable immune system of antibodies, which are protein substances produced by cells called lymphocytes, that destroy antigens that invade the body, such as viruses and bacteria. This system can become supersensitive to such foreign particles as flea saliva, pollen, house dust, and wool, however, and this supersensitivity can produce chemicals that cause an *allergy*, a severe inflammatory reaction.

Allergic inhalant dermatitis has been well documented in dogs. It is caused by a supersensitivity to certain particles in the air, such as pollen from trees, ragweed, grass, and other plants, house dust, feathers, and wool. The allergy follows a predictable history:

1. It is inherited, so if the parents had it, the offspring probably will, too.

2. It is seasonal—the signs appear about the same time every year.

3. The signs begin between six months and three years of age.

4. The signs include severe biting and scratching, licking the paws, sneezing, rubbing the face, and generalized redness of the skin.

Home Treatment

Home treatment is directed toward symptomatic relief and avoiding the foreign particle, or allergen. If the offending allergen is thought to be house dust, vacuuming daily and using Dust-seal (L. S. Green Associates, 162 W. 56th Street, New York, NY 10019) in the environment may help. If wool or feathers are thought to be the culprits, eliminating as many things composed of wool or feathers as possible is recommended.

Bathing your dog with a mild shampoo (such as baby shampoo) will soothe any skin inflammation and remove any allergens on the hair coat. Calamine lotion or Domeboro® solution can be applied to the irritated skin. Hydrogen peroxide (3 percent) and antibiotic ointments are also helpful.

If the signs persist, see your veterinarian. Other skin diseases that may cause similar signs are flea bite dermatitis (page 168) and contact dermatitis (page 170).

What to Expect at the Veterinarian's Office

Your veterinarian will take time to get a good history. He or she may be able to identify the allergen in your pet's environment.

If allergic inhalant dermatitis is the problem, two avenues of treatment are possible—steroids or hyposensitization. Most veterinarians, at this time, use a low dose of steroids to relieve the signs. *Note:* Steroids should *not* be given for long-term treatment because they have some very serious side effects.

The other type of treatment involves testing for the allergy. It can be a long and sometimes frustrating treatment, however, since the dogs seem to keep developing allergies to new and different foreign particles.

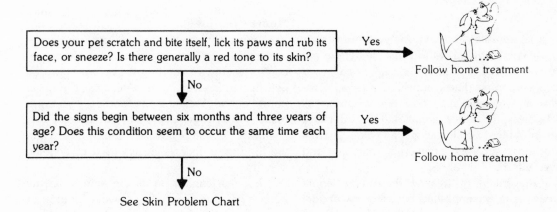

Does your pet scratch and bite itself, lick its paws and rub its face, or sneeze? Is there generally a red tone to its skin? → Yes → Follow home treatment

No ↓

Did the signs begin between six months and three years of age? Does this condition seem to occur the same time each year? → Yes → Follow home treatment

No ↓

See Skin Problem Chart

Flea Bite Dermatitis

Internal parasites aren't the only parasites your dog has to contend with in this life: There are numerous insects that would like to call your pet's skin home. These are called *external parasites* and include such dastardly creatures as ticks, fleas, mites, lice, and flies. They can cause severe itching, skin infections, and even internal problems, such as tapeworms, anemia, and even a form of paralysis.

Preventing or treating these unwelcome creatures is accomplished by using insecticidal preparations. Understanding their life cycles will give you an edge in this battle, and the following discussion should be beneficial. Ticks and mites are discussed separately (see page 176).

Any dog older than six months of age can develop an allergy to flea saliva. Fleas are thin, wingless, brown insects that are extraordinary jumpers and move through the hair coat rapidly. The flea injects its saliva under the dog's skin as an aid in retrieving its meal (the dog's blood). The saliva acts as foreign material that can cause your pet to itch and bite itself profusely. Even people may be bitten by hungry fleas; their favorite human areas are ankles and waists, and the bites are very itchy.

Hair loss and skin infection are characteristic, especially on the lower back, neck, and inner thighs, favored flea feeding sites. The hair loss usually has a pattern: a triangular patch on the lower back and patches at the tail base, on the neck, and on the inner thighs. You may even see fleas jumping or moving in these areas, although often you won't see fleas on your dog. Flea droppings are the black specks (digested blood) found primarily on the hairs of the lower back. To test, place the droppings on white paper and moisten them with water. If they turn red, they are flea droppings; if not, they are simply dirt.

Before treating for fleas, check to see if your dog might have allergic inhalant dermatitis or contact dermatitis.

Home Treatment

You must control fleas on all animals in the household and in the environment. A natural control agent that can be tried *before* your dog gets fleas is Brewer's yeast. Mixing 0.1 gm. per pound of body weight in the food daily seems to make some dogs "distasteful" to fleas. Other "naturals": Onion or garlic salt can be mixed with the food, and cedar shavings used as bedding may help.

For flea control on all the animals in the household, you can use flea powders or dips, or flea collars or medallions. When using dips, read the directions carefully. Sponge your pet with the dip, avoiding the eyes, and repeat as the directions indicate. *Note:* Do *not* apply dips to open sores.

If you use a flea collar, use the recommended size for your dog. The flea collar must be aired for a few days before you place it around your pet's neck. If the skin underneath the flea collar becomes red and hair is lost, *remove* the collar. Some animals are sensitive to the chemical. *Note:* Do *not* combine flea collars or medallions with other insectides. For example, don't dip your dog and then put on a flea collar.

There has recently been some discussion about the wisdom of animals or their owners inhaling the vapors in the collars. If your pet sleeps on your bed, it might be prudent to remove the flea collar until the morning.

Since fleas spend most of their life cycle *off* your dog, controlling or treating the environment is most important to avoid that frustrating "Where are the fleas coming from? I sprayed my dog a month ago!" routine. Vacuum weekly for a few months, especially rugs, upholstery, cracks and crevices, and closets. Throw the vacuum bags away after vacuuming; otherwise, the fleas will hatch in your vacuum, closets, etc. Wash or

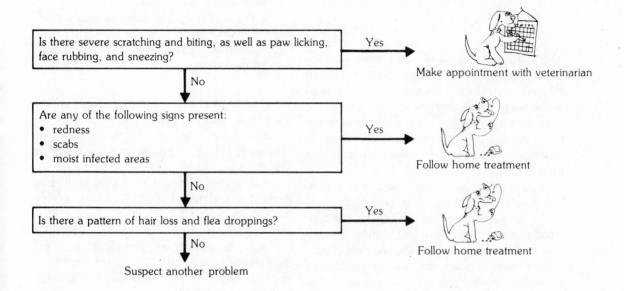

Is there severe scratching and biting, as well as paw licking, face rubbing, and sneezing? — **Yes** → Make appointment with veterinarian

No ↓

Are any of the following signs present:
- redness
- scabs
- moist infected areas

Yes → Follow home treatment

No ↓

Is there a pattern of hair loss and flea droppings? — **Yes** → Follow home treatment

No ↓

Suspect another problem

throw away the dog's bedding. Finally, a commercial insecticide should be sprayed around your house periodically for a few months. If you think it might stain something, test by spraying only a small area first.

Your dog should be treated from the end of the winter through the first frost if you live in a varied climate.

What to Expect at the Veterinarian's Office
If you have tried everything and your dog is still scratching, see your veterinarian. He or she will make sure that none of the "rule-outs" are present. If a flea bite allergy is suspected, corticosteroids, which can reduce or stop the itching, will be prescribed. If there are open sores, your doctor may give you antibiotics, a medicated shampoo, and topical ointment to use. Be sure to discuss flea control for the pet *and* the house to avoid a recurrence of the problem.

Contact Dermatitis

Reddened, itchy areas of skin can be seen on any dog that comes in direct contact with an irritating substance. Hairless or thin-coated areas, such as the abdomen, the armpits, the inner thighs, the chest, the area between the toes, and the scrotum are usually affected. In addition, irritation around the neck is common from flea collars.

Common irritants are soaps, insecticides, flea collars, wool (particularly wool rugs), dyes (especially those used in nylon carpets), paint, or wood preservatives. Have any of these entered your dog's life recently? Poison ivy, poison oak, pollens, and grasses can also cause contact dermatitis. If your pet is on a new drug, this could be the source of the problem.

Home Treatment
First, try to identify the offending substance. If you think you have found the culprit, try to eliminate it from your dog's environment.

To relieve the itching, apply calamine lotion to the red areas three times daily. Cool compresses of Burrough's solution (Domeboro®), applied for fifteen minutes every six hours, is an alternative. Dogs can be given antihistamines, but check with your veterinarian.

If the lesions are extensive, if home treatment is ineffective, or if the skin infection seems to be getting worse, a visit to your veterinarian may be necessary.

What to Expect at the Veterinarian's Office
Your veterinarian will get a complete history in order to discover the identity of the offending substance. He will, of course, first rule out other skin diseases.

An antibiotic-steriod cream applied four times daily and steroid tablets work well, even if the culprit cannot be identified. Treatment is usually necessary for one to two weeks. Steroids should not be used for long periods of time, but if the condition recurs, steroids can be used for a short time again. Your doctor may advise medicated baths and cold applications of Burrough's solution.

Prevention
Air out a new flea collar for three days before using it, and buy the recommended size for your dog. If a neck irritation is seen, do not use a flea collar.

Contact Dermatitis

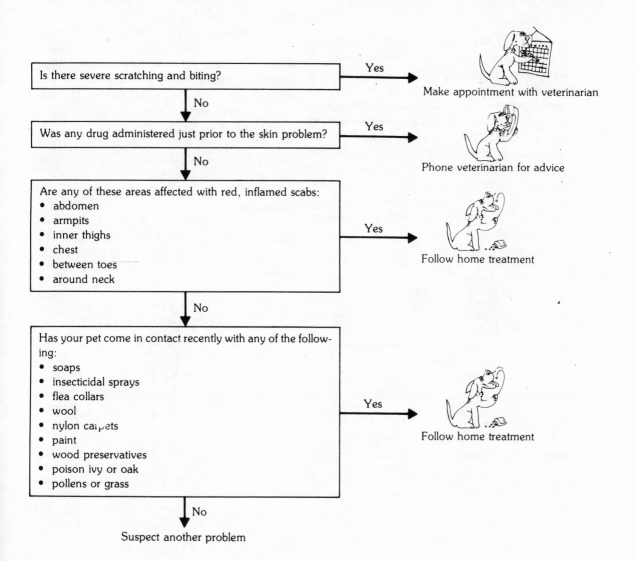

Is there severe scratching and biting?

Yes → Make appointment with veterinarian

No

Was any drug administered just prior to the skin problem?

Yes → Phone veterinarian for advice

No

Are any of these areas affected with red, inflamed scabs:
- abdomen
- armpits
- inner thighs
- chest
- between toes
- around neck

Yes → Follow home treatment

No

Has your pet come in contact recently with any of the following:
- soaps
- insecticidal sprays
- flea collars
- wool
- nylon carpets
- paint
- wood preservatives
- poison ivy or oak
- pollens or grass

Yes → Follow home treatment

No

Suspect another problem

Mange

The mite *demodex canis* is found on almost all dogs and is responsible for demodex mange in *susceptible* young dogs (three months to one year old). Any breed can get mange, although there does seem to be a *hereditary predisposition*—i.e., the pup's genes are programmed to react to the mite. The mite is acquired from the mother during the nursing period.

The skin lesions are characterized by hair loss and slight redness and are found around the eyes, at the mouth corners, and on the front legs. In a few instances, the disease spreads all over the body. It does not itch.

Home Treatment
If the lesions are small and do not get larger, no treatment is necessary. The dog will "out-grow" the disease. If the lesions *do* get larger, see your doctor.

Ringworm (see page 178) can be confused with mange.

Demodex mange is not infectious to humans, and other dogs in the household, if mature, are usually not susceptible to the disease.

What to Expect at the Veterinarian's Office
The mites' presence can be confirmed by a skin scraping and microscopic examination. The mite is cigar-shaped and has four pairs of legs. Ask if you can see it under the microscope.

Your doctor may recommend a topical insecticide to be applied to the affected area. Hair should regrow in about a month or two.

Prevention
Always contact the breeder. The bitches who have pups with demodex mange should not be bred. Of course, your dog should also not be bred.

Mange

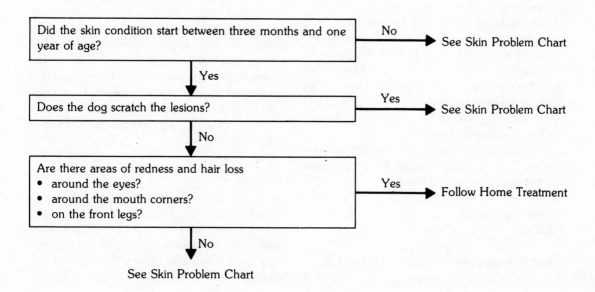

Did the skin condition start between three months and one year of age? → No → See Skin Problem Chart

↓ Yes

Does the dog scratch the lesions? → Yes → See Skin Problem Chart

↓ No

Are there areas of redness and hair loss
- around the eyes?
- around the mouth corners?
- on the front legs?
→ Yes → Follow Home Treatment

↓ No

See Skin Problem Chart

Scabies

Scabies is a severely itchy infestation of the skin that is highly infectious, both between dogs and between dog and man. The mite burrows into the dog's skin to lay eggs. Favorite locations for this are the ear margins and the elbows, although any area can be affected. These areas become reddened, and intense itching, hair loss, and crusting will follow. If left untreated, the entire body will be affected.

The mite does not burrow into human skin, but small, itchy bumps appear. Favorite areas are the abdomen and forearms.

Home Treatment
No treatment is effective.

What to Expect at the Veterinarian's Office
The mite or its eggs can be detected by a skin scraping and by microscopic examination. The mite is a round parasite with four pairs of legs.

Your doctor will prescribe a dip to be used once weekly for a month. Chemicals effective against the mite are *lindane, malathion, dichlorvos,* and *ronnel.* All dogs in the household should be treated to avoid reinfestation.

To prevent your dog from itching and chewing itself raw, steroids will be prescribed. If there is a bacterial infection (from skin injury), antibiotics will be dispensed, as well.

A long-haired dog should be clipped to make treatment easier.

Prevention
Keep your dog away from dogs who are being treated for scabies. Board your dog in clean, well-ventilated facilities. Always ask to see the cages and runs beforehand. If you are buying a pup that scratches a lot, have it checked by a veterinarian before introducing it into your house.

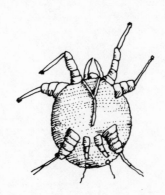

Scabies

Is there severe scratching? — No → See Skin Problem Chart

Yes ↓

Are there reddened, crusty lesions on the ear margins and/or the elbows? — Yes →

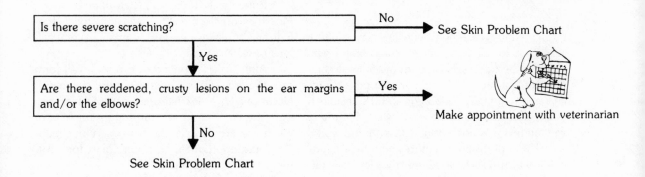

Make appointment with veterinarian

No ↓

See Skin Problem Chart

Ticks

I don't think even Albert Schweitzer, who had a reverence for all living things, could find a purpose for the tick's existence. In my opinion, any parasite that sucks your own or your pet's blood, lays approximately 5,000 eggs, and transmits a fatal disease to humans (Rocky Mountain spotted fever) is not a good citizen of the world!

These disgusting creatures bury their heads in the skin and suck blood until they look like fat, brown beans. At this point, probably because it is so fat that it can't hold on any more, the tick falls off the host and lays the 5,000 or more eggs. The eggs hatch one or two months later. The next two phases in the development of the tick are called the larval and nymph stages. These stages may last quite a long time, because different ticks need different hosts to feed on. In the dormant stages, the ticks can patiently wait for months—or even hibernate during the winter—under bushes, in the ground, or in your own home until a suitable host comes along.

Ticks seem to be more common on dogs than on cats. This may be due either to a distinct chemical attraction to the dog or to the cat's fastidious grooming habits.

Ticks can be found anywhere on the skin but they prefer the ear flaps, interdigital areas (between the toes), head, neck, and shoulder areas.

Home Treatment

Tick removal is surrounded by many myths and old wives' tales. Some of the popular methods—using a match to burn off the tick or using gasoline or kerosene—are overkill: They will get rid of the tick, but they may also injure your dog! Instead, just grasp the tick close to where it is embedded with your fingers or tweezers and firmly pull it out. (By the way, a tick does *not* get its whole body under the skin!). Soaking the tick with alcohol or nail polish remover (*acetone*) will plug up its breathing holes and make removal easier.

Burn the tick with a match *after* removal. Please do not flush one tick down the toilet; ecologically, it makes no sense to waste several gallons of water on one tiny insect.

After a tick is pulled out, a scab will form over the area. (This is not the tick growing back!) Occasionally, a tick bite may get infected—not from the bite, but from your dog's scratching or biting the area where the tick was embedded. Read the appropriate Decision Chart for treatment of skin infections.

Since female ticks can lay 5,000 or more eggs, you can see that if those eggs are laid in your home or kennel, a serious infestation will occur. (The sight of thousands of ticks crawling up the walls is enough to tick anybody off!) Your veterinarian can dispense products to use in the home environment. The commercial products found under flea bite dermatitis, page 168, can also help keep the tick infestation under control.

An exterminator may be necessary for heavy tick infestations, because ticks can live for a long time in the cracks and crevices of floors, woodwork, and walls without having a blood meal.

"Chiggers" is the popular name for the red or Harvest mite. In its larval stage, it is orange or red, the size of a pin head, and parasitic on most mammals (dogs, cats, humans). The larvae hitch a ride on your leg or your pet's leg in the woods. Their bite causes severe redness and itching. Chiggers can be found anywhere on the body, but their favorite hangouts are the head, neck, ear canals and flaps, and abdomen. After getting a good blood meal, the larvae drop off and become nymphs. Later they develop into adult chiggers, which feed on plants. The adult chigger lays eggs that develop into larvae, which are the only parasitic form.

If only the ears are affected, use the same treatment for ear discharges (page 190). Your veterinarian will dispense a safe insecticidal prep-

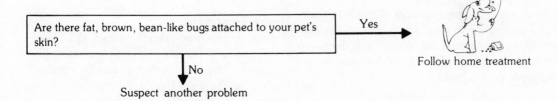

Are there fat, brown, bean-like bugs attached to your pet's skin?

Yes → Follow home treatment

No

Suspect another problem

aration if a generalized infestation is present. An antibiotic-steroid cream will control the itching.

You can prevent chigger problems on your dog by using an insecticidal preparation during warm weather (the same as for fleas, page 168).

The white mite known as "walking dandruff" is large enough to see. This mite causes itching and can affect dogs, humans, and cats. The same insecticides administered for fleas, used for about three weeks, are effective.

The adult fly and its larvae (*maggots*) occasionally cause skin problems. Maggots develop from eggs that are laid by flies. If they are in wounds, remove them with tweezers. Clean the area with Phisohex® and apply an antibiotic ointment to the wound.

Lice look like very small white oval specks that are seen best with a magnifying glass. They are spread by direct contact and cause severe itching. They spend their whole life cycle on the pet. Fortunately, lice are not seen very often on dogs. A bath is effective. After drying, an insecticide can be used.

Ringworm

Ringworm is a fungus infection of the skin that can be transmitted to your dog by other infected animals, by humans, or by contact with the soil. Pets under one year old and children are more susceptible than adults.

Ringworm lesion

The classic ringworm lesion is a rapidly-spreading, circular, hairless, scaly area sur- rounded by an outer edge that is red. However, ringworm lesions do not always take on the classic form. Your doctor has further tests to verify this diagnosis.

Home Treatment
A single fungus lesion can be treated with *tolnaftate* (Tinactin®), which you can purchase in the drugstore. The pet's bedding, combs, brushes, leashes, and collars should be sterilized or discarded, since reinfection from fungus spores is a constant danger. Clean and vacuum your house and throw the vacuum bag away. If there is more than one small lesion on your dog, see your doctor.

What to Expect at the Veterinarian's Office
Your doctor will use an ultraviolet light (one type of fungus will fluoresce green), a skin scraping, and/or a fungal culture to diagnose ringworm. The treatment of choice for ringworm is topical Tinactin® or Conofite® combined with *griseovulvin*, an oral medication, for at least one month.

Ringworm

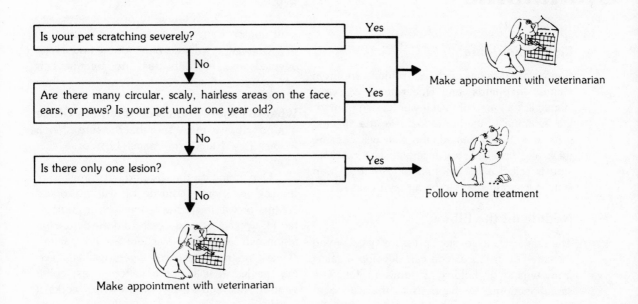

Is your pet scratching severely? — Yes → Make appointment with veterinarian

No ↓

Are there many circular, scaly, hairless areas on the face, ears, or paws? Is your pet under one year old? — Yes → Make appointment with veterinarian

No ↓

Is there only one lesion? — Yes → Follow home treatment

No ↓

Make appointment with veterinarian

Nodule/Lick Granuloma

Lick Granuloma

Some large dogs, such as retrievers, Great Danes, shepherds, and Dobermans, will constantly lick an area of their lower foreleg or hindleg. Eventually, the hair is lost over the affected area and, if not treated, the skin will become thick and firm and will ulcerate. The resulting sore is called a *lick granuloma*. Boredom and lack of exercise seem to be a major cause.

Nodule on the Elbow

The skin reacts to constant pressure by becoming thicker. For instance, you can develop a callus from writing or holding a tennis racket. The same phenomenon happens to the skin over bony pressure points. A thickened, gray, wrinkled, and hairless area may develop on the outside of the elbow or hock, especially on large or obese dogs or those that spend a lot of time lying on hard surfaces, such as cement or wood.

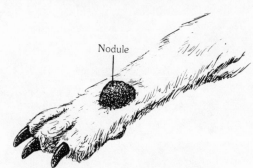

Nodule

Home Treatment

Since boredom seems to be a major factor, more exercise or more companionship (human or canine) may help.

If the area is not severely inflamed, spray *around*—not on—the lesion with Bitter Apple® (sold in pet stores) four times daily. Try buying a cream called Variton® (sold by your veterinarian). It tastes terrible and is anti-inflammatory.

If the dog continues to lick the sore, see your doctor. Early lesions are easier to cure.

Unless the wrinkles of an elbow nodule get infected and fill with pus, no treatment is necessary.

What to Expect at the Veterinarian's Office

Your doctor will make sure that the sore is not a fungus (see Ringworm, page 178) or a skin tumor.

Depending on the size and inflammation of the lick granuloma, your doctor will use topical creams or will inject the lesion with a corticosteroid, which is very successful if done before the lesion gets large. The injections are not painful. A new treatment that works very well is injecting the lesion with cobra venom—yes, cobra venom. Although we don't know why it works, it is safe.

Lick granulomas that are not treated early may require surgery or radiation therapy. Recurrence in the same or a different area is common if the boredom factor is not resolved.

For an infected callus, your doctor will prescribe a cleansing shampoo. Antibiotics may also be dispensed, especially for a severe infection. If this treatment is not successful, surgery to remove the infected areas may be necessary.

Prevention

Longer walks and vigorous exercise in parks reduces the boredom of large dogs, as will more human companionship and play. A new puppy as a playmate may divert your dog from its licking fixation. Can you take your dog to work with you?

If nodules are forming, encourage your dog to lie on soft surfaces. Foam rubber pads and blankets can help prevent further insult to the affected area.

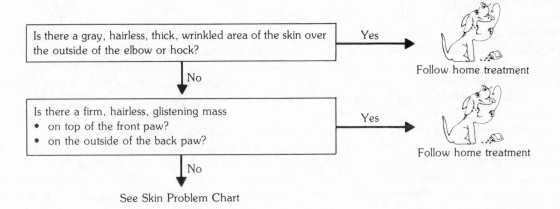

Is there a gray, hairless, thick, wrinkled area of the skin over the outside of the elbow or hock? — **Yes** → Follow home treatment

No ↓

Is there a firm, hairless, glistening mass
- on top of the front paw?
- on the outside of the back paw?

— **Yes** → Follow home treatment

No ↓

See Skin Problem Chart

Abscesses

An abscess is a walled-off collection of pus caused by a bacterial infection. (Pus is a collection of live and dead bacteria, dead tissue, white blood cells, and other cells called on to defend your pet's body.) Any damage to the skin, especially lacerations or puncture wounds, can admit bacteria into the underlying tissue. If the dog's body cannot fight the bacteria, tissue will be damaged and an abscess will form. An abscess is potentially dangerous: If prompt medical and/or surgical attention is not provided, the infection can spread to the chest, brain, heart, kidneys, or liver via the blood stream.

An abscess is characterized by a warm swelling that is painful to the touch. Your dog may also be lethargic and have a fever.

Skin Scab Abscess

Sometimes a dog is brought to the office with a lameness and lethargy that has become worse over a few days. Pressing on each area of the limb, hip, or shoulder may elicit pain. The owner thinks the dog's leg is broken, but a swelling and a scab over a healed bite wound can be felt. The dog's rectal temperature can be 104° to 105°F.

Home Treatment

EMERGENCY A dog that has an abscess should be seen by your doctor, since the potential for tissue damage or death from bacterial toxins is high unless proper wound cleaning and/or surgery and antibiotic treatment are done.

If it is impossible for you to see a veterinarian, you will have to treat the abscess at home. If the abscess is open and draining, probe and clean the wound with a cotton-tipped applicator. Remove any hair, wood slivers, or other matter that may be in the wound. Pour a small amount of hydrogen peroxide (3 percent) into the wound, three times daily, or use an eye dropper or turkey baster. Press on the swelling to help the hydrogen peroxide flush the wound.

If the abscess has not burst, apply hot towels to the area to help bring it to a head. When you can feel a soft spot in the swelling, use a clean razor blade to nick the swelling. The pus should drain out easily. Probe and flush the wound as explained above. Try to get your dog on antibiotics as soon as possible.

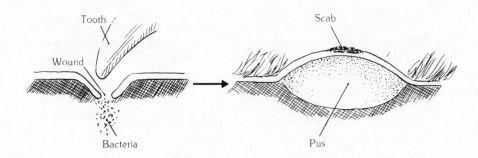

Tooth

Wound

Bacteria

Scab

Pus

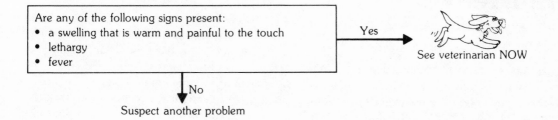

Are any of the following signs present:
- a swelling that is warm and painful to the touch
- lethargy
- fever

Yes → See veterinarian NOW

No
Suspect another problem

What to Expect at the Veterinarian's Office
Your doctor will probe the wound for dirt, debris, and foreign material and may flush the abscess with antibiotic, sterile saline, or hydrogen peroxide solutions or surgically *debride* (remove dead and infected tissue) the area. A drain may be left in the wound to allow flushing of the wound for a few days. Antibiotics will be given for one week.

Prevention
Cleaning wounds promptly with soap and water or hydrogen peroxide and gently probing for hair, dirt, or foreign material will prevent many infections (see Cuts and Wounds, page 100).

Lumps and Swellings in the Breasts

Breast tumors are seen in female dogs older than seven years of age. The incidence may be greater in dogs who have not been spayed (also called an ovariohysterectomy) before their first heat (see Preventing Pregnancy, page 239).

A nursing female can develop an infection in one or more breasts (*mastitis*) in which the breast becomes red, hot, hard, and painful. This may be accompanied by fever and loss of appetite. The dog may lose interest in the puppies, who in turn become restless and weak because of the infected milk.

A mother dog can have engorged breasts after weaning, but they will not be red, hot, hard, or painful. In addition, the dog will remain alert and active and will still eat well.

The breasts may enlarge about two months after the heat period. If the dog is not pregnant, this is due to normal hormone changes. Milk can be produced and other signs of false pregnancy (page 231) can occur.

Home Treatment

If the mother dog has mastitis, your doctor will prescribe antibiotics. *Note:* Do *not* let the puppies nurse, since the antibiotics in the milk could be toxic. This means hand-feeding very young puppies (under two or three weeks old). See page 236 for directions.

Also keep the puppies away if the mother has engorged breasts after weaning, since nursing will stimulate the milk production. Apply cold compresses to the breasts. Improvement should be seen in one to three days; if not, contact your doctor. No treatment is necessary for the slight breast swelling seen in females during the heat cycle.

What to Expect at the Veterinarian's Office

Breast tumors can range in size from smaller than a pea to masses involving the whole gland. They can also be benign (not cancerous) or malignant (cancerous), so see your doctor *early*—do *not* wait for the nodules to get larger. Your doctor will palpate the breast and the adjacent lymph nodes for evidence of malignancy. If the nodule is thought *not* to be a cyst, a radiograph of the chest will be taken to check for the possible spread (*metastasis*) of a malignant tumor. If the X ray is normal, your doctor may recommend surgical removal of the nodule and a biopsy (microscopic examination of a tissue sample) of both it and the adjacent lymph nodes. If the nodule is malignant, further therapy will be considered (see Cancer, page 253).

Mastitis is usually treated successfully with antibiotics.

Lumps and Swellings in the Breasts

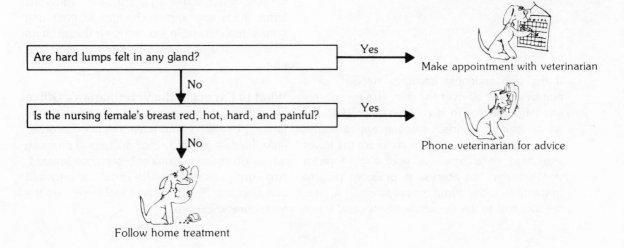

Are hard lumps felt in any gland? — **Yes** → Make appointment with veterinarian

No ↓

Is the nursing female's breast red, hot, hard, and painful? — **Yes** → Phone veterinarian for advice

No ↓

Follow home treatment

Lumps and Bumps on the Skin

If the face suddenly becomes swollen, or if bumps appear all over the skin, this is probably an allergic reaction to insect bites (page 104). If a warm, painful, reddish swelling appears anywhere on the skin (common areas are the lower legs, head, or tail base) and your dog is feverish and lethargic, an abscess is probably present (page 182). If the bump moves freely—i.e., it is not attached to the skin underneath—and is not painful or enlarging, follow the Home Treatment.

Home Treatment

If none of the above signs are seen, watch the lump. If its appearance changes or your dog seems uncomfortable, contact your doctor. If no change is seen, ask about the lump on your next visit.

What to Expect at the Veterinarian's Office

If the tumor is benign, such as a *lipoma* ("fatty tumor") or a *sebaceous adenoma* (a cauliflower-gray, hairless growth), your doctor will probably advise no treatment unless it becomes irritated. Any suspicious skin growths should be removed and biopsied. Skin tumors, if malignant, are the most curable cancers.

Lumps and Bumps on the Skin

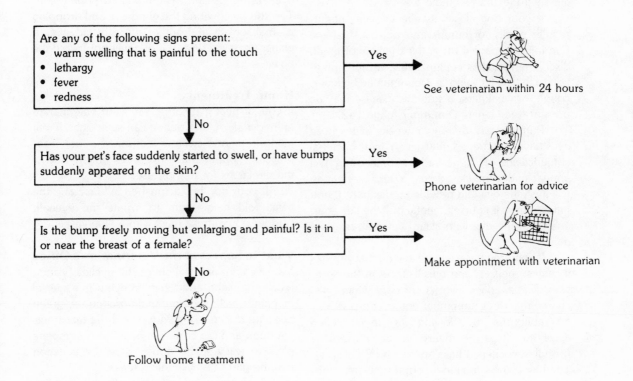

Are any of the following signs present:
- warm swelling that is painful to the touch
- lethargy
- fever
- redness

Yes → See veterinarian within 24 hours

No

Has your pet's face suddenly started to swell, or have bumps suddenly appeared on the skin?

Yes → Phone veterinarian for advice

No

Is the bump freely moving but enlarging and painful? Is it in or near the breast of a female?

Yes → Make appointment with veterinarian

No

Follow home treatment

Eye Discharges

Your dog has only two eyes. Therefore, a seemingly minor eye problem could rapidly turn into a major catastrophe. See your veterinarian *immediately* if the chart so indicates.

If your dog closes its eye in pain, has irregular pupils, or bumps into objects, first see Eye Injuries, page 114. A thick yellow or green discharge indicates conjunctivitis, an inflammation of the eyelid lining. If accompanied by fever, cough, or weakness, a systemic disease may be present (see Canine Distemper, page 142).

Puppies less than two weeks old whose eyes have not opened may get an acute bacterial conjunctivitis. A large reddened swelling will appear under the closed lids. Your veterinarian will flush the eye and provide medication. If you have to treat it yourself, gently pull the lids apart and flush the eye with clean water three times daily.

If your dog has a watery eye discharge, licks its paws, sneezes, and rubs its face on the floor, see Allergies, page 166. A constant watery discharge that does not bother your pet is probably an abnormal overflowing of tears called *epiphora*. It is hereditary in certain breeds (poodles, cockers, Lhasa apsos, and Shih Tzus). The hair in the eye's inner corner is always moist and stains a dark brown. Its causes are misplaced eyelashes, blocked tear ducts, nasal fold hairs irritating the eye, or eyelid defects.

Glaucoma

Glaucoma results from increased fluid pressure within the eye, which damages the retina. Bassett hounds, cockers, poodles, Norwegian elkhounds, malamutes, and wire-haired terriers are particularly prone to this condition. In the normal eye, fluid is continually produced to keep the eyeball firm; any excess fluid is drained. An increase of fluid or a blockage to its outflow dangerously raises the pressure in the eyeball.

There are a number of signs: Your dog will experience severe pain, will constantly close its eye, and will seem especially sensitive to light. Excessive tearing occurs. The eyeball will be larger than normal, and the blood vessels in the white area will be red and swollen. The cornea will look cloudy and the pupil will remain dilated, even in bright light. There will be poor vision. Test this by covering the good eye and dropping a small object in front of the affected eye. If glaucoma is present, the eye will not follow the object.

Home Treatment

If you suspect glaucoma, see your veterinarian *immediately*. Quick action can save sight. Treat mild irritations with Neosporin® or Neopolycin® *ophthalmics* (for eyes only!). Follow the directions for human use.

If your dog has a "pushed-in" face and the nasal fold hairs seem to irritate the eyeball, smooth down these hairs with a little vaseline.

What to Expect at the Veterinarian's Office

Your veterinarian will check the eyelids, vision, reaction to light, and the inner eye with a special magnifier called an *ophthalmoscope*. A green dye, *fluorescein*, is used to see if the tear ducts are open and the cornea is healthy. A complete physical will also be done, since the infection may be part of a systemic disease.

Antibiotic eyedrops or ointments are frequently given for eye infections. Cortisone-type medicine should be prescribed very infrequently, since it can cause certain infections (such as herpes) to worsen. If herpes is diagnosed, special eyedrops are needed.

Misplaced eyelashes or eyelid defects may have to be corrected surgically. Blocked tear ducts may need to be flushed out if the medication is not working.

The treatment for glaucoma involves improving the flow of fluid from the eyeball, decreasing the fluid volume, and reducing the amount of fluid formed, using oral and intravenous medication. Once the pressure is reduced, your doctor can determine whether

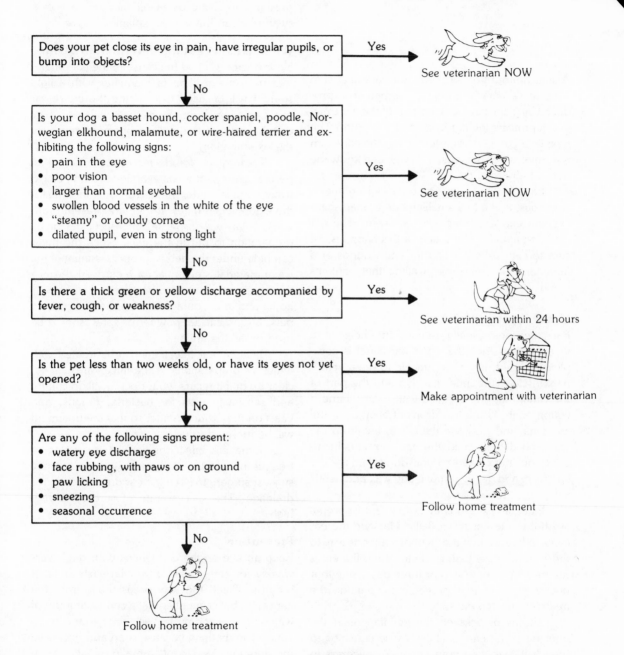

Does your pet close its eye in pain, have irregular pupils, or bump into objects?

Yes → See veterinarian NOW

No ↓

Is your dog a basset hound, cocker spaniel, poodle, Norwegian elkhound, malamute, or wire-haired terrier and exhibiting the following signs:
- pain in the eye
- poor vision
- larger than normal eyeball
- swollen blood vessels in the white of the eye
- "steamy" or cloudy cornea
- dilated pupil, even in strong light

Yes → See veterinarian NOW

No ↓

Is there a thick green or yellow discharge accompanied by fever, cough, or weakness?

Yes → See veterinarian within 24 hours

No ↓

Is the pet less than two weeks old, or have its eyes not yet opened?

Yes → Make appointment with veterinarian

No ↓

Are any of the following signs present:
- watery eye discharge
- face rubbing, with paws or on ground
- paw licking
- sneezing
- seasonal occurrence

Yes → Follow home treatment

No ↓

Follow home treatment

Prevention

To diagnose glaucoma before its signs are present, measure the eye pressure in the predisposed breeds during the regular yearly examination.

medical or surgical treatment will be necessary to prevent recurrence.

A small amount of light-brown waxy material in your dog's ears is probably normal. It is produced by glands in the outer part of the ear canal and it protects the ear canal and ear drum. The next time you visit your doctor and the ear exam is normal, smell the ears. You will then know the odor of a normal ear.

Ear infections may exhibit a slight redness, some pus, and a foul-smelling odor. Head shaking and ear scratching are also seen. The ear may be painful to the touch. If this happens, be sure to check the ear flap for bite wounds or a *hematoma* (a tumor or swelling that contains blood).

Home Treatment
Ear infections usually require the help of a veterinarian, since the dog's ear canal is complexly shaped. If you are unable to see a veterinarian, clean the inner ear flap and the part of the canal that you can see with baby oil and a cotton swab. Use a few drops of baby oil in the ear canal and massage the ear to break up the wax and debris. Hold the ear flap straight up over your pet's head so you don't damage the ear drum and gently remove any wax and debris with the cotton swab.

Place a few drops of 70 percent isopropyl alcohol in the ear twice daily. Massage the ear canal to be sure that the alcohol makes its way to the bottom of the L-shaped ear canal. If there is no improvement in two or three days, see your doctor. If there is improvement, continue the treatment for ten days.

Thorns or ticks on the ear flap or at the opening of the ear canal can cause your dog to scratch its ear. Use your fingers or tweezers to remove any irritants. Apply 70 percent isopropyl alcohol to the irritated area so that it won't become infected.

If there are no signs of ear infection and a small amount of light-brown waxy material is present, use baby oil or alcohol and a cotton swab to clean the ear as explained above.

What to Expect at the Veterinarian's Office
Your doctor will find the cause of the ear inflammation. An *otoscope* (a magnifier with a light source) will be used to examine the entire ear canal and ear drum. Some pets with very sore ears have to be tranquilized or anesthetized for this examination.

If ear mites (*otodectes cyanotis*) are suspected, your doctor will examine the dry, black, waxy material under the microscope, looking for the eight-legged mites. If they are present, your veterinarian will dispense an insecticidal or oil preparation to put in the ears. Since the mites can hide under the debris, proper cleaning of the waxy material is essential for a cure. Also, since the mites may live on other parts of your pet's body and are contagious to other household pets, an insecticidal powder or spray should be used on all the animals.

Bacterial ear infections can be treated with antibiotic preparations. If the infection does not clear up or if it recurs, your doctor will do culture and sensitivity tests for bacteria, fungus, and yeast on the *exuded* matter so that the treatment will be more effective.

Some ear infections can be frustrating to treat. If the infection is chronic, your doctor may suggest surgery to keep the ear dry and enhance drainage. The success rate of surgery is very high.

Prevention
Keep an eye on the ear! Check your dog's ears weekly for early signs of trouble, such as slight redness. Clean the wax occasionally from the ear canal, but remember that a certain amount of wax is normal and protective. Place cotton in the ears before bathing because soap and excessive moisture may lead to inflammation. Place cotton in the ears also if your dog is going to run through bushes that have thorns. Remember to remove the cotton afterward!

Ear Discharges

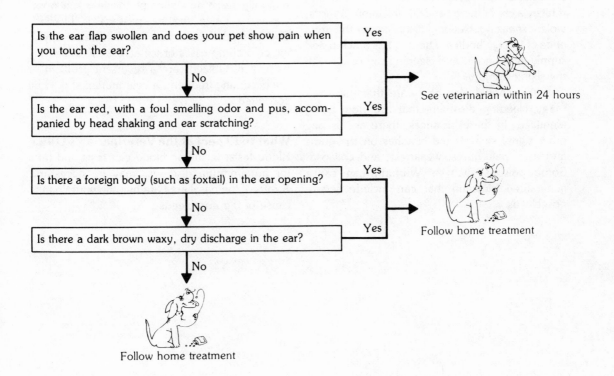

Is the ear flap swollen and does your pet show pain when you touch the ear? — **Yes** → See veterinarian within 24 hours

No ↓

Is the ear red, with a foul smelling odor and pus, accompanied by head shaking and ear scratching? — **Yes** → See veterinarian within 24 hours

No ↓

Is there a foreign body (such as foxtail) in the ear opening? — **Yes** → Follow home treatment

No ↓

Is there a dark brown waxy, dry discharge in the ear? — **Yes** → Follow home treatment

No ↓

Follow home treatment

Nosebleeds

Nosebleeds can occur from trauma (if your dog is hit by a car or has a bad fall), infection, tumors, violent sneezing, bleeding disorders, or the presence of foreign bodies. The dog has a rich blood supply in the nose, and bleeding can occur with the slightest injury.

You should also be aware that there are many bleeding disorders that are now being identified. In these instances, there are usually other signs, such as red blotches on the gums and ears, pale gums, weakness, and collapse. Some poisons such as Warfarin can cause generalized bleeding that can include severe nosebleeds.

Home Treatment

The dog's nose consists of a bony part and a soft part (the *turbinates*). The area of the nose that is usually involved in nosebleeds lies within the soft portion. Dogs are nose breathers, so they will naturally resist any attempt to clear the nose, especially when the air passage is blocked. Squeezing the nostril for a few minutes or applying cold compresses or ice across the nose may help. If nosebleeds are a recurrent problem or are becoming frequent, a veterinarian should be consulted.

What to Expect at the Veterinarian's Office

Blood tests, including blood clot tests and tests for autoimmune diseases, may be necessary. X rays of the nasal area are helpful in finding the cause of the nosebleeds.

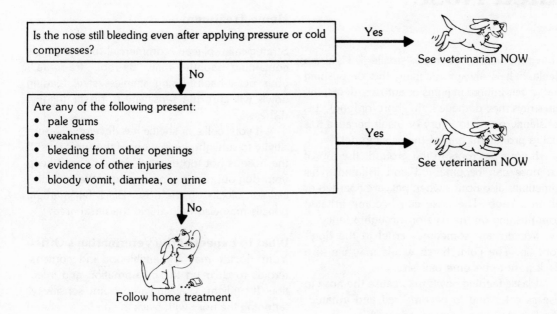

Is the nose still bleeding even after applying pressure or cold compresses?

Yes → See veterinarian NOW

No ↓

Are any of the following present:
- pale gums
- weakness
- bleeding from other openings
- evidence of other injuries
- bloody vomit, diarrhea, or urine

Yes → See veterinarian NOW

No ↓

Follow home treatment

Red or Irritated Nose

Your pet's nose is not only a "smeller," it is also a "feeler": It is always touching this or pushing that; it gets injured in fights or auto accidents; the sun's rays may damage it. In short (or long), it is constantly prone to injury or insult because it is such a prominent part of the moving pet.

If your pet roots in the ground, the top of the nose can become red and irritated. This sometimes also occurs when pets are boarded or left in a cage: The nose can become irritated from pushing on the bars or through a fence.

Winters are sometimes cruel to the dog's front tip: The cold, harsh winds may cause a black nose to become pinkish.

Plastic feeding bowls may cause the nose to lose its color and to become red and irritated. The lips may also become inflamed.

Collies and shelties can develop an extreme sensitivity to sunlight. This reddening of the nasal area seems to be hereditary.

Any slow-growing swelling in the nasal area of older pets may be a serious condition such as a tumor.

Home Treatment
Chew toys or playmates may cure the rooter. Strategically placed commercial pet products containing naphtha may "de-root" (re-route?) your pet's habit. Using stainless steel feeding bowls will cure the sensitivity to plastic feeding dishes.

If your collie or sheltie has developed a sensitivity to sunlight, keep it out of the sun's rays. If the nose is not too irritated and you can't keep your dog out of the sun, try one of the commercial sun blocks on the nose. Black felt marking pencils may also help shield the nasal area.

What to Expect at the Veterinarian's Office
Your doctor may try antibiotics and corticosteroids to clear up the inflammation and infection. If sunlight is causing an extreme sensitivity, tattooing the nose with black ink under a general anesthesia works very well. This procedure may have to be done two or three times for the desired results to be completely effective.

Red or Irritated Nose

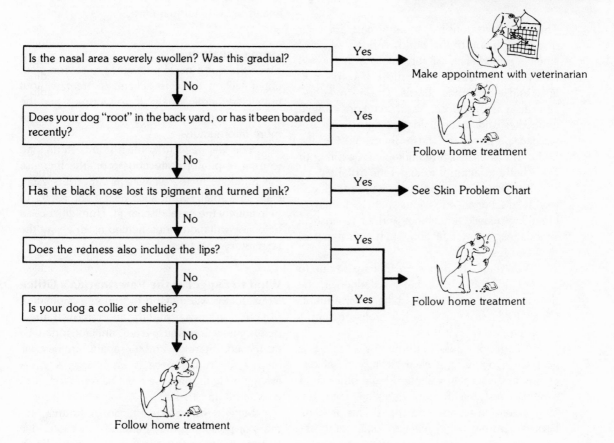

Is the nasal area severely swollen? Was this gradual? — Yes → Make appointment with veterinarian

No ↓

Does your dog "root" in the back yard, or has it been boarded recently? — Yes → Follow home treatment

No ↓

Has the black nose lost its pigment and turned pink? — Yes → See Skin Problem Chart

No ↓

Does the redness also include the lips? — Yes → Follow home treatment

No ↓

Is your dog a collie or sheltie? — Yes → Follow home treatment

No ↓

Follow home treatment

Runny Nose

The nose is responsible, in large part, for your dog's perception of the world. A dog's sense of smell is remarkable. All the smells of the world filter through it—but so do viruses, bacteria, pollens, and, sometimes, thorns. These "invaders" can cause a runny nose. Nasal secretions contain antibodies and tissue fluid that fight these unwanted particles and flush them outside the body. The sneeze is a remarkable reflex in your dog's body to attempt to expel the irritant.

If your dog's nose and eyes have a thick yellowish discharge and your pet is lethargic, breathing heavily, coughing, and/or feverish, a serious respiratory infection, such as distemper, may be present.

A discharge from one nostril may be due to a thorn or other object that has lodged in the nose as your dog inspected its environment. Older dogs can have sinus infections or tumors involving one side of the nose.

A common cause of runny noses in dogs is allergies. Dogs with a clear, watery nasal discharge and sneezing will often have other signs simultaneously, such as paw licking, face rubbing, watery eyes, and scratching. This problem lasts longer than a viral infection (often for weeks or months) and occurs most often seasonally, when pollen particles or other allergens are in the air. House dusts and molds may aggravate the allergic runny nose.

Whether your pet's nose is cool and moist or warm and dry is not a good indication of its health or body temperature.

Home Treatment

Since the dog's nasal passages are so complex, any infection there is difficult to treat without your veterinarian's help. If you suspect that the problem may be an allergy, see that section for more information.

You will need to contact your veterinarian to treat respiratory infections properly. Increase the humidity in the air with a vaporizer, especially in a small room, such as the bathroom, to help liquefy the nasal discharge. Humidifiers also help stop irritation when heated air dries out the respiratory passages.

What to Expect at the Veterinarian's Office

Your doctor will make a thorough examination of your dog's nose, mouth, and throat. If a respiratory infection is suspected, antibiotics may be dispensed. Steroids and/or antihistamines will help if the runny nose is an allergic sign. A foreign body in the nose must be removed, with or without anesthesia.

Severe respiratory infections, trauma, tumors or poisoning may demand more intensive treatment, laboratory tests, and radiographs (X rays).

Runny Nose

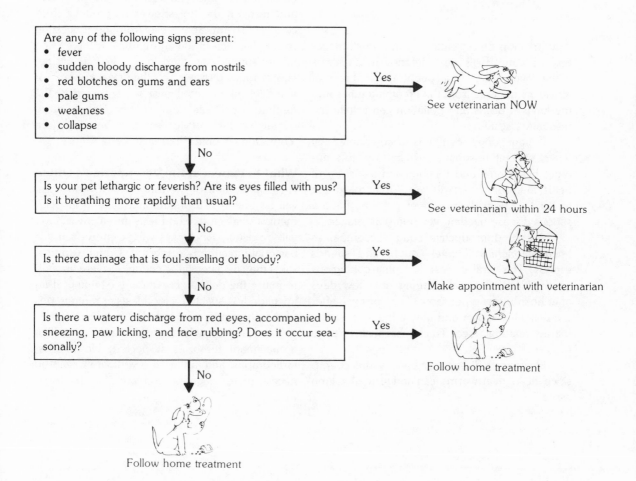

Are any of the following signs present:
- fever
- sudden bloody discharge from nostrils
- red blotches on gums and ears
- pale gums
- weakness
- collapse

Yes → See veterinarian NOW

No

Is your pet lethargic or feverish? Are its eyes filled with pus? Is it breathing more rapidly than usual?

Yes → See veterinarian within 24 hours

No

Is there drainage that is foul-smelling or bloody?

Yes → Make appointment with veterinarian

No

Is there a watery discharge from red eyes, accompanied by sneezing, paw licking, and face rubbing? Does it occur seasonally?

Yes → Follow home treatment

No

Follow home treatment

Coughs

Any irritation of the breathing tubes will trigger one of your dog's best defense mechanisms —the cough reflex. In a cough, a violent rush of air cleans material from the breathing tubes and the lungs. Pollens and pollution can irritate the respiratory system.

If your dog's cough is accompanied by fever, difficult breathing, weight loss, low energy, blue gums and tongue, and a history of heart murmur, heart disease, or a malignant tumor, see your doctor. Your pet may have a serious disease needing veterinary assistance.

A dry, unproductive cough accompanies *tracheobronchitis* (kennel cough) and sounds serious. This viral disease is highly contagious among dogs, especially during or a few days after boarding or a pet show. The dogs gag after the coughing spasm and may bring up a white, foamy material (see Tracheobronchitis, page 46).

Heartworm disease can begin with a cough, since dead heartworms can lodge in the lung tissue.

Home Treatment

To help clear the unwanted material from breathing tubes, use a cool mist vaporizer in the bathroom or take your pet into the bathroom and turn on the hot shower to produce thick clouds of steam. Some relief from the congestion should be seen in fifteen minutes. If there is no improvement, see your doctor. If your pet becomes more distressed in the "steam room" or when using the cool mist vaporizer, stop the treatment and see your doctor. Cough syrup containing just guaifenesin can be used (see Your Dog's Home Pharmacy, page 75).

What to Expect at the Veterinarian's Office

An examination of the throat, neck, and chest will be made. If a pneumonia or lung involvement is suspected, blood tests and a chest X ray will be taken. Antibiotics will be prescribed if a bacterial infection is suspected. Cough suppressants may be given if the cough is severe enough to injure the delicate breathing tube lining. If an infection is suspected, blood tests or radiographs of the chest may be needed.

If a heart problem or metastasis (spread) of a malignant tumor is suspected, blood tests, radiographs and an electrocardiogram will be necessary to diagnose and monitor the treatment.

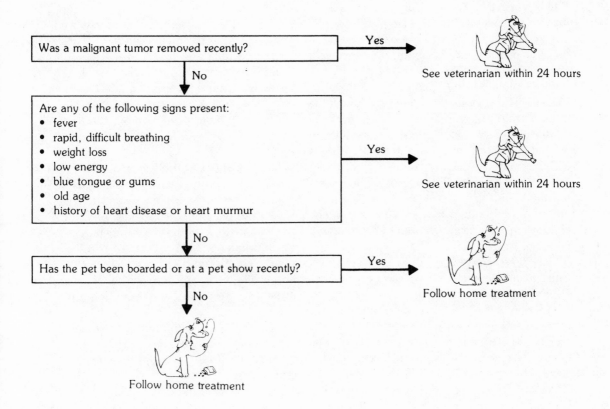

Was a malignant tumor removed recently? — **Yes** → See veterinarian within 24 hours

No

Are any of the following signs present:
- fever
- rapid, difficult breathing
- weight loss
- low energy
- blue tongue or gums
- old age
- history of heart disease or heart murmur

Yes → See veterinarian within 24 hours

No

Has the pet been boarded or at a pet show recently? — **Yes** → Follow home treatment

No

Follow home treatment

Mouth Odor

Bad breath in dogs is commonly due to problems involving the teeth and gums. Dogs develop *plaque* (the mucus film that develops if you don't brush your teeth) just as humans do. Since very few owners brush their pets' teeth, the plaque hardens into a brownish material called *tartar* or *calculus*. The tartar that you *don't see* (under the gum) loosens the delicate membranes that hold the teeth in their sockets, and infections develop around the receding gums and teeth. This is called *periodontal disease*, and it is not easily missed by the owner: The odor is quite powerful, the tartar is prominent on the canine teeth and molars, and the gums are red and swollen. In addition, your dog may drool or have trouble chewing.

Tumors and overgrowth of gum tissue will cause a foul mouth odor. The dog needs veterinary care.

A very sweet mouth odor combined with lethargy and increased water intake, urination, and appetite may indicate diabetes. See your doctor and take a urine sample to be checked for sugar.

Dogs rarely need to have a cavity filled because they don't get cavities very often.

Home Treatment

Don't worry if your puppy is only a few months old and has "garlic breath"; this is normal. It is caused by certain "good" bacteria that live in the mouth. In a few months this odor will disappear.

Prevention of periodontal disease is important, since chronic mouth infections constantly spread bacteria and toxins to the kidneys and other organs. In time, this takes its toll on your pet. If the tartar is just forming, you can scrape it off with your fingernail, but keep in mind that the culprit is the tartar that you *don't see*, under the gum.

What to Expect at the Veterinarian's Office

If the mouth odor is caused by dental tartar and gum inflammation, a teeth cleaning (and possibly an extraction) is necessary. Very few dogs will tolerate their teeth being scraped by the special instrument called a tartar scraper—and *no* dogs will tolerate the ultrasonic teeth cleaners—while they are awake, so sedatives or anesthesia are necessary. If your dog is middle-aged or older, your doctor may perform a blood test to check the health of the kidneys before using a sedative or anesthesia. The heart will be monitored before, during, and after the teeth cleaning.

If teeth need to be extracted or if the teeth and gums are very unhealthy, your doctor will prescribe antibiotics. Since the bacteria can spread through the bloodstream, antibiotics will prevent an infection from developing in the mouth or in some distant organ (the liver or kidney, for instance). They may be started a few days before the teeth cleaning.

Prevention

The time to prevent future dental problems is before tartar forms, or after your doctor cleans the teeth. Cleaning your dog's teeth at least twice weekly with a children's tooth brush or gauze pad is the ideal way of increasing the time interval between professional teeth cleanings.

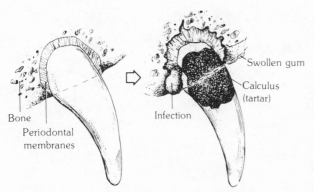

Bone

Periodontal membranes

Infection

Swollen gum

Calculus (tartar)

Mouth Odor

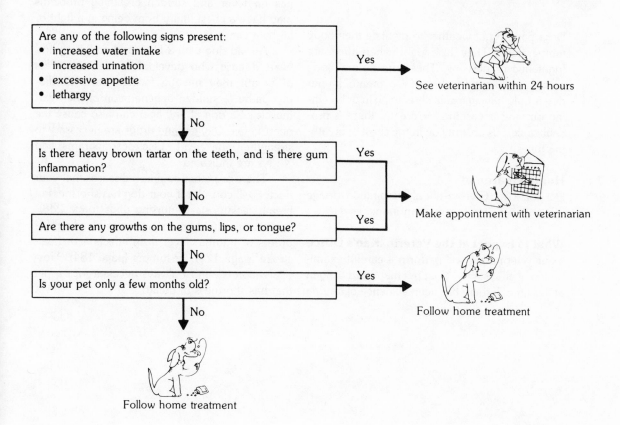

Are any of the following signs present:
- increased water intake
- increased urination
- excessive appetite
- lethargy

Yes → See veterinarian within 24 hours

No

Is there heavy brown tartar on the teeth, and is there gum inflammation?

Yes →

No

Are there any growths on the gums, lips, or tongue?

Yes → Make appointment with veterinarian

No

Is your pet only a few months old?

Yes → Follow home treatment

No

Follow home treatment

Most dogs don't like the foaming and fizzing of human toothpastes, so use a salt-water or bicarbonate of soda solution to clean the outer surface of the gums and teeth. The inner surface collects tartar much more slowly, and since most pets resist the process, don't bother cleaning it. It is best to start this routine when your pet is a puppy. Handle firmly but gently. You can clean the outside of the teeth rapidly, in about thirty seconds. Set up a regular teeth cleaning schedule with your veterinarian and have him send you a reminder card. Some dogs need a teeth cleaning every six months; others can go a year or two between cleanings.

I'm not a big believer in hard bones, hard rubber toys, dry food, or hard biscuits that purport to clean teeth. If these *were* helpful, I'm sure your dentist would suggest that you chew on a soup bone while you're watching television or when you're caught in a traffic jam.

Shortness of Breath

Dogs pant in hot weather to regulate their body temperature. They also pant when they are frightened or nervous. These are normal body reactions and are *not* shortness of breath. If your dog is truly having trouble breathing in or breathing out and is gasping for breath, there is probably a serious obstruction in the chest or breathing tubes.

Home Treatment
EMERGENCY Give artificial respiration (page 90) and see your veterinarian immediately.

What to Expect at the Veterinarian's Office
Your veterinarian will perform a careful examination of all systems. Your pet may need oxygen at this time. If there has been evidence of trauma (such as an auto accident), X rays will be taken when your dog is stabilized. An outdoor pet that has no fever and sudden breathing problems may have a chest injury from being in a fight or hit by a car.

An old dog with a history of coughing and heart disease who develops sudden shortness of breath may have a failing heart. Cardiomyopathy (a sudden degeneration of the heart muscle of a dog at any age) can also cause the heart to fail. Oxygen and drugs are necessary to strengthen the heart. Electrocardiograms and X rays are indicated.

There are other common diseases that your doctor will consider if your dog has shortness of breath: eclampsia in nursing dogs (page 238), anemia, internal hemorrhage from bleeding disorders or trauma, fever from infection or heatstroke (page 124), or tumors (page 184). Hospitalization is almost always necessary for a pet that has shortness of breath.

Shortness of Breath

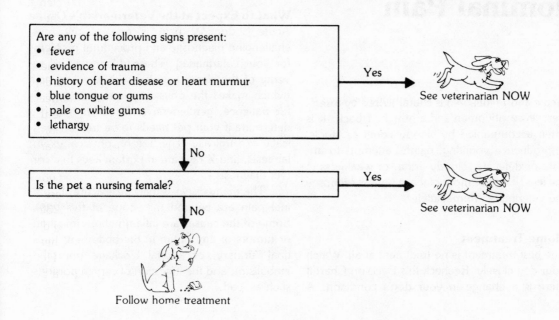

Are any of the following signs present:
- fever
- evidence of trauma
- history of heart disease or heart murmur
- blue tongue or gums
- pale or white gums
- lethargy

Yes → See veterinarian NOW

No ↓

Is the pet a nursing female?

Yes → See veterinarian NOW

No ↓

Follow home treatment

Acute Abdominal Pain

Acute abdominal pain is characterized by a tender, tense abdomen and a hunched back. It is often accompanied by bloody vomit or stools, unproductive vomiting, painful attempts to urinate or defecate, bloody urine, or weakness in the legs. If one or more of these signs is seen, see the veterinarian *immediately*.

Home Treatment

The best treatment is no treatment at all. Watch your dog closely. Recheck this Decision Chart if there is a change in your dog's condition. A phone call or visit to your veterinarian may be necessary.

What to Expect at the Veterinarian's Office

Acute abdominal pain is one of the most challenging diagnostic and procedural problems for your veterinarian. The suddenness and severity of the signs, coupled with a pet in pain (which makes the physical exam difficult) calls for patience, gentleness, and thoroughness to determine if your pet needs to be treated medically or surgically. The history, physical exam, lab tests, and X rays are important keys to a correct diagnosis.

The many diseases that cause acute abdominal pain are beyond the scope of this book. Some of the causes are inflammation, infection, or tumors of any organ in the abdomen; intestinal, urinary, or arterial blockage (thromboembolism); and the ingestion of certain poisons, such as lead.

Acute Abdominal Pain

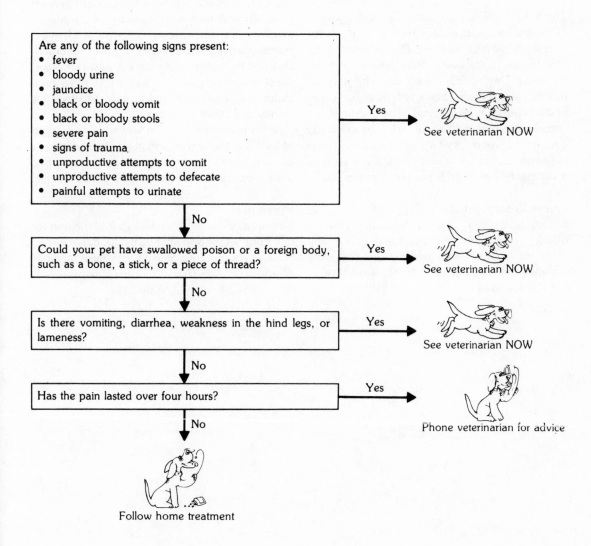

Are any of the following signs present:
- fever
- bloody urine
- jaundice
- black or bloody vomit
- black or bloody stools
- severe pain
- signs of trauma
- unproductive attempts to vomit
- unproductive attempts to defecate
- painful attempts to urinate

Yes → See veterinarian NOW

No ↓

Could your pet have swallowed poison or a foreign body, such as a bone, a stick, or a piece of thread?

Yes → See veterinarian NOW

No ↓

Is there vomiting, diarrhea, weakness in the hind legs, or lameness?

Yes → See veterinarian NOW

No ↓

Has the pain lasted over four hours?

Yes → Phone veterinarian for advice

No ↓

Follow home treatment

Stomach Dilatation/Torsion

This is an extreme emergency. Stomach (gastric) dilatation/torsion is usually seen in large, deep-chested dogs such as Great Danes, shepherds, bloodhounds, retrievers, Irish setters, and St. Bernards. The cause is not known. The stomach distends enormously as air and fluid accumulate, and it twists on itself (torsion). The abdomen becomes very large and painful. The dog will vainly attempt to vomit, salivate profusely, become very restless, breath heavily, and, if not seen by a veterinarian promptly, will collapse and die.

Home Treatment
EMERGENCY See your veterinarian *immediately*. Transport the dog gently, since any rapid movement—even making the dog walk any distance—may cause it to go into irreversible shock and die.

What to Expect at the Veterinarian's Office
The veterinarian will try to insert a stomach tube to allow the gas to escape. Antibiotics, steroids, and massive amounts of intravenous fluids are needed to stabilize the dog's condition.

If the veterinarian cannot insert a stomach tube, the stomach will have to be decompressed by a surgical technique called *gastrostomy*—a local anesthesia is given and the stomach is exposed through an incision in the abdomen. Other veterinarians decompress and reposition the stomach using general anesthesia and a large abdominal incision. Blood is drawn to monitor kidney and other functions.

An important factor in survival is the length of time that the dog experienced the dilatation or torsion before receiving veterinary care. See your veterinarian at the first sign of trouble!

Prevention
Strenuous exercise should be spared the dog for one hour before and after giving food and water. Small, frequent (four or five times daily) feedings of a low-fat, soft, bland diet may help prevent this sad and frustrating disease.

Stomach Dilatation/Torsion

Are any of the following signs present:
- enlarged abdomen
- painful abdomen
- unsuccessful vomiting
- profuse salivation
- extreme restlessness
- heavy breathing
- collapse

Yes →

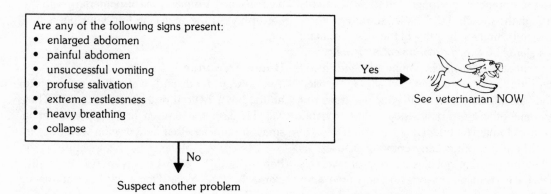

See veterinarian NOW

No ↓

Suspect another problem

Vomiting

Vomiting is a reflex by which your dog forcibly expels stomach or upper intestinal contents through the mouth. Dogs have "sensitive" stomachs and vomit easily. Most of the time, vomiting is triggered by a mild irritation called *acute gastritis*, commonly caused by eating garbage, moist dog food that stays in the bowl all day, spoiled food, tin foil, and bones. If your pet does not have any other signs of illness you can probably use the Home Treatment.

There are other fairly common causes, as well: Any pet that gobbles its food or overeats may have vomiting episodes a short time after eating. Excess salivation and vomiting during a car ride is called motion sickness (see Traveling With Your Dog, page 60).

Two misconceptions should be mentioned here. First, dogs sometimes gag and bring up a small amount of foamy, white material but remain normal afterward. This is usually caused by irritation in the throat area and is *not* vomiting. Second, if your pet eats grass and does not vomit, it usually means only that your pet likes grass, not that there is something wrong.

See your veterinarian if the Decision Chart advises a visit. Vomiting can indicate inflammation of the pancreas, the presence of foreign bodies, intestinal obstructions, liver disease, kidney failure, or infections such as distemper, hepatitis, or leptospirosis. See Stomach Dilatation, page 206, if you have a deep-chested dog whose abdomen is swollen and who has made unsuccessful attempts to vomit.

If your dog is on medication and is vomiting, call your doctor, since the medication may be causing it. Vomiting will also interfere with the absorption of the medicine that your pet is taking.

Home Treatment

Take away food *and* water for twenty-four hours, but give your dog ice cubes to lick. They will decrease the nausea and supply water in small amounts so that dehydration won't occur.

Maalox®, Mylanta®, Kaopectate®, or Pepto-Bismol® can be given to coat the stomach. See Your Dog's Home Pharmacy, page 75.

Once the vomiting has stopped, feed small amounts of chicken broth, boiled chicken, *boiled* hamburger (with the fat poured off), or baby food. If your dog does not vomit, repeat the feeding in two hours. Water can also be reintroduced. You can begin the regular diet again the next day.

What to Expect at the Veterinarian's Office

The doctor will conduct a complete history and physical exam. If your dog is dehydrated, fluids will be given subcutaneously or intravenously. Blood tests, a stool sample, a urinalysis, and X rays may be necessary to determine the cause of the vomiting.

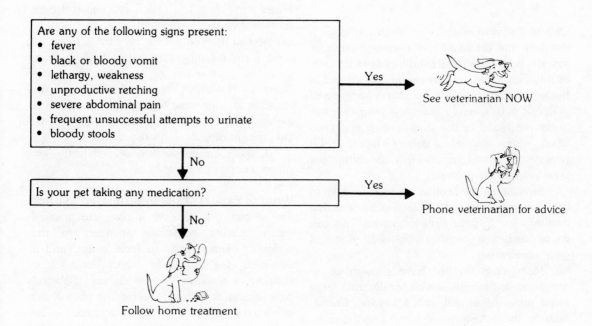

Are any of the following signs present:
- fever
- black or bloody vomit
- lethargy, weakness
- unproductive retching
- severe abdominal pain
- frequent unsuccessful attempts to urinate
- bloody stools

Yes → See veterinarian NOW

No ↓

Is your pet taking any medication?

Yes → Phone veterinarian for advice

No ↓

Follow home treatment

Diarrhea

One of the most common problems in dogs is diarrhea, the elimination of watery, runny, or soft stools. Usually, the condition lasts for only twenty-four to thirty-six hours and treatment at home is enough, unless the diarrhea persists and your pet gets severely listless. If your dog has bright red blood in the stools, black and tarry stools, severe abdominal pain, or fever, or if it persistently vomits or attempts to vomit, see your veterinarian promptly.

Sometimes medication such as antibiotics can change the number and kind of bacteria that normally live in your pet's intestines. This can cause diarrhea. If your dog is on medication, call your veterinarian.

Many dogs do not have enough of an enzyme called *lactase*, which breaks up a large sugar molecule in milk called *lactose*. Consequently, the lactose "pulls" water into the intestinal tract to soften the stools.

Very often diarrhea is caused by diet—that is, by eating "exotic" things, such as garbage, tin foil, candy, the family's table food (especially spicy foods), and bones. Excess fat in the diet, or sudden pet food changes, can sometimes cause diarrhea as well.

Worms and other intestinal parasites can irritate the intestine and cause diarrhea that is sometimes bloody.

If you suspect a chemical or plant to be the cause, see Swallowed Poisons, page 126. However, neither is a common cause of diarrhea.

Home Treatment

You can manage diarrhea by changing the diet and giving Kaopectate® to coat the intestinal tract and firm the stools. Except for puppies, who have only a small caloric reserve, no food should be given for twenty-four hours. *Note:* Do *not* take away water. Puppies with diarrhea may quickly develop severe fluid losses, so be sure to maintain adequate fluid intake. Dehydration is discussed on page 33.

After the one-day fast, you can give small, frequent feedings (four to five small meals) of *boiled* hamburger or chicken with boiled rice for four or five days. Cooked eggs and cottage cheese can then be added. Be sure to bring the food to room temperature before feeding, since food that is too hot or too cold can cause diarrhea. The small, frequent feedings give the intestine enough time to digest the food. Over the next few days, mix this diet with an increasing amount of your dog's regular food.

If the diarrhea persists beyond forty-eight hours, contact your veterinarian.

What to Expect at the Veterinarian's Office

The doctor will conduct a complete physical exam, paying particular attention to the abdomen. Blood tests, a fecal exam, and a urinalysis may be needed if an infectious (distemper) or systemic (kidney disease, diabetes, pancreatitis) disease is suspected. A plain X ray or a barium series may be necessary to define the area of inflammation or the intestinal obstruction (such as string or a rubber ball). Sometimes, *intussusception* (the telescoping of a loop of the bowel into an adjacent bowel loop) is obstructing the digestive tract. Intestinal obstruction is not uncommon in puppies and usually requires surgery. Tumors of the intestinal tract in dogs can be seen in leukemia.

If your dog is dehydrated, fluids may be administered intravenously or subcutaneously.

Prevention

Do *not* give your dog table food (especially spicy food) or milk, if it causes loose stools. Do *not* feed it bones. They serve no useful purpose but they *do* splinter, and the razor-sharp pieces can cut or perforate the intestines.

Have your veterinarian check your dog's stool samples for worm eggs often—particularly at vaccination time.

Do *not* let your dog play with yarn, string, or any toys that can be chewed up or swallowed. These can cause a fatal intestinal blockage.

Diarrhea

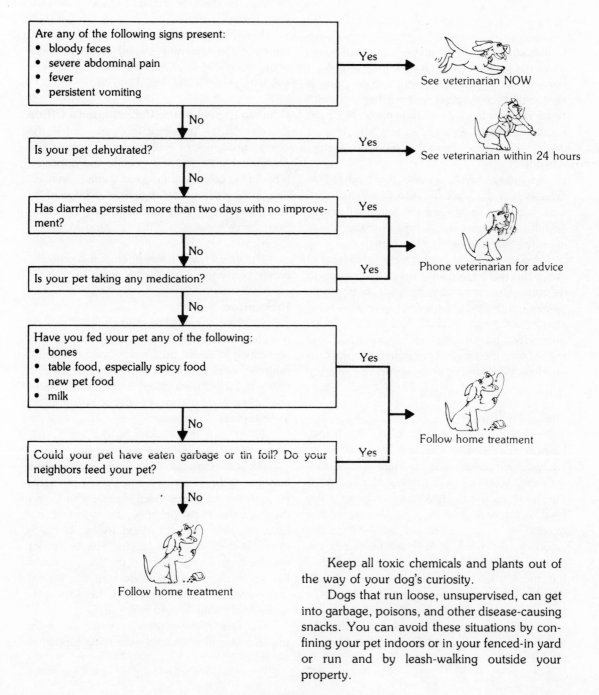

Are any of the following signs present:
- bloody feces
- severe abdominal pain
- fever
- persistent vomiting

Yes → See veterinarian NOW

No ↓

Is your pet dehydrated?

Yes → See veterinarian within 24 hours

No ↓

Has diarrhea persisted more than two days with no improvement?

Yes → Phone veterinarian for advice

No ↓

Is your pet taking any medication?

Yes → Phone veterinarian for advice

No ↓

Have you fed your pet any of the following:
- bones
- table food, especially spicy food
- new pet food
- milk

Yes → Follow home treatment

No ↓

Could your pet have eaten garbage or tin foil? Do your neighbors feed your pet?

Yes → Follow home treatment

No ↓

Follow home treatment

Keep all toxic chemicals and plants out of the way of your dog's curiosity.

Dogs that run loose, unsupervised, can get into garbage, poisons, and other disease-causing snacks. You can avoid these situations by confining your pet indoors or in your fenced-in yard or run and by leash-walking outside your property.

Constipation

Constipation is characterized by straining to move the bowels or by having infrequent bowel movements. If your dog is not straining and is alert, active, and eating well but has not defecated in two or three days, don't panic. Not even Amtrak is always on time, so why should your dog's bowel movements be on such a strict schedule?

Ingesting bones, wood, or other indigestibles is the leading cause of constipation. Less common causes are the ingestion of hair balls from cleaning themselves and the slower intestinal movements of older animals.

A dog that has *impacted feces* (hard feces in the colon) makes frequent, straining attempts to defecate. The animal may be listless or *anorectic* (without appetite) and may vomit or pass small amounts of blood-streaked, foul-smelling feces. Some long-haired dogs get feces stuck and matted over their anus. Consequently, they cannot defecate. This is called *pseudocoprostasis*.

Home Treatment
Take your dog's temperature (page 34). It may be normal or slightly elevated. You can try to relieve mild constipation by adding over-the-counter laxatives such as Metamucil® or Mucilose® to the food. Adding water to a dry food diet may also be helpful. Also try adding mineral oil, which lubricates and softens the stools, to the food. Add 1 teaspoon per ten pounds of body weight, but don't give mineral oil for more than three days—prolonged use decreases the absorption of vitamins. *Note:* Do *not* administer it directly into the mouth, as it is very bland and may pass into the respiratory system before your dog can cough. Mineral oil in the lungs will cause a pneumonia.

If your dog is straining to pass small amounts of blood-streaked, foul-smelling feces, you can try a pediatric Fleet® enema if your veterinarian recommends it. Follow the directions on the package and stay in touch with the veterinarian.

Pseudocoprostasis is cured very simply by trimming the hair and matted feces from the anus, using scissors. Bathe the area and apply a soothing cream if the skin is irritated.

What to Expect at the Veterinarian's Office
If your dog has impacted feces trapped in the colon, your doctor will perform a complete physical. He or she will palpate the impacted feces in the colon and do a rectal exam. In addition, your doctor may suggest a radiograph to study the extent and cause of the impaction. Sometimes a piece of bone is found lodged in the rectum.

Repeated warm water enemas will probably be necessary to relieve the blockage.

Prevention
Do *not* give your dog bones to chew. Bones do not clean the teeth. If you *must* give your dog something to chew, try a nylon bone or a large marrow bone, but take it away when it starts to splinter. Steak, pork chop, and chicken bones are taboo. They can cause obstructions and cut the intestines like a razor.

Keep your dog's water bowl filled. Dehydrated pets can have hard, dry feces.

As your dog ages, so does the muscle in the intestine. It becomes lazy and moves the feces through the intestines much slower. The longer the feces stay in the intestine, the more water is removed from them, making the stool much drier. Give an oil-based gel and mix stewed or raw fruits and vegetables in the food—prunes live up to their reputation! Be sure that an old dog's water bowl remains filled, because adequate fluid intake is very important.

To help prevent pseudocoprostasis, keep the anal area of your long-haired dog clipped of excess hair.

Constipation

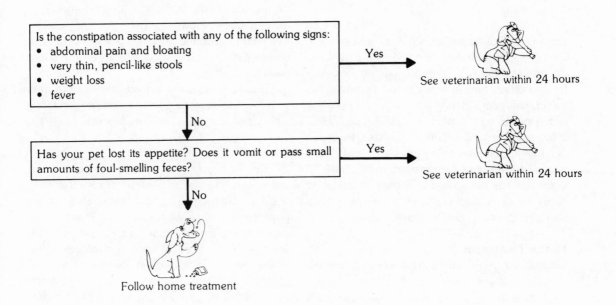

Is the constipation associated with any of the following signs:
- abdominal pain and bloating
- very thin, pencil-like stools
- weight loss
- fever

Yes → See veterinarian within 24 hours

No ↓

Has your pet lost its appetite? Does it vomit or pass small amounts of foul-smelling feces?

Yes → See veterinarian within 24 hours

No ↓

Follow home treatment

Swallowed Foreign Objects

Dogs (especially puppies) can chew and swallow enough paraphernalia to stock a moderate-sized department store. If your dog has swallowed a foreign object and is vomiting or attempting to vomit, coughing, bleeding from body openings, or having abdominal pain or breathing problems, a blockage or perforation of the digestive tract (esophagus, stomach, or intestine) may have occurred. See your veterinarian *immediately*. If your dog has swallowed a known chemical or medicine or a suspected poisonous plant, see the appropriate Decision Charts.

Home Treatment
EMERGENCY You will usually need veterinary assistance. If you cannot reach a doctor, feed a large meal of dog food and bread or cotton balls soaked in milk or broth to coat the object and cushion its passage through the digestive tract, so that it passes out in a bowel movement without causing injury. This is especially important if you suspect that a pin or piece of glass has been swallowed. Check with your doctor as soon as possible and check the feces daily for the object.

What to Expect at the Veterinarian's Office
Your doctor may take plain and barium radiographs to determine the position of the foreign object. Surgery is necessary if the object is too large or too sharp to pass out in the feces. Sometimes the doctor can remove foreign bodies in the esophagus or stomach without surgery, by using a scope. However, these are very expensive instruments and are usually only available at university veterinary medical centers or some central hospitals.

Some doctors will expect the object to pass with no problem and will discharge your dog with instructions to check the feces daily.

Prevention
Do *not* give your dog chewable toys that are small enough to be swallowed or toys that may splinter. Keep string and yarn away from puppies (a string obstruction of the intestine is a *very* serious surgical emergency). Do *not* give your pet bones to chew since they are also a frequent cause of digestive inflammation and obstruction. Watch your puppy carefully during the teething stage since anything is "fair game" for swallowing. If you have a young child *and* a puppy in the house, you have double trouble —you need four eyes. After a play period, be sure that all your child's playthings—especially pacifiers—are accounted for and have not been chewed by your pet. After sewing, account for all thread and needles.

Swallowed Foreign Objects

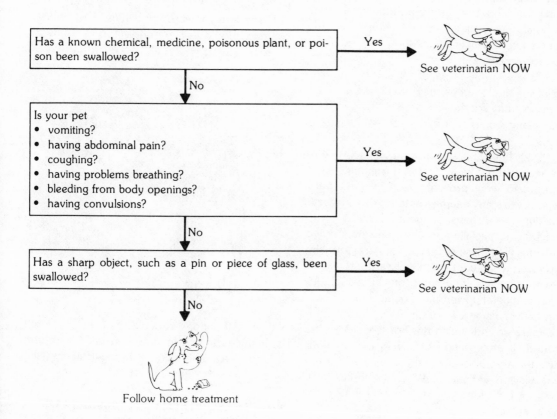

Has a known chemical, medicine, poisonous plant, or poison been swallowed?

Yes → See veterinarian NOW

No ↓

Is your pet
- vomiting?
- having abdominal pain?
- coughing?
- having problems breathing?
- bleeding from body openings?
- having convulsions?

Yes → See veterinarian NOW

No ↓

Has a sharp object, such as a pin or piece of glass, been swallowed?

Yes → See veterinarian NOW

No ↓

Follow home treatment

Anal Problems

Older male dogs (over eight years of age) commonly develop slow-growing nodules around the anal area called *perianal adenomas*. Although they can ulcerate and look very red, they are rarely malignant.

Tapeworms (see page 53) can cause itching of the anal area as they pass out the anus. Your dog may lick the anal area or "sleigh-ride": slide along on its rear-end with the back legs lifted.

Dogs have anal sacs located on each side of the anus that are equivalent to the skunk's scent glands and were probably used by your pet's ancestors to spray enemies or to mark a territory. The fluid has a sharp, pungent odor.

Dogs (especially toys and miniatures) have problems with these sacs. The sacs are normally expressed when your pet exercises vigorously or moves its bowels. If the secretion in the anal sacs is not emptied by exercise or defecation, impaction and infection can occur. Your pet will lick the anal area and "sleigh-ride" or scoot along the ground. If an infection occurs in one or both sacs, the area adjacent to the anus will become red, swollen, and painful. When the abscess ruptures, pus or blood-tinged fluid may drain from the opening.

An irritation of the anal area can also develop from diarrhea, since the fluid is acidic and can scald the anus.

Home Treatment
If the anal sac becomes infected, your veterinarian should treat it.

You may try to treat an impacted anal sac at home. *Note:* Cover the anal area with a tissue or gauze pad when expressing the anal sacs. If the secretions get on your rug or clothes, the smell can be very difficult to remove. Place your thumb and index finger at the 3 o'clock and 9 o'clock positions outside the anal area. Squeeze firmly toward the center. The anal sac contents should exit from holes on the anus.

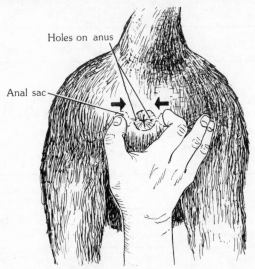

Anal irritations from diarrhea can be treated by bathing the area with a medicated soap and applying calamine lotion, white petroleum jelly, or an antibiotic ointment.

What to Expect at the Veterinarian's Office
Anal sac infections can be treated by flushing the sac with sterile water and antibiotics. Your doctor may hospitalize your pet for a few days or may treat the animal on an out-patient basis. Anal abscesses need more vigorous therapy.

Chronic anal sac infections are best treated by removing the sacs surgically.

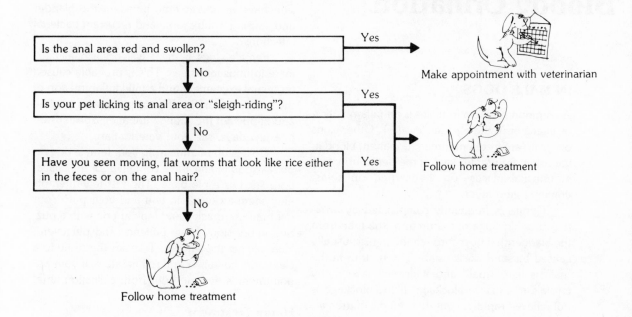

| Is the anal area red and swollen? | **Yes** → Make appointment with veterinarian |

No ↓

| Is your pet licking its anal area or "sleigh-riding"? | **Yes** |

No ↓

| Have you seen moving, flat worms that look like rice either in the feces or on the anal hair? | **Yes** → Follow home treatment |

No ↓

Follow home treatment

Perianal adenomas are best treated by surgery or *cryosurgery* (freezing the nodule for removal). Radiation therapy is an alternative method and is successful. Hormone therapy is not a very successful treatment, since the nodule will get larger when therapy is stopped. The mass should be biopsied to confirm that it is benign. Castration seems to reduce the recurrence rate and to restrict new nodule growth.

Prevention

Since dogs express the anal sac while running, regular exercise is very important.

If your pet is prone to impactions, frequent expressing of the sacs by you or your doctor will lessen the chances of anal infections or abscesses developing.

Flea control will prevent tapeworms (see page 168).

Painful, Frequent, or Bloody Urination

IN MALE DOGS

A common problem in males is an inflammation or infection of the bladder (*cystitis*). Other signs of cystitis are frequent, urgent urination; blood in the urine; frequent licking of the penis; urinating in unusual places—on the carpet, on sofas; vomiting; and fever.

Cystitis is frequently complicated by *urolithiasis*, a blockage of the urethra (the tube from the bladder that goes through the penis), usually caused by sand-like crystals. The urethra in the male is very small, and it doesn't take many crystals to cause a blockage. If the blockage is not relieved rapidly, your dog can die of *uremia*, a condition in which the toxic products that are normally eliminated in the urine build up in the blood. Loss of appetite, vomiting, weakness, and dehydration are ominous signs of a very serious situation, such as impending kidney failure or death.

Trauma, such as being hit by an auto or being kicked, can injure or rupture the bladder. You may see blood in the urine, but sometimes the evidence can be checked only microscopically, by your doctor.

If your pet is urinating more than usual and is drinking excessive amounts of water, diabetes or kidney disease may be the cause.

IN FEMALE DOGS

The previous discussion, for males, applies with just a few qualifications. The female's urethra has both an advantage and a disadvantage: The urethra is more distensible (the advantage); therefore, the stones and crystals that form can be passed easier and generally without blockage. However, the urethra is also much shorter (the disadvantage); therefore, bacteria from the outside have an easier time invading the bladder and causing troublesome and recurrent bacterial infections.

Female dogs in heat will occasionally urinate in unusual places. This is probably caused by sexual excitement and a mild inflammation of the urinary opening. If your pet seems healthy and happy but the strange urination doesn't stop in a few days, see your veterinarian.

Collection of urine from your female dog requires good timing and a container for the collection, such as a pie plate. The first few attempts may seem awkward to you and your pet: Your pet may *rise* quickly and look at you with a puzzled expression. Have patience and persevere. You *will* get the sample. Transfer the urine to a clean, dry container and refrigerate it, if your appointment is over an hour from collection time.

Home Treatment

EMERGENCY   If your dog is straining to urinate, seek veterinary aid *immediately*: A dog that hasn't been able to urinate for twenty-four hours may die. If your male dog is urinating a good stream, but there is blood in the urine, you should see your veterinarian. It may be only an inflammation or infection of the lower urogenital tract (bladder, prostate, or urethra), but it could lead to a blockage. Give your pet vitamin C or cranberry or tomato juice to drink to acidify the urine (see Your Dog's Home Pharmacy, page 75). The juice or vitamin C will act as a natural antibiotic if bacteria are present.

What to Expect at the Veterinarian's Office

Your veterinarian will perform a complete physical examination. If your pet is a male dog, your doctor will do a rectal exam to check the size and shape of the prostate gland. If there is a partial or complete obstruction of the urethra, the bladder may be as large as an orange and painful to the touch. In this case, your dog will

Painful, Frequent, or Bloody Urination

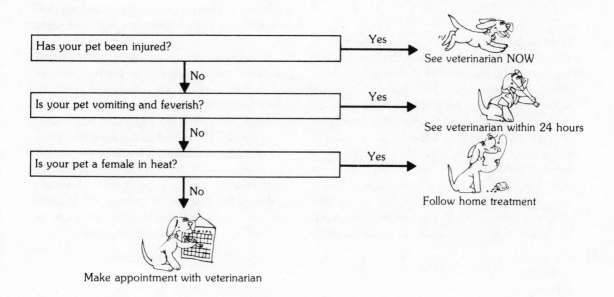

Has your pet been injured? —— Yes → See veterinarian NOW

No ↓

Is your pet vomiting and feverish? —— Yes → See veterinarian within 24 hours

No ↓

Is your pet a female in heat? —— Yes → Follow home treatment

No ↓

Make appointment with veterinarian

Painful, Frequent, or Bloody Urination

(cont.)

have to be *catheterized* (i.e., a sterile tube is placed into the urethra) and the blockage of crystals will be dispersed by flushings with sterile water. This procedure is sometimes done under sedation. The health of the kidneys may be determined by blood tests before the anesthesia is given. At the time of catheterization, a sterile urine sample may be collected to determine if bacteria are causing or complicating the cystitis and, if so, what antibiotic will be effective. X rays may be taken of the bladder to rule out bladder stones or tumors. Fluids are usually given intravenously or subcutaneously to increase urine flow and to remove the toxic products that were retained during the obstruction. Antibiotics, *antispasmodics* (to relax the muscles of the bladder and relieve pain), and urinary acidifiers (if the crystals are found only in neutral or alkaline urine and the kidney tests are normal) will be used. It is necessary to hospitalize and carefully monitor your pet's kidney function and urination.

Urolithiasis is one of the most frustrating conditions that your veterinarian has to treat, and the blockage can recur very easily. It takes only a few crystals to block the small urethra in the male. Recurrent blockages are best treated with a surgical procedure called a *urethrostomy*, in which a larger opening is made in the urethra. This does not cure the disease but it provides a larger hole for the passage of the crystals and decreases the chance of another blockage. If there are stones in the bladder, they can be removed by *cystotomy* (bladder surgery).

If a bacterial infection is present, an antibiotic should be prescribed. Months of treatment may be necessary to clear up the infection. Many times, infections can move up the urinary tract and remain "silent" while slowly deteriorating your dog's kidneys. Bacteria can move up into the kidney or *seed* (multiply) in the bladder wall and can be difficult to eradicate. Culture, sensitivity, and urine tests—not just the outward appearance of a cure—are important follow-ups.

If your dog has been injured and there is visible or microscopic blood in the urine, your doctor will want to monitor the damage and repair to the urinary system with blood tests and urinalyses.

Prevention
Recurrence of bacterial infections and/or bladder stones may be prevented by antibiotics, acidifiers, or alkalinizers, depending on the type of bacteria isolated and the type of stone formed.

Painful, Frequent, or Bloody Urination

(cont.)

Unfortunately, recurrence of these problems is high.

Long-term urinary acidifiers may be recommended. Two acidifiers that can be purchased in drug stores or your pet store are DL-Methionine (250 mg. three times daily) or ascorbic acid (vitamin C) tablets. Vitamin C (250 mg.) three times daily should acidify the urine. Any long-term medicine should only be given with your doctor's consultation. Litmus paper can be used to check the effectiveness of the acidifiers.

Tomato juice and cranberry juice are also urinary acidifiers. See Your Dog's Home Pharmacy, page 81.

Penis Discharge

A discharge from your dog's penis may be the first sign that something is wrong in the urinary tract. If blood is dripping from the penis, an inflammation of the prostate gland or an irritation of the urethra or bladder may be present. See your veterinarian.

Many male dogs have a yellowish discharge from the prepuce, the flabby skin covering the penis. This is a normal secretion.

A bloody discharge from the penis and frequent attempts to urinate is a serious problem that needs immediate veterinary attention. Male dogs have a small urethra, and crystals or stones can block the tube. Retention of urine can result in uremia and death. See Painful, Frequent, or Bloody Urination, page 218.

Home Treatment
If the yellowish discharge from the prepuce becomes excessive, flush the prepuce with a feminine douche solution (ask your doctor to recommend one) or use an antibiotic ointment. The structure of the prepuce makes this a recurrent problem. I find that frequent douches (once weekly) usually control the discharge.

What to Expect at the Veterinarian's Office
Your doctor will do a urinalysis and a rectal to check the size and sensitivity of the prostate gland. If a urinary or prostate infection is suspected, a culture and sensitivity of the urine (collected by sterile catheterization) may be done. Survey radiographs or specialized radiographs involving air or dyes in the urinary tract may be required to make a diagnosis.

Penis Discharge

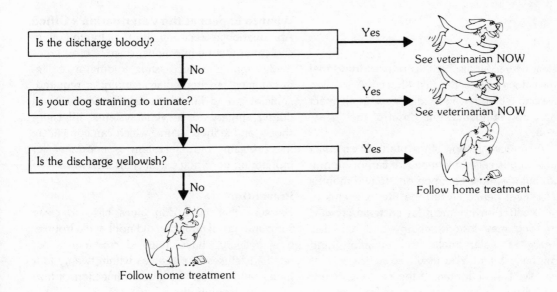

Is the discharge bloody? — Yes → See veterinarian NOW

No

Is your dog straining to urinate? — Yes → See veterinarian NOW

No

Is the discharge yellowish? — Yes → Follow home treatment

No

Follow home treatment

Vaginal Discharge

A clear or yellow discharge is present in normal female dogs before the first "heat." A swollen vulva and a bloody vaginal discharge in an intact female dog announces the onset of the "heat" period.

A serious infection of the uterus in an intact female dog is called *pyometra*. It can occur any time, but it is more common one to two months after a heat period, when the uterus seems to have a better environment for bacterial growth. Your dog may lose its energy and appetite, increase its water intake and urination, and vomit fairly often. You may also notice a fever and a swollen abdomen. If the cervix is open, there will be a yellowish or greenish foul-smelling vaginal discharge. If the cervix is closed and there is no vaginal drainage, rapid deterioration or death can occur. See your doctor immediately. Uterine infections can also be seen a few weeks after the birth of puppies. A red or brownish discharge is present, along with some of the signs seen in pyometra. Again, see your doctor as soon as you can.

An infection of the vagina is not very common in dogs.

Home Treatment
No treatment is necessary for the slight mucus discharge of the female just entering or in heat. For other discharges, professional care is necessary.

What to Expect at the Veterinarian's Office
An ovariohysterectomy is the treatment of choice for uterine infections, since in most cases medication is unsuccessful. Pyometra is life-threatening, so immediate surgery is required. Antibiotics and fluids are usually administered during surgery to prevent systemic infection, shock, and kidney failure, which can complicate the problem. Hospitalization is important for monitoring your dog's vital signs afterward.

Prevention
Be sure that your dog gives birth in clean surroundings. If your dog did not have a trouble-free delivery, have your doctor check for retained fetuses or placentas within twenty-four hours, and ask him to give an injection of hormones to involute the uterus.

Watch your dog carefully for one to two months after a heat period. If any signs of pyometra are present, see your doctor immediately.

If you do not intend to breed your dog, schedule an ovariohysterectomy *before* the first heat. Besides eliminating the chance of contracting pyometra, having the procedure done this early may prevent breast cancer (see Breast Cancer, page 258).

Vaginal Discharge

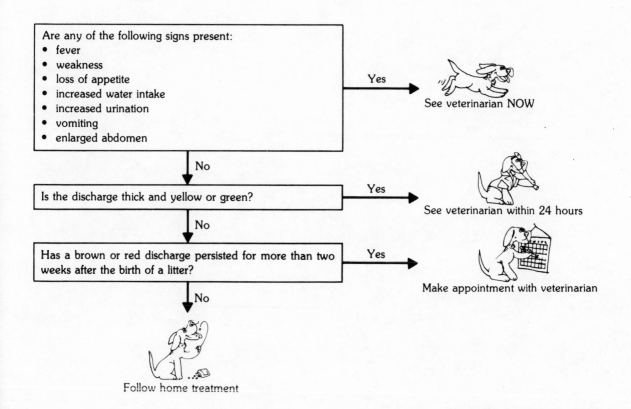

Are any of the following signs present:
- fever
- weakness
- loss of appetite
- increased water intake
- increased urination
- vomiting
- enlarged abdomen

Yes → See veterinarian NOW

No ↓

Is the discharge thick and yellow or green?

Yes → See veterinarian within 24 hours

No ↓

Has a brown or red discharge persisted for more than two weeks after the birth of a litter?

Yes → Make appointment with veterinarian

No ↓

Follow home treatment

Chapter 9

Breeding and Reproduction

Breeding, pregnancy, delivery, and nursing require a healthy mother dog. This section is provided to make your care easier and more organized before and during breeding and when the dog is pregnant. If all the steps are followed, delivery should be very easy. Most dogs have no problems during delivery and nursing, but just in case, charts are provided to inform you of the general processes and to let you know situations when your veterinarian's help might be needed.

BREEDING AND MATING

Once you have decided to breed your dog, the first step is to have it examined by the veterinarian. Besides updating vaccinations (see page 42) and checking for internal and external parasites (see page 47), your doctor will also be on the lookout for any genetic traits or diseases that might be a problem in the puppies. Your veterinarian might also suggest that both dogs be tested for brucellosis. If you have picked your dog's mate, it's wise to collaborate with the other owner so that all pertinent information is available for the physical examination. If the mate hasn't been chosen, ask your veterinarian to recommend a good breeder.

Ideally, the two dogs should meet at least once before they mate, preferably at the breeding site. The female will not let the male mount unless the male is dominant, and this needs to be determined before breeding. Since male dogs can be finicky about breeding away from familiar surroundings, I recommend breeding at the male's home.

Brucellosis

Canine brucellosis is a bacterial disease that can cause both males and females to become sterile. In addition, infected bitches can abort, usually between the 45th and 55th days of pregnancy. The most common means of transmission is by contact with the vaginal discharge of an infected bitch that has aborted. The bacteria can live in the male dog's prostate gland and testicles, causing infection (*orchitis*) and infertility. Many male and female dogs appear normal but may be carriers of the disease.

A rapid screening test can be done in your veterinarian's office, but a diagnosis *cannot* be made on this test alone, since it can show a false-positive result. Further testing is necessary to confirm the presence of brucellosis. A serum test or cultures of the blood, lymph, bone marrow, vaginal discharge, or prostate fluid is necessary before a final diagnosis can be made. In many unfortunate instances, dogs have been unnecessarily treated (and even euthanized) without confirmation that the disease was present.

If you plan to breed your dog, the following suggestions should be helpful:

1. The stud dog should have been tested within the last three to six months.
2. All the breeding bitches associated with the male dog while in the kennel and afterward should be negative.
3. Your bitch should be serologically negative one month prior to breeding.

Treatment of an infected pet may be attempted, but discuss the pros and cons, including the public health risk, with your veterinarian. Neutering is important to avoid transmission to offspring. Few antibiotics have been successful in treating the infection.

Note: The bacteria *can* cause disease in humans, through contact with infected dogs. The Center for Disease Control in Atlanta, Georgia, reported four confirmed cases in 1974. Many more probably go undiagnosed since, in mild cases, the symptoms are similar to those of the flu—fever, chills, weakness, headache, backache, joint aches, and a spontaneous recovery or a recovery after antibiotic (especially tetracycline) therapy. A positive diagnosis in humans is difficult to get, because the serum test can be easily misinterpreted and the bacteria are difficult to culture from blood or tissue.

Sexual Maturity

The onset of sexual maturity (puberty) varies greatly among different breeds of dogs. In general, puberty occurs between six and eighteen months. Smaller breeds seem to reach sexual maturity earlier than larger breeds, such as Great Danes or Irish wolfhounds.

The female usually has two "heat" periods per year. Again, there is wide variation: some bitches have three "heats," while the basenji has only one per year—the same number as its wild relative, the dingo. Each heat is incorporated in a cycle consisting of proestrus, estrus ("heat"), metestrus, and anestrus.

The Estrus Cycle

During proestrus, which occurs just before the "heat," the vulva, or lips of the female's vaginal opening, swell and a bloody discharge is excreted. The female teases the male, standing still for inspection with its rear end raised but running at the first sign of advance. The male will be eager to mount and will lick the swollen vulva with gusto.

Swollen vulva (lips of vagina)

In the next phase, estrus, ovulation occurs and the egg is released to meet the sperm. This period lasts about three weeks. The exact time of ovulation cannot be determined, but it is usually between the ninth and fifteenth day after the bloody discharge and the swelling of the vulva are seen. Breeding on the ninth, eleventh, or thirteenth day after proestrus begins will cover the average ovulation times of most females. The bloody discharge stops and the female accepts the male. As in the earlier teasing, the female presents itself with the rear end up, tail to the side, and the vulva twitching up and down (called *winking*).

The experienced male will mount from the rear, holding the female's waist with its front legs so that the female can't sit down. After a few pelvic thrusts, the penis enters the vagina, ejaculation occurs, and the pelvic thrusts stop.

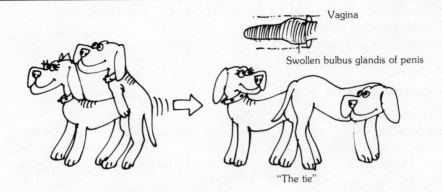

Vagina

Swollen bulbus glandis of penis

"The tie"

The swollen bulbus glandis of the penis and the muscles in the vaginal area cause a delay in separation called "the tie." The male will usually swing one leg over the female so that they are facing in opposite directions. The "tie" is not necessary for fertilization, since the major ejaculate is in the first few pelvic thrusts. When the swelling subsides, the male will dismount. The entire mating routine can last from ten to thirty minutes.

Metestrus is the two-month phase after estrus. In the final phase of the cycle, anestrus, the ovaries rest from egg production for two to three months.

PREGNANCY

Your female is now probably pregnant, but you should look for certain telltale signs to be sure. First of all, your dog's appetite and body weight will increase. After thirty-five days, the belly and breasts will start to enlarge. A physical exam at this time will confirm pregnancy and monitor the health and nutritional status of the dog. Your doctor should also tell you when to expect the puppies, and he or she should help you formulate an emergency plan, in case problems arise during delivery. Pregnancy lasts an average of sixty-three days after conception. After fifty days milk production will begin, and a few days before your dog gives birth, the breasts may secrete a milklike substance.

If the pregnant bitch does not seem to be in good condition, your doctor may perform a few blood tests, such as hemoglobin and serum protein, and suggest supplementing the daily balanced diet. Undernutrition is a major factor in the birth of puppies that are too small to survive the postnatal period. Also, an undernourished bitch may not care for the pups properly, and the milk production may be inadequate.

For healthy dogs, a normal commercial dog food diet should provide adequate nutrients, although supplements of high-quality proteins, such as milk products and cooked eggs, certainly won't hurt. Vitamin and mineral supplements are a rather controversial topic; I suggest you discuss this with your dog's doctor.

The primary difference in the pregnant dog's diet is that the bitch needs more food, more calories, and more protein during the second month of pregnancy. Divide the total daily ration into three or four smaller meals to aid digestion (see Nutrition, page 36).

Exercise is beneficial—it will keep your dog from getting too heavy and having a difficult delivery. Therefore, do not at first restrict exercise, but don't let the dog roam far without supervision. Most bitches will themselves limit their exercise as the pregnancy progresses, but you should restrict all strenuous exercise three days before the expected delivery.

Drugs taken during pregnancy are potentially dangerous to the fetuses. Consult your veterinarian before giving your pregnant dog any medication. Some medications to avoid are aspirin, acetaminophen, antihistamines, antibiotics (especially tetracycline, kanamycin, streptomycin, and sulfa drugs), hormones, tranquilizers, and most worming medications. An exception seems to be the heartworm preventative, diethylcarbamazine, which can be administered during pregnancy and after whelping. But I advise to have all the necessary medical treatment done before breeding.

False Pregnancy

Although it is rare, some females may experience a false pregnancy: They have all the signs of the "real thing"—even labor pains—but no puppies are born. In their place, the "mother" will drag slippers, socks, or other soft objects into the "nest," wherever it is. In fact, the "babies" may even be shredded clothing or newspaper.

To check the reality of your bitch's signs, palpate the abdomen very gently after thirty-five days have elapsed. If you can't feel anything, or if your dog is espe-

Breeding Checklist

☐ Schedule a veterinary exam, for:

    ☐ intestinal parasites

    ☐ vaccinations

    ☐ brucellosis

    ☐ genetic diseases

☐ Choose a responsible breeder

☐ Introduce the dogs before they mate, if possible

☐ Let them breed in the male's home, if possible

☐ Breed during entire "heat" period or on 9th, 11th, or 13th day after bloody discharge begins

Pregnancy Checklist

☐ Feed high quality food:

    ☐ well-balanced commercial food

    ☐ high protein (milk products, cooked eggs) supplements

☐ Divide the daily ration into 3 or 4 smaller meals

☐ Discuss vitamin supplements with your veterinarian

☐ Schedule a midgestation veterinary exam, for:

    ☐ confirmation of pregnancy

    ☐ health check

☐ Let exercise continue, but not unsupervised

☐ Avoid drugs

☐ Prepare for delivery:

    ☐ arrange nursing box

    ☐ have this book handy, open to the Delivery Chart

    ☐ have all utensils handy

    ☐ have emergency plan

    ☐ stop strenuous exercise 3 days before due date

cially large or fat, your veterinarian can help you tell for sure. An X ray may be necessary to determine the existence of puppies.

If the pregnancy is false, hormone injections can be given to lessen or alleviate the signs, but I suggest that you just wait it out and let your dog "nurse" your slippers. The less hormone therapy, the better, because hormones can affect so many different body processes. However, I recommend spaying to prevent the almost certain recurrence of false pregnancy—probably after the very next heat.

PREPARING FOR DELIVERY

Introduce your bitch to the whelping box two weeks before whelping. It should be large enough for the dog to stretch out and nurse the puppies comfortably. The sides should be high enough to keep the puppies inside, but low enough for the mother to get in and out. Line the bottom with several layers of newspaper, towels, or sheets, but whatever is used, clean the box regularly. Be sure that any material that lines the bottom goes to the edge of the box so that the newborn pups will not get caught underneath and smother.

The temperature in the whelping box should be about 80°F, because chilling is a frequent cause of puppy mortality. Since newborn pups have a difficult time regulating their own temperature, position a 250 watt infrared (heat) bulb above the box so that half of the area is heated. (Otherwise, a nearby radiator or electric heater may be adequate.) Attach a thermometer to the box to monitor the temperature. The "delivery room" should be a familiar area—perhaps the dog's regular sleeping area—as long as it's warm and draft-free. Place the maternity box there.

The "delivery room" should also be supplied with:

- this book, open to the delivery section
- thread dipped in alcohol
- scissors dipped in alcohol
- warm, rough towels
- a bowl of water for the mother
- your veterinarian's phone number

WHELPING

In general, your assistance won't be required, but it's a good idea to be there, if the mother dog will endure your presence, to monitor the process in case something goes wrong. Keep the area quiet, especially if this is your dog's first time; talk in whispers and avoid bright lights.

When the pup is born, it may or may not be enclosed in the amniotic sac. The mother dog should chew open the sac immediately, so that the pup can breathe, and stimulate the puppy by licking it. The mother should then chew apart the umbilical cord. After birth, the bitch may eat the placenta—that's OK.

If your dog does not chew open the sac immediately, gently tear it open yourself and clean the mucus from the puppy's mouth with your finger. Wait a few minutes to see if the mother chews the umbilical cord. If not, tie it tightly with a piece of thread that has been dipped in alcohol about one inch from the pup's abdomen. Using scissors that have been dipped in alcohol, cut the cord on the mother's side of the thread. Rub the puppy gently with a clean, soft towel to stimulate circulation and respiration.

Puppies, like humans, may enter this world head first or feet first. If only a part of the pup shows, wrap a clean cloth around the slippery newborn's body and, as the mother strains, pull it gently all the way out. Relax when the bitch does. Call your doctor if you are not able to deliver the pup.

If a puppy is not breathing, wrap it in a warm towel with its head down (but support the head so it doesn't wobble) and shake it downward. This should stimulate respiration and remove fluid from its breathing tubes. If a breath *still* is not taken, gently blow into the pup's nose until its chest expands, and try rubbing it in a warm, rough towel to stimulate respiration.

The mother dog may rest anywhere from fifteen minutes to two hours between deliveries. After all the puppies are born, the mother will stop straining. Instead, your dog will comfortably lick and clean the new pups.

Within twenty-four hours after the delivery, which in most cases occurs with no problems, the mother and puppies may be examined by your doctor. Be sure to keep the puppies warm if a trip to the office is necessary. A snug blanket placed in a box is perfect.

The doctor will palpate the bitch's abdomen to make certain all the pups were delivered. The mother will be given an injection of a hormone (*oxytocin*) to involute (shrink) the uterus and to stimulate milk flow from the breasts. Your veterinarian will determine the little ones' sexes, weigh them, and check for birth defects, such as cleft palates, harelips, heart problems, and umbilical hernias.

If there are any problems at all during delivery, *telephone your doctor*. If a puppy is stuck in the birth canal and you have tried gentle help, professional manipulation may unstick the problem. Sometimes an *episiotomy* (an incision between the upper end of the vagina and the anus that enlarges the vaginal opening and eases the birth of the puppy) is necessary.

Occasionally, *uterine inertia* (weak contractions of the uterus) will occur during delivery. If the mother is obese, old, upset by many people in the room, or has been straining for a long time, the uterus may become tired and stop squeezing the puppies out efficiently. Injections of oxytocin may help.

In some instances, a *caesarean birth* (surgical removal of the puppies through the abdominal wall) is necessary. Timing is very important, but the surgery is generally fast and safe. After recovery from the anesthesia, the mother can nurse the puppies and go home. The sutures are removed in ten days.

Whelping

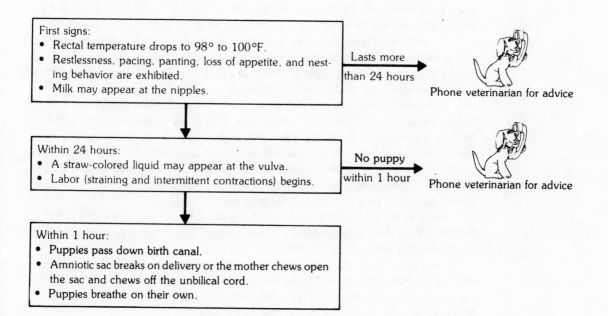

First signs:
- Rectal temperature drops to 98° to 100°F.
- Restlessness. pacing. panting. loss of appetite. and nesting behavior are exhibited.
- Milk may appear at the nipples.

Lasts more than 24 hours → Phone veterinarian for advice

Within 24 hours:
- A straw-colored liquid may appear at the vulva.
- Labor (straining and intermittent contractions) begins.

No puppy within 1 hour → Phone veterinarian for advice

Within 1 hour:
- Puppies pass down birth canal.
- Amniotic sac breaks on delivery or the mother chews open the sac and chews off the unbilical cord.
- Puppies breathe on their own.

THE NURSING PERIOD

Usually, this is pleasant for all concerned—mother, puppies, and you. Remember not to disturb your new dog family any more than necessary for about three days. But you *do* have a few important jobs during this time: cleaning the maternity box and the mother's breasts, watching for signs of illness or malnutrition, and initiating solid foods (*weaning*).

The puppies will soil the maternity box, so on the third day, when the mother goes to relieve itself, change the newspapers or towels. Wash the bitch's breasts once daily with warm water and a clean wash cloth, but do *not* use soap.

The milk produced during the first twenty-four hours is called *colostrum* and is rich in antibodies that protect the puppies from such diseases as distemper for a few weeks. But if you see any signs of illness, see your veterinarian *immediately*. Most puppy illnesses need professional attention.

Appearance and milk production are the best indication of the mother's nutritional status. A well-balanced, commercial dog food is adequate for lactating bitches. If necessary, supplement this with high protein foods, such as milk products and cooked eggs. A general rule is to feed an additional 100 calories per pound of puppy. By the end of the lactation period, your dog may be eating three times the prebreeding level. Vitamin and mineral supplements and extra calcium should be fed to heavy lactaters with large litters.

Using an ounce or gram scale, weigh the pups about two weeks after birth. At that time they should be double their birth weight. Their eyes will open about ten days following birth.

Later in nursing, the pup's teeth and nails may irritate the breasts, and their mother will lose patience and leave them for longer periods of time. Although you can help by trimming the pups' nails, this is actually nature's ways of telling the pups to try some solid food. That is the time to try weaning.

Hand-feeding

Hand-feeding the pups may be necessary if the mother becomes ill or dies, if a puppy is too weak to nurse, or if the litter is unusually large. Borden's Esbilac® is a very good commercial milk substitute. Cow's milk does not contain the level of protein, calcium, phosphorus, or calories needed by the puppies, but in an emergency, you can use one cup of homogenized milk mixed with two egg yolks, one-half teaspoon corn syrup, and a pinch of salt. The puppies should be fed three times a day at eight-hour intervals:

Daily Calorie Needs of Puppies
(per pound of body weight)

1st week—70 calories

2nd week—70 to 80 calories

3rd week—90 calories

4th week—100 calories

The Nursing Period

Are any of the following signs present in the mother:
- nervousness
- crying
- staggering and trembling
- fever
- convulsions
- straining to urinate
- weakness
- loss of appetite
- foul-smelling reddish or puslike discharge

Yes → See veterinarian NOW

No ↓

Is one or more breasts hot, hard, swollen, discolored (red or purple), or painful?

Yes →

No ↓

Are any of the following signs present in one of the litter:
- diarrhea
- weakness
- crying
- loss of appetite
- pale gums

Yes → See veterinarian within 24 hours

No ↓

Does the mother ignore the young?

Yes →

No ↓

Does the pet under two weeks old have swollen eyes or an eye discharge?

Yes → Make appointment with veterinarian

No ↓

Are your pet's breasts being scratched and irritated by the litter?

Yes → Follow home treatment

No ↓

Follow home treatment

First, warm the formula to body temperature (100°F). Feed the small pups using a doll-sized baby bottle with a nipple or a Pet-Nip®, which is sold in pet stores or by your doctor. A regular baby bottle with an anticolic nipple can be used for larger breeds. *Note: Never* use an eye dropper for feeding. The pup may aspirate the milk into the lungs and get pneumonia. The formula should drip out slowly when the bottle is inverted; a heated needle can enlarge the hole in the nipple, if necessary. Place the pup on its stomach, open its mouth with your finger, and position the nipple on top of the tongue. As an extra treat, place a towel within reach so the pup can knead. The pup will suck vigorously and be very happy. At the end of a feeding, its abdomen should be enlarged, not bloated.

The pup should be burped and stimulated to urinate and defecate after each feeding. Burp the pup as you would a human baby. Hold it against your shoulder and gently pat its back. A warm, moist cotton ball washed against the anal, genital, and abdominal areas will simulate the mother's tongue (which normally would do this) to initiate urination and defecation. The bowel movements should be yellow and formed.

If the puppies are orphaned, the environmental temperature must compensate for the mother's absence. The whelping box should be kept at 85° to 90°F for the first week, 80°F for the second week, 75°F for the third and fourth weeks, and 70°F thereafter. A heating pad on "low" draped over one side of the box and covering a few inches of the bottom will suffice. This way the puppies can choose to be near the heat source or, if too warm, to crawl away to the cooler side. The heating pad should be covered with a sheet or towel to avoid burns. Whatever external heat source is used, be sure it doesn't burn or overheat the puppies.

If you find that the puppies' skin is getting irritated from sucking on each other, separate them for a week.

Nursing Problems

There are some serious problems during nursing that require immediate cooperation between you and your doctor.

Since pregnancy and milk production may demand more calcium than the mother can spare, *eclampsia* (low blood calcium) may be seen during nursing. The signs are nervousness, crying, stiffness, staggering, fever (as high as 107°F), and muscle spasms and convulsions. Eclampsia usually develops within the first three weeks of the nursing period and is a life-threatening medical emergency. See the veterinarian *immediately*. If the rectal temperature is 106°F or over, place ice packs between the dog's thighs to lower the fever during the ride to the doctor's office.

Intravenous calcium solutions will usually stop the signs. As the solution is injected, the convulsions cease, the muscles stop twitching, and the dog stops panting. The mother dog will not have to be hospitalized unless it does not respond to treatment (this is rare). Upon returning home, nursing should be stopped or at least restricted. If the puppies are older than three weeks, start them on solid food. Younger pups will have to be hand-fed to prevent a recurrence of the disease. Your doctor may also prescribe a calcium supplement for the next few weeks.

A malfunction in the organ that controls calcium metabolism (the parathyroid gland) is thought to cause eclampsia. To prevent it, consult your doctor before you breed your dog. He will advise you on the proper calcium, phosphorus, and vitamin D supplements. Eclampsia can recur in a female who has had it once and is re-bred. To prevent this, have your dog spayed.

A bacterial infection of the uterus called *acute metritis* is another emergency. A physical exam, blood tests, and possibly X rays may be necessary for diagnosis. If retained fetuses are seen on the X rays, an immediate ovariohysterectomy is the best treatment. If you want to breed again and there are no retained fetuses, a less acceptable and risky choice is to do culture and sensitivity tests and to use the specific antibiotic for the infection. Flushing the vagina with general antibiotics may also be tried. An injection of oxytocin within twenty-four hours after delivery may prevent uterine infections. Good hygiene and appropriate care are also important.

Mastitis is a bacterial infection of one or more of the breasts. If your dog develops this, hand-feeding the pups is necessary, because the infected milk may sicken them. In addition, the antibiotics used to treat the infection will be passed in the milk. Again, proper hygiene and care may prevent its development.

Puppies are also susceptible to some problems that can be fatal. For instance, simple diarrhea can dehydrate them quickly. Overfeeding could be the cause, but check with your doctor. Undernutrition from ineffectual nursing can make a puppy cry constantly, but so can other problems, so again—contact your doctor.

Weaning

At three weeks of age, place a shallow saucer of formula on the floor. Dip your finger into the formula and let the puppies suck on it. Repeat this a few times until their noses get closer to the formula. They will probably walk into the saucer, but have patience; you'll be amazed at how fast the pups will pick up your message. Moistened commercial puppy food or high protein pablum can be added to the formula to make a thin gruel.

The mother dog will still let the puppies have a free lunch until they have all their baby teeth (about five weeks of age), but then their teeth will start to irritate the breasts, so the mother will be happy to cooperate with your weaning program. Keep the dog away from the pups for a few hours during the day. After a week, just let them be together at night. At the same time, decrease the mother's food intake accordingly, to decrease milk production. If the breasts become engorged, which does occasionally happen, compresses may help. Contact your doctor if things don't improve in two or three days.

PREVENTING PREGNANCY

If you do not want to breed your dog, *please* have it neutered, for its own health and as a contribution to reducing the pet population. It is *not* true that neutering causes obesity and laziness; overeating and getting too little exercise are usually to blame.

The best time for the female's ovariohysterectomy is *before* the first heat (but not before five or six months of age). The estrogens secreted during the heat period may prime the breast tissue for later tumor development, and approximately 50 percent of them are malignant. Spaying early may help prevent tumors from developing.

The ovariohysterectomy is the surgical removal (*"ectomy"*) of ovaries (*"ovario"*) and the uterus (*"hyster"*) through an abdominal incision. The size of the incision does *not* indicate your doctor's surgical skill. Some doctors make small incisions and others like to have good exposure of the surgical area. The size of the organs to be removed will vary among animals, as well.

Spaying is common surgery, but every pet is unique, and special care will be taken. A careful and thorough preoperative exam will determine your dog's ability to undergo surgery. Modern anesthesia (gas or inhalants) is very safe: An anesthetic death is extremely rare in a healthy pet. Your doctor will instruct you not to feed your dog for twelve hours before surgery, which will allow the stomach to empty. If there is food in the stomach during surgery, it may be vomited and pass into the breathing tubes and lungs, and an aspiration pneumonia could occur. If the monitoring equipment (which keeps track of breathing and heart functions during surgery) indicates a potential problem, your dog can be made lighter or brought out of the anesthesia in a few minutes. Many veterinary hospitals have the same heart monitors used for humans in hospital intensive care units. Emergency fluids and drugs, which are rarely needed, are readily available.

Postoperative complications (such as infection) are also very rare because of aseptic surgical techniques: The operating room is well sterilized, as are the instruments, drapes, caps, masks, and gowns. Modern anesthetics allow most dogs to be on their feet minutes after surgery, which also probably lessen the postoperative discomfort. Your dog may be home the same day or the next day, depending on the veterinary hospital's procedure.

Home care after surgery consists of keeping the incision clean (don't allow your pet to lie on dirt), exercise restriction (short walks on a leash), and checking the incision for swelling, redness, or discharge. If any infection develops, call your doctor. The sutures can be removed in a week.

Castration of male dogs is also done to stop or reduce objectionable behavior, such as extreme aggression, "marking territory" in the house (sometimes this is a urinary problem—see page 218), and roaming. If it is done before puberty, the dog will not develop these sexually related behaviors. Some dogs that are castrated after puberty will still roam (usually for food and out of curiosity), mark territory, and mount, but they cannot impregnate. This may be caused by a very small amount of male hormones being secreted by other glands, such as the adrenals.

Sometimes a male dog will have only one testicle (*monorchid*) or none at all (*cryptorchid*) in the sacs (*scrotum*). Although sperm will not be produced in the undescended testicle, male hormones will still be manufactured: Your dog will continue to strut around like the neighborhood lover. One problem with undescended testicles is that they frequently form a large *sertoli cell tumor* after your dog reaches seven years of age.

Birth Control Medication

If you are considering breeding your bitch at a later date but do not want it to have a heat for a while, talk to your doctor about two new drugs to stop the heat—Checque® and Ovaban®.

If your female dog has been *mismated* (accidently bred), an estrogen injection followed by estrogen tablets given at home is usually successful at preventing pregnancy *if* given within twenty-four hours of the breeding. The injection makes the uterine environment hostile to the sperm and egg; therefore, implantation won't occur. Estrogen can have toxic side effects, however, so this treatment is discouraged. Unless you really want to breed your dog, I recommend an ovariohysterectomy.

Chapter 10

Cosmetic Surgery

Dewclaws, the appendage on dogs comparable to the human thumb, are present on some paws but not on others. Some dogs, such as Great Pyrenees, have double dewclaws (the Pyrenees' are needed for show purposes). If you do not have your pet's dewclaws removed, be sure that you keep the nail trimmed. Since it doesn't touch the ground, it does not get worn down like the other nails. If allowed to grow long, it will penetrate the footpad and cause a painful infection. The dewclaws of hunting dogs and "woodsy" dogs can get caught and torn easily in underbrush, and even small house pets can catch their dewclaws on the carpeting as they stalk the "great white rawhide." Dewclaws should be removed at tail docking time, which is about three days of age.

Ear cropping is usually done after your puppy has the vaccination series, at about fourteen weeks of age. Every show person and veterinarian has an opinion of ear cropping. In Canada and England, for instance, show dogs' ears are *not* cropped, the opposite of the U.S. show practice. Personally, I feel that every breed of dog has more character with its natural ears.

The correct length of the tail is determined by the official standard for the breed. The best time for *tail docking* or for amputation of any part of the tail is three days of age. The tail is clipped and sterilized, and a tourniquet to prevent bleeding is applied. A clamp is then placed at the length of tail desired, and a scalpel is used to cut off the "puppy dog tail." A few sutures prevent bleeding and speed up healing. The tourniquet is removed and the little tail may be bandaged. A tail that is not docked properly may ruin your puppy for show purposes, so be sure that you and your veterinarian agree on the length desired. Remember: It can't be reattached!

If you don't expect to show your dog, or if you have a beautiful mutt, please consider not docking the tail or cropping the ears. Again, I think the tail and ears that your dog is born with are its proper parts. But discuss this with your veterinarian.

Chapter 11

Genetics and Hereditary Diseases

The Austrian empire in the mid-1800s was *the* important center of the arts, literature, and music. At the same time that Brahms produced his brilliant *Variations on a Theme by Händel* (1861), another genius, an Austrian monk named Gregor Mendel, was making one of the most important biological discoveries ever made: An organism's traits, such as height, are regulated by two particles we now know as *genes* (Greek for "to give birth to"), one particle contributed by the female and the other by the male. Mendel performed his experiments on the garden pea plant. He noticed that when he bred tall pea plants to short pea plants, all the offspring were tall. Mendel called this characteristic the *dominant* trait, and the characteristic that "seemed to disappear" he termed *recessive*.

When Mendel bred the offspring to each other, the result was three tall pea plants for every short pea plant—a ratio of three to one. Mendel surmised that each offspring of the first breeding carried one dominant and one recessive particle and that in the breeding of the offspring, one short pea plant should be produced for every three tall pea plants.

Unfortunately, Vienna and the rest of the world neither understood nor cared about the biological sciences, which were considered antireligious. Gregor Mendel's papers were burned after his death in 1884 and his great findings were not rediscovered until the beginning of the twentieth century.

What is this genetic material, which determines that like shall beget like? Genes are composed of *deoxyribonucleic acid* (DNA). This DNA is found in long strands called *chromosomes* in the nucleus of the billions of cells in your pet's body. Every cell of your dog contains thirty-nine pairs of chromosomes.

Each gene controls the synthesis of one protein. Protein makes up about three-fourths of the body solids and is the building block of life. The majority of proteins are enzymes that regulate the chemical reactions in the cells. Blood, bone, hair, and muscle are primarily protein. Hormones such as insulin are also proteins. Structural protein called *connective tissue* gives the skin its elasticity and the hair its form.

Throughout a lifetime there is a constant turnover of cells—daily wear and tear destroys skin, hair, and blood cells, but they are constantly being replaced, thanks to the cells' ability to duplicate themselves. Before the cell divides, the chromosome forms a replica of itself (a process called *replication*). Each new cell has the exact number and order of genes as the original cell. Thousands upon thousands of activities occur and renew themselves daily in your pet's body, thanks to a biological "blueprint," called the *genetic code,* in the chromosomes.

Every part of your pet's body (and even its temperament, to a large extent) is dependent on the chromosomes that were combined when its parents mated. The fertilized egg is a complete cell containing all the information that determines hereditary make-up. That cell divides in the mother dog's uterus, and the developing embryo contains the identical genetic make-up.

Let's suppose that you bred your female black-coated Labrador retriever to a brown-coated Chesapeake Bay retriever. What color coat would you expect in the pups? Black is dominant, and brown is recessive. If the female has two dominant genes for a characteristic, such as a black coat, the dog is called *homozygote* for that trait. Let's use the letters BB. When a dominant gene is paired with a recessive gene, the dog is called *heterozygote* (Bb) for this trait, but it still produces black coats. Since brown is a recessive trait, it can appear only if it is paired with another recessive hair coat gene. Let's use the letters bb. Using a chart called Mendel's Checkerboard, you can predict the probability of certain genetic traits in the offspring of pea plants, dogs, cats, or any living thing.

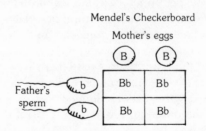

Mendel's Checkerboard

All the puppies will be heterozygote and they all will have black hair coats, just as Mendel's tall and short pea plants produced all tall plants in the first generation. The next generation could produce some brown dogs, since all have at least one recessive gene.

By now, you're probably wondering what all this has to do with your dog's health. It has a *lot* to do with it! As you already know, one gene carries the message for the production of one protein. But if the DNA gets mixed up, the gene carries an abnormality known as a *mutation,* a change from the normal pattern of inheritance that appears as a new or altered characteristic.

Inbreeding (mating closely related individuals, such as mother to son, father to daughter, or brother to sister) or *linebreeding* (mating more distant relatives, such as cousins) increases the chance of defects that require two recessive genes to come together or defects that require a polygenic union. Before breeding, the male and female should be checked by a veterinarian for defects or diseases that have a hereditary basis.

The OFA, the Canine Eye Registry Foundation, and the International Registry of Bleeding Disorders are important in coordinating the information on many inherited disorders. If you are purchasing a pet whose breed has a high incidence of an inherited disorder, an added assurance is a certification that the parents and close relatives are free of the disease or defect.

A disease called *globoid cell leukodystrophy* is reported primarily in Cairn terriers and West Highland white terriers. A genetic enzyme deficiency causes progressive degeneration of the nervous system and death in puppies between two and six months of age. It has a *recessive pattern of inheritance* — that is, a puppy must receive two abnormal genes to produce the disease. A dog that has one normal gene and one abnormal gene is called a *heterozygote carrier* and will appear normal, but it can pass the abnormal gene to its offspring.

Conscientious golden retriever and Labrador retriever owners delay breeding until the dogs are two years old because of two genetic disorders, cataracts and hip dysplasia, that can develop before that age. If one or both occur, the breeder will consider not mating the dog. Cataracts in the golden and Labrador retrievers has a *dominant pattern of inheritance* — only one of the pair of genes must be abnormal to produce cataracts. The cataracts are usually visible with the aid of an ophthalmoscope between one and two years of age.

Hip dysplasia has been diagnosed in almost all breeds of dogs, but it is more common in the large breeds, such as retrievers and German shepherds. The hip joint is a ball and socket—put your fist into the cup of your other hand to get the idea. Dogs with hip dysplasia develop varying degrees of bony changes in the femoral head and the pelvic socket (*acetabulum*). The hip joint may be obliterated in some dogs—equivalent to putting a knobby fist into the *flat* palm of your hand. Hip dysplasia has a *polygenic mode of inheritance* — that is, the cumulative effect of many abnormal genes results in the disease.

In the October, 1975 issue of *Purebred Dogs — AKC Gazette,* Dr. Donald F. Patterson, Chairman of Veterinary Medical Genetics at the University of Pennsylvania School of Veterinary Medicine, likened this cumulative effect to a balance in which one pan contains "good genes" (producing normal hip development) and another pan contains "bad genes" (tending to produce hip dysplasia). If there are enough "bad" genes, the balance will be tipped towards the abnormality. If there is a large number of "bad" genes, the balance will be tipped towards severe hip dysplasia. Dr. Patterson further stated that "some dogs can have normal or marginally normal hips by X-ray examination but have a large number of dysplasia-promoting genes. Such individuals, though themselves outwardly within normal limits, can transmit hip dysplasia-predisposing genes to their offspring. If two such "balanced" individuals are mated, the chances are great that at least some of the offspring will receive enough dysplasia-producing genes to tip the balance toward the hip dysplasia side. The more severely affected dogs tend to produce the highest percentage of affected offspring. Likewise, the more severely affected are the parents, the more severe is the degree of hip dysplasia in the offspring."

Normal hips

Severe
hip dysplasia

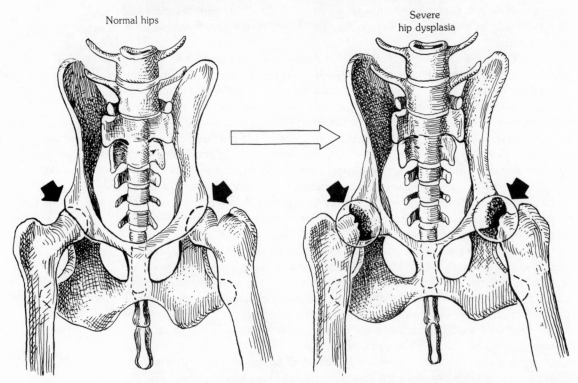

Environment may modify the effect of the polygenic defects. Dr. Wayne H. Riser, also of the University of Pennsylvania, has demonstrated that "the incidence of hip dysplasia in German shepherd pups is greatest in those which show early rapid growth and weight gains, suggesting that nutrition might have some influence on the disease—the heavier the dog, the greater the degree of biomechanical imbalance."

The outward signs of hip dysplasia are varied (also see Lameness, page 158). Some dogs have a lower exercise tolerance, difficulty in rising after lying down, and wobbly hind quarters, and they drag the rear toenails when walking or have pain in the hip joints. The only reliable method of diagnosing hip dysplasia is by radiography. Your dog's hip X ray can be further evaluated and certified by the Orthopedic Foundation for Animals. Write to:

University of Missouri—Columbia
Columbia, MO 65201

You will receive an OFA certificate attesting to the health of the hips and increasing the worth of your dog for breeding. If your dog has a mild degree of hip dysplasia but has outstanding intelligence, good disposition, good conformation, and good behavior (other inherited qualities), breeding may still be considered. Discuss it with your veterinarian and the breeders or dog clubs in your area.

The Canine Eye Registry Foundation has been established to certify that your dog does not have a hereditary eye disease. For more information, write to:

P.O. Box 15095
San Francisco, CA 94115

Dr. Patterson, Dr. Peter Jezyk, and their co-workers are studying the "fading puppy syndrome." In human neonates and infants, genetic enzyme defects such as *phenylketonuria* (PKU) have been identified. Newborn infants can be screened for these hereditary metabolic defects and treated before mental retardation, liver or kidney dysfunction, or death occurs. Neonatal puppies that fail to thrive (they lose weight, have problems moving, and can't maintain body temperature), may have similar disorders. Dr. Patterson states that "small pups can be tested as early as the first few days of life by collecting a few drops of urine on filter paper." The dried urine specimen is mailed to their laboratory and analyzed by a number of different techniques to determine whether abnormal chemical compounds are present.

Metabolic screening is a new and important procedure in veterinary medicine. As Dr. Jezyk points out, "In human medicine, 5 to 10 percent of all admissions to pediatric hospitals are for disorders which are clearly genetic, while another 10 to 15 percent are for conditions with some genetic component." The development of veterinary clinical specialties such as neurology, cardiology, dermatology, and ophthalmology has increased the accuracy of diagnosis and the recognition of genetic diseases. Improved methods of both prevention and treatment of parasitic, nutritional, and infectious diseases have decreased the importance of these illnesses and brought to light diseases that are entirely or partially genetic in origin.

Dr. Patterson has catalogued approximately 100 disorders in dogs in which the hereditary nature is well established. Many of these diseases have their counterpart in human diseases. Veterinarians have been instrumental and will continue to be active in identifying and curing diseases common to our pets and to humans. For instance, an underlying inherited defect that seems to make boxers susceptible to tumors may possibly be important in understanding and curing various forms of human and animal cancer.

The International Registry of Animal Models of Thrombosis and Hemorrhagic Diseases, chaired by Dr. W. Jean Dodds, was established to study, treat, and coordinate the worldwide research of bleeding diseases in animals. For more information, write to:

Griffin Laboratory
New Scotland Avenue
Albany, New York 12201

Inherited blood clotting disorders such as hemophilia A have been identified in most breeds of dogs, including collies, German shepherds, beagles, shelties, greyhounds, weimaraners, Chihuahuas, Samoyeds, vizslas, miniature poodles, Labrador retrievers, and even mutts. The American spaniel clubs and several otterhound breeders have launched a vigorous testing and registry campaign to identify affected dogs. In Canada, the Ontario Veterinary College in Guelph also has research in progress, and in Europe, the State University of Utrecht in The Netherlands is active in studying bleeding disorders.

Some of the most common genetic disorders, and the breeds they affect, are listed in the following table.

Disease or Defect	Breeds Affected	How Inherited	Random Facts
CANCER			
All types	Boxers	Not known	See Cancer, page 253
Bone cancer	Large and giant breeds		
SKELETAL			
Hip dysplasia	Primarily large breeds	Polygenic	Parents should be OFA-approved
Intervertebral disc degeneration ("slipped disc")	Beagles, dachshunds, cocker spaniels, Pekingnese	Probably polygenic	
HEART			
Patent ductus arteriosus	Poodles; possibly collies and Pomeranians	Polygenic	
Subaortic stenosis	Newfoundlands; possibly German shepherds, boxers	Polygenic	
Conotruncal septum defects	Keeshonds	Polygenic	
Pulmonary stenosis	Beagles	Polygenic	
Persistent right aortic arch	German shepherds, Irish setters	Polygenic	
Degeneration in the heart's electrical activity	Dobermans	Not known	Sudden collapse and death occur
DIGESTIVE SYSTEM			
Cleft palate (split in the roof of the mouth)	Bulldogs, beagles, dachshunds, cocker spaniels, Shih Tzus	Probably polygenic	
Chronic progressive hepatitis*	Bedlington terriers	Possibly recessive	The terrier seems to be "wasting away"

*This is similar to a human disorder called Wilson's disease, which can be controlled by *penicillamine*.

Disease or Defect	Breeds Affected	How Inherited	Random Facts
EYES			
Cataracts	Miniature schnauzers	Recessive	The cataract usually does not progress, therefore vision is OK; the eye can be dilated with atropine two or three times weekly if the cataract impedes vision
	Afghan hounds (to 3 years old), standard poodles (to 1½ years old)	Recessive	
	Golden and Labrador retrievers (to 1½ years old)	Dominant	
Glaucoma	Basset hounds, cocker spaniels, wire-haired fox terriers	Not known	Can be treated medically or surgically
Progressive retinal atrophy (generalized)†	Miniature and toy poodles (5 to 7 years old), Norwegian elkhounds (2 to 3 years old), Irish and Gordon setters (less than 1 year old), American cocker spaniels (3 to 4 years old), English cocker spaniels (3 to 7 years old), Welsh Corgis	Recessive	Night blindness is the first sign and can be diagnosed before sexual maturity by examination with an ophthalmoscope Cataracts are a common complication; no treatment is available
Progressive retinal atrophy (central)	Golden retrievers, Labrador retrievers, English springer spaniels	Not known	Seen between 3 and 7 years of age; impaired vision is the first sign; dilating the pupil with atropine helps for a while
"Collie eye"	Collies	Recessive	90% of all collies have some degree of "collie eye"; have your veterinarian check the retina with an ophthalmoscope—if the retina is out of focus, the pup will develop retinal detachment and will be blind, but retinal "collie eye" does not always progress to detachment

†Dr. G. D. Aguirre and Dr. L. F. Rubin of the University of Pennsylvania Veterinary School have demonstrated that this can be diagnosed in pups as young as twelve weeks old (Irish setters), using a technique called *electroretinography*.

Disease or Defect	Breeds Affected	How Inherited	Random Facts
NERVOUS SYSTEM			
Epilepsy	Miniature poodles, dachshunds, German shepherds, golden retrievers	Not known	See Convulsions and Seizures, page 106
SEX ORGANS			
Cryptorchid or monorchid (one or both testicles do not descend into the scrotum)	Any breed	Probably recessive	This can lead to a midlife sertoli cell tumor Although not usually malignant, it can cause feminine signs to develop in your male dog—large breasts, hair loss around the lower abdomen, and male dogs will be attracted to your dog Remove the tumor before it gets large, becomes malignant, or causes illness or the feminine development
SKIN			
Allergic inhalant dermatitis (*atopy*)	Poodles, wire-haired fox terriers, Dalmatians, West Highland white terriers	Not known	See Allergies, page 166
URINARY SYSTEM			
Uric acid stones in the bladder	Dalmatians	Recessive	

Chapter 12
Cancer–
A Chronic Disease

The improvements in the prevention and treatment of infections, parasites, and nutritional diseases have lengthened the lifespan of our pets. Consequently, a dog living into its middle and later years will develop other health problems. Probably the most dreaded disease of mid- and later life is cancer (although there are some cancers, such as bone cancer, that affect primarily younger dogs). Yearly, there are almost 400 new cases of cancer per 100,000 dogs.

Cancer begins as a biologically abnormal change in a single cell in one of your pet's organs. This cell divides repeatedly, producing more abnormal cells. These new cells also divide at an extremely rapid rate and cannot be stopped by your dog's normal internal monitoring system, which makes normal cells behave. These abnormal cells are biologically destructive: They form solid tumors and invade and destroy surrounding tissue. Malignant tumors produce chemical substances that aid the cellular destruction and help stimulate a blood supply (to obtain oxygen and nutrition) for the tumors. Malignant cells frequently spread throughout the body by way of veins or lymph vessels and thus bring their destructive ways to other organs in your dog's body. This process is called *metastasis*.

WHAT IS CANCER?

Why should normal cells in your dog's body suddenly transform into malignant cells? Researchers feel that cancer is caused by one or more of the following factors:

contact with harmful environmental agents, heredity, viruses, immunologic factors, or body hormones.

Harmful Environmental Agents

Chemical *carcinogens* (agents that produce cancer) are being identified in our air, water, and food. Our pets share this unhealthy environment and share the carcinogens, most of which alter cellular genetic material. Asbestos workers and heavy cigarette smokers have a high incidence of lung cancer. Since dogs don't smoke and don't work—especially around asbestos—they have a very low incidence of lung cancer. However, dogs living in urban, air-polluted areas have a higher incidence of cancer of the tonsils than do their country relatives.

Heredity

Certain breeds seem to have a predisposition for and a high incidence of specific cancers. Others seem cancer-free. For example, the giant breeds, such as Great Danes and St. Bernards, have a greater incidence of *osteosarcoma* (bone cancer); boxers are walking tumor factories; yet beagles have the lowest incidence of tumors.

Viruses

Tumor-causing viruses are being identified. These viruses change the genetic code in cells, transforming them into malignant cells. The most publicized cancer-inducing virus is the feline leukemia virus.

Immunologic Factors

Tumor cells have antigens (see page 42) on their surfaces. Your dog's immune system (antibodies, lymphocytes, and *macrophages*) recognizes these "foreign" cells and attempts to destroy them. It has been speculated that our pets (and our own) bodies produce cancer cells quite often but the immunologic defenses in healthy humans and dogs destroy these cells before they can get established. This is called *immunologic surveillance*. If the immune system fails for any reason, the cancer cells can start their destruction.

Body Hormones

It is well known that having an ovariohysterectomy *before* the first heat may help to avoid breast cancer in later years.

Cancer will be prevented only when we understand how and why these factors cause normal cells to transform into cancer cells. For example, if air pollution and smoking induce lung cancer in humans, why don't *all* exposed humans develop cancer?

If your pet develops cancer, don't feel that all is hopeless. In many cases, modern veterinary medicine, just like human medicine, has therapy available to help your pet. The chance for a cure or *remission* will depend on the type of tumor, its location(s), the type of therapy used, and your dog's general health (for example, whether general anesthesia or chemotherapy can be tolerated).

First, you and your doctor must be *sure* that your dog has cancer. Most types of cancer cannot be diagnosed by looking at your pet. Some of the signs, such as loss of appetite, gradual weight loss, weakness, lumps in the abdomen, and even ugly skin growths, could indicate a simpler problem. Your doctor must perform certain tests and take radiographs to verify that cancer is present, to determine the type and extent of the cancer, and to decide on the best type of treatment, if any, for the malignancy (see Laboratory Tests, page 69 and X rays, page 72). Your veterinarian may select some or all of these diagnostic tools to give you clear assessment of your dog's situation.

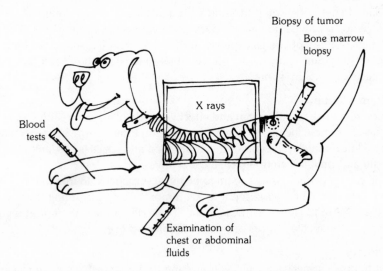

Once the lab tests and X rays have been studied, the doctor can determine the next step. If there is cancer and it is treatable, you should receive the following information so that you and your doctor can reach a common understanding and decision in your dog's best interests.

- What are the chances for a cure or remission?
- If you can expect a remission, how much time does this give your dog to live free of pain and discomfort?
- What type of therapy will be used?
- What are the side effects of the therapy?
- What is the cost of the therapy?
- How much of your time will be taken up by visits to the veterinary hospital for therapy and follow-up exams?
- Is there any new cancer therapy that will not cause your dog discomfort and that may benefit it and contribute to current human cancer studies?

THERAPY

At the present time, there are five modes of therapy, effective either singly or in combination, used in the treatment of various cancers in different stages of development: surgery, chemotherapy, radiation therapy, cryosurgery, and immunotherapy.

Surgery

This is the major method to diagnose and treat cancer. The major drawback is that a microscopic number of tumor cells may be left behind, which can spread and cause a relapse. If there is a high risk of relapse, or if the entire tumor cannot be successfully removed, one or more of the other modes of therapy may also be used.

Chemotherapy

The hope of chemotherapy is in using a drug or chemical agent that will kill tumor cells while doing as little damage as possible to your dog's healthy cells. The drawbacks of chemotherapy are its expense (unless the therapy is supported by government grants to a university or private veterinary medical center) and the potential toxic effects on healthy tissue.

Radiation Therapy

Radiation therapy is an important and effective mode of cancer treatment in human medicine. It is now being recognized as an important form of general cancer therapy. Unfortunately, the cost of the equipment and facilities has limited its use to university and private veterinary medical centers.

The cells of certain tumors seem to be more susceptible to therapeutic doses of *ionizing radiation*. These *ions* seem to kill tumor cells by disrupting their "code of life"—the DNA and chromosomes. The cells die when their attempt at division is ineffective. Susceptible tumors are termed *radiosensitive*.

Cryosurgery

Certain tumors—especially some skin and mouth tumors—have been successfully treated with cryosurgery. This is a technique using liquid nitrogen or a compressed gas such as nitrous oxide to kill tumor cells by alternately freezing and thawing the tissue. A temporary but odorous and oozing wound is the main disadvantage until healing results.

Immunotherapy

A new form of therapy that seems to hold some promise, especially when combined with surgical treatment, is immunotherapy. Your own and your pet's immune system protects the body against "foreign" cells such as bacteria, viruses, and tumor cells. In cancer, the immune system is suppressed or blocked from destroying the tumor cells. Certain biological and chemical substances called *immune adjuvants* are being used to stimulate the immune system in hopes of getting remissions in breast cancer.

Early diagnosis and treatment is most important if therapy is to be successful. If your dog is over five years old and you suspect the presence of cancer, see your veterinarian.

Most dog owners are willing to prolong their pet's life if it will be free of pain and suffering. If you and your veterinarian reach a common understanding that this is not possible, it is in your pet's best interest to administer euthanasia (page 259). In this way, pets do not have to suffer through the pain and misery of cancer that has spread throughout the body. But please consider euthanasia only as one option. Just like heart disease, cancer can be considered a chronic illness that can, in many cases, be controlled—your dog can live free of pain and discomfort. Euthanasia should be used only if treatment has failed or if your dog has a form of cancer that is completely hopeless.

Skin cancer, lymphosarcoma, and breast cancer are three forms of cancer commonly seen in dogs.

SKIN TUMORS

Any growth in or on your dog's skin should be examined by your veterinarian. Most skin tumors, such as those described below, are benign, but any growth that increases rapidly in size and infiltrates the surrounding tissue may indicate malignancy. Early surgical removal is curative for the majority of skin tumors.

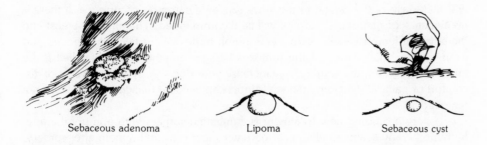

Sebaceous adenoma   Lipoma   Sebaceous cyst

Sebaceous Adenoma
This skin growth looks very much like a cauliflower: There are several small clumps of grayish matter growing from a common base. If the adenoma gets irritated, it may become red and ulcerated. You should be able to get your fingers around the growth because it does not infiltrate adjacent tissue.

Lipoma
The more common term for this growth is "fatty tumor." It grows under the skin, but you can feel it. A lipoma can get very large, although it grows slowly. Again, it should move freely because it does not spread to surrounding cells.

Sebaceous Cyst
This is similar to a lipoma in that it is a freely moving growth under the skin. However, this cyst is composed of cheeselike matter and remains fairly small, around the size of a marble. This, too, does not harm adjacent tissue.

LYMPHOSARCOMA (Leukemia)

Lymphosarcoma is the third most common cancer in dogs. Unlike cat lymphosarcoma, the cause is not known. It is usually seen in dogs over five years old. Without treatment, it is rapidly fatal. Remission for six to eighteen months may be possible with surgery, chemotherapy, radiation therapy, and/or immunotherapy, either singly or in combination.

BREAST CANCER

Breast cancer is a disease of middle-aged and old female dogs. Fifty percent of dog breast tumors are malignant. Any hard lump near a nipple and under the skin of a breast should be examined by your veterinarian. Early diagnosis and aggressive therapy of malignant breast tumors may prolong your dog's life.

The cause of breast cancer is not known; however, it is very possible that breast cancer may be averted if your dog is spayed before the first heat. So if you do not plan to breed your dog, it may be a good idea to have the ovariohysterectomy done early.

If the lump is suspicious, your veterinarian will probably recommend two procedures—a radiograph of the chest and a biopsy of the lump. If malignancy is present, metastasis of the cancer to the lungs is a fairly common occurrence. If there is no evidence of metastasis, surgery will be recommended. The affected breast and the adjacent lymph vessels, veins, and lymph nodes will usually be removed and examined for malignancy. If the tumor is benign, breathe a sigh of relief! If the tumor is malignant, the surgery may increase your dog's life span and free it of discomfort or pain. *Note:* Some benign tumors can become malignant if they are not removed.

A very promising new treatment is combining surgery with immunotherapy. Immunotherapy seems to eliminate the few cancer cells that remain after surgery, and the survival time seems to increase considerably. In one study, at the veterinary cancer unit of the Animal Medical Center in New York, it increased by more than seventeen months.

As you can see, cancer is a very complex chronic disease that, in many instances, *can* be treated. Early diagnosis is *very* important, as is close cooperation with your veterinarian during treatment. The decision between euthanasia and treatment should be made only after serious consultation with your veterinarian, always keeping in mind your dog's well-being.

Chapter **13**

Euthanasia: When It's Time to Say Goodbye

This is the hardest decision to make. I know, because I had to make that decision for our dear, fourteen-year-old miniature poodle, Pepe, who was suffering with pancreatic cancer. All life is precious, but euthanasia has its time and place. If your dog has an incurable disease or is vicious and dangerous, euthanasia is usually recommended. An intravenous overdose of an anesthetic that is fast and painless is used.

Many owners want to be present when their pet is "put to sleep," and most veterinarians will assent. Although the injection is fast and painless, you should be aware that there are involuntary reflexes for a few minutes after your pet has departed.

Albert Schweitzer's reverence for life was a great influence on me when I was very young. Consequently, I will not euthanize a healthy animal or an animal that has a curable disease. Most veterinarians feel the same way. If you cannot afford the necessary care, discuss it with your veterinarian. He or she may work out a long-term payment plan or may not charge you for the time.

Final arrangements for the remains should be made prior to euthanasia. Your veterinarian may suggest cremation or a pet cemetery. Many areas have public ordinances against backyard burials.

It's very hard to lose a pet that has given you love and companionship. But you'll always have the memories, and as soon as you feel ready, I recommend finding a new family member to share your love. You'll be happy you did.

Index

265